IM SO WITHIN IM NEVER WITHOUT

BY ELLEN GRIGGS

Text © Ellen Griggs 2017

Author contact:
ellensusangriggs@hotmail.com
IG: im_so_within_im_never_without

In loving memory of my angel, forever your KingL

Disclaimer

This book is a memoir. It reflects the author's present recollections of experiences over time. The events are portrayed to the best of Ellen Griggs's memory. While all the stories in this book are true, some names and identifying details have been changed to protect the privacy of the people involved. I have tried to recreate events, locales, and conversations from my memories of them. In order to maintain their anonymity in some instances I have changed the names of individuals and places, I may have changed some identifying characteristics and details such as physical properties, occupations, and places of residence. I have been completely honest with myself and portrayed everything as I remember. Human memory is subjective as we are all influenced by our own perceptions, which is also influenced by many other factors during growth. I understand that perceptions along with memories can vary from person to person, not all memories or perceptions of the events foretold may be the same. I state that regardless of what may have happened, all characters based on real people are upstanding citizens. We all make mistakes, and all are able to learn and grow.

I was born into a place that I do not belong
I want to be in a place that has no form

Where people don't think, instead they feel
Where people don't act, instead they're real

I was born into a place that I do not belong
Instead of crumble I've decided to be strong

I try to lead by example with love and care
Willing to help anyone in the world out there

I will love deeply with no regrets
And within my efforts I will try my best

I choose to love every human, animal, and piece of
land
Tearing down the old constructs of man

I was born into a place that I do not belong
I want to be in a place that has no form

Where people don't think, instead they feel
Where people don't act, instead they're real

"What is more powerful than the darkness? The light"

Table of Contents

Preface

We are our own saviours, only we can save ourselves. This can happen when we look within, learning to heal from our traumas and working on all our flaws to become better than we were yesterday. Changing ourselves will change the world.

I am writing this book because at one point in time, my soul felt such an urge to spread an important message, and all that would flow through my mind were images of pages and pages of my own book, that would inspire, motivate, and empower anyone who would read it.

The original inspiration that accelerated the idea of this book was from a situation of sexual coercion while I was staying in Jamaica for three months. After the incident, I decided that it is an important message to show people. Even when someone can make you feel like you are left with no other choice, except the one that person is offering. When you believe in yourself and you decide what you genuinely want, you can take your power back, and an option can materialise, even if you cannot yet see how. You are your own hero. I believe that sometimes when your life is relatively comfortable and there is not so much conflict or disruption within your environment, it is easier to follow and carry on living your life on autopilot. Never needing to question your world and environment or sometimes never even wanting to gain consciousness and a peace within, because you can see no reason as to why you need to. From a young age I had experienced traumatising situations, with no support around me, even with family there, they were so unconscious they could not support or help me. I had nowhere and no one to turn to, it was me against the world and at first with all the demons I had gained, through the negative experiences I had gone through, it was not easy.

I have included my true-life stories to show people that bad things happen all the time, even if you're the one doing it. I learnt that it is not what happens to you that defines you, but what you do after. It can be difficult, and I did follow a self-destructive pattern, but after time I began to learn. After experiencing all the pain, it enabled me to learn of true compassion, empowerment, and many life lessons of which now I am aware a lot of religions try to preach. Unfortunately, with religion also comes negative connotations from labelling yourself as part of a group, it divides, I see us all as coming together, we are all one. Regardless of religion, certain lessons are a way of life, like choosing to live honestly, and some things you will never deeply appreciate or understand, until you have learnt what it is like to be completely without them, like for example love or basic care.

The first part of this book talks of my life experiences and the lessons I have come to learn from them, I want the reader to apply it to their own lives and to find their own solutions, to their life situations. An internal journey, personal development, growth, how to find your power, your light, and to be the best you can possibly be. Aimed at helping you go beyond self, that is your conditioned self, that is moulded by expectations, family, societal and cultural standards thrusted onto you from birth, the self that lives through internalising discriminations, labels, and repetitive negative patterns. The self that has gained all your demons from society like fear, low self-esteem, unreasonable standards, pressure, pain, jealousy, no confidence, self-violence, hate, aggression, envy, needing everything to be perfect, if you can heal this self then you can truly live.

Negative life experiences and negative social information can dim your light, your power on an individual and societal level. I want to tell you how to reignite, because we may feel that external forces take our power but really that is impossible, only we can give it away willingly or unknowingly.

The second part of the book is based on a true story of sexual coercion that happened when travelling alone to Jamaica. How to overcome a situation where you think you are left optionless, with no favourable outcome for yourself. Detailing how this predator used his platform as a host, to target vulnerable young girls, and try to convince them to be his friend with benefits. This young woman overcame his predatory trap, thrived in a situation where she was cornered, she destroyed his plans, making him learn that he cannot take what he wants. Developing lifelong friends, living in Jamaica, connecting with the culture, nature and creating memories and bonds like no other.

The third part of the book draws on the types of oppression within society, it shows how the oppressors are maintaining the prejudice and discrimination within the world. The mainstream education system reinforces many oppressions within society, maintaining the status quo, individualising, and normalising oppressions. To overcome the institutionalised aspect of oppression, we must combat the disease that is negative prejudice, to educate, to become more consciously aware, and to be active anti-discriminators in all areas of society. Imagine building so much, where you do not depend on your oppressors for media, food, shelter, money and so on, this will loosen their grip of control. Highlighting how oppression can be internalised and can influence negative emotions, and when individuals decide to feel worthy. Self-love can reignite the power we have always possessed, which can create greater avenues of inner and external growth. Drawing on psychological literature, we can discuss and account for educational sources that has led us on the path of discrimination, so we can see and ultimately break the chain. To educate all individuals on the prejudices they may give out, or experience, and the discriminations which fuel oppressions, in hopes to bring awareness and as much social change and justice as possible. There would be much more information that could go into this subject, I have used what I know to the best of my ability, trying to eradicate any biases I may have.

The last chapter is on empowerment, showing how we have lost our power on an individual and collective level. How we can work to regain our power, how to make our lives and the world we live in, externally and internally at one.

Introduction

Although I feel like I have grown so much throughout my life, I was put into a situation that made me feel at first like, I had no other option other than the one you could say the dominator was offering. The sexual coercion came from a white Jamaican man who was abusing his position. He was classed as a super host on a widely used accommodation booking site and used language like, 'welcome to our lovely family home.' It was something you would not see coming because of how profound and professional the booking site made him look. After letting it disrupt my thoughts, emotions, and allowing it to make me feel powerless. I was sitting on the beach within my own void, all I could hear were these words repeat themselves over and over. "The most powerful person in your life is you, you just have to let yourself be." After, I sat there, and I really started to think about the words that had replayed in my mind. The deeper I would think, the clearer of an understanding I would receive, the more I could see the strength and truth within the words. I had realised I had willingly given him power over my life, letting his actions and words disrupt my mind, emotions, and behaviour. It made me feel worried, anxious, and violated; disgusting inappropriate thoughts were flooding my mind, I felt sick and emotionally low. I had so many factors to worry about, it seemed that he had everything, and I had nothing.

That time on the beach became my saviour, as I became aware that it was me giving him my power over my life, was the exact moment I was able to take it back. Realisation creates awareness, that in turn creates self-power. That is exactly what happened, I thought to myself I am a strong, smart, honest, a real individual and I will not let this person and situation dictate my life, I will stick to my truth and get myself out of it one way or another. After this realisation, I took my power back and became two steps ahead of him the whole time. This story is a detailed memory of coerced sexual harassment and so much more than that, it shows the predatory instinct within some individuals, mixed with intellect can create a well devised trap.

One of which they are ignorant to know that there can be a way out, they may underestimate our power as their position makes them feel as though they are above it. Their prejudice and ignorance along with their ego, will always leave them in a weak position. Being aware, rational, calm, and most importantly taking time to think, instead of impulsively reacting within the moment, will keep you one step ahead.

We live in a world where human beings are sexualised, both men and women within many platforms within society, such as the media, education, music, culture and for entertainment. Even children have been subject to sexualisation within platforms that wish to exploit and coerce an agenda, of which dominates the lives of these individuals. It is a violation of a person's most private and intimate parts of their body, adults being sexualised okay were adults, but children. It goes deeper, there is child sex slavery in which children are being trafficked to extremely rich individuals and used for sex and other abusive acts, no one has the right to take a child's virginity. Sex is true and pure, when two individuals have an uncontrollable attraction, which within sharing time and space can develop into a true connection, the sex becomes a wave of spiritual and physical pleasure with the two having only each other's best interest in mind. Any sex that is coerced, forced, or emotionally detached, creates a negative energy field around the situation or experience, the participants will consume this energy, either knowingly or unknowingly. When you constantly feed yourself negative thoughts and behaviours, or surround yourself with negative people, you will constantly be emanating a low vibration, of which you will see the side effects from the negative experiences that enter your life. This is also true if you emanate a high vibration and only indulge in others on the same wavelength. If you think positive thoughts and carry out positive behaviours, you will grow and see more positive experiences and people enter your life.

The intention of this book is to empower any individual who wishes to read it, to show you that you are the most powerful person in your life, to expose corruption within society and individuals of which have been continuing for many years. This is reinforced with the beliefs that are thrust upon men and women. I want to expose the ways of some sexual predators and how they use certain organizations like booking sites for accommodation or properties, to give themselves a platform to prey on vulnerable individuals.

I want to show everyone the power they hold within, how they may have lost it and how they can regain it. I am going to give a detailed account of my origins, experiences, achievements, beliefs, attitudes, and ideologies. I want you to look at the lessons I have learnt from my experiences, and to try and see the lessons within your own life. I also believe this to be important as you, the reader, can get a better image of who I am and my history, so you can see how everything in Jamaica played out.

Some experiences are hard to admit to yourself but know that you are not alone, there are so many people that have been through similar experiences, sometimes worse, but the best way for us to reclaim our power is to own it, learn from it and grow from it.

My last intention for this book is to show and discuss the different types of oppression in this world, to educate individuals, to create a space and opportunity of social change and social justice in a positive way. To highlight and recognise the individuals who have fought against oppression, suggesting that we have an obligation to listen to those who are directly affected by oppressions we may not experience, and to exercise empathy with one another. To show the reader how to be the best they can be, by learning to live through self-empowerment and growth.

Part 1

<u>Who are you?</u>

Who are you is a very deep subjective question, only you can answer, people can draw their own conclusions by the stereotypes you fit into, the aspects of life you enjoy, and how you come across as an individual, but deep down only you know your truth! When you think about it deeply, who are you? Are you shaped by your family, or by your environment? Do you live your truth, or do you live through trends? Do you learn your lessons when bad things happen and try to grow, or do you continue a journey without reflection and change? The best way for me to describe my truth to you, so you can get an image of who I am, is to share some of my experiences, environmental influences, my family unit, my life lessons, beliefs, and attitudes. The aim of life I believe, is to look within ourselves to understand our experiences and how they have made us feel? What could we possibly learn from them, to do better and grow?

We are beings destined for growth, and if we do not ask ourselves these questions we will never heal and learn, your life circumstance will stay as it is. We are in control of our own lives, for some, everyday life will be harder due to the pre-existing structures within society, also some situations are a lot more painful than others, so it is easier to be overtaken by them. Although all of this is true, I have faith, I urge you to be there for yourselves, whatever background, whatever life situation, I urge you to love yourself, every beautiful human being out there. Love does not need to be sexualised, love is respect, kindness, empathy, understanding, positivity, you can love anyone, you must choose too, but most importantly first you must love yourself; how can you truly love another if you do not love yourself. I am not saying it will be a pretty path or an easy one, but the rewards of finding universal truths within yourself are unfathomable. Discovering the importance and magnificence of yourselves will uncover limitless possibilities.

Who am I?

My name is Frankie Lee Dunnam, I was born in North London Islington, in Whittington Hospital on Friday 17th December 1993 at 8:15am. My dad was adopted, I only found out later in life and I have no ties to his biological family, so I do not know of my dad's origins except that he was born in the same hospital as me, 29 years prior. My mum was born in The Mothers Hospital in Hackney London, my mums grandma was a Russian Jew who got disowned by her Russian family, due to marrying an Englishman, who happened to be very abusive. As far as I am aware the rest of my mum's side of the family is English. Although considering for thousands of years, humans have been travelling and changing. So, who really knows their exact true origins? Does it really matter if we are living in the moment, if we are living now?

My mum was a conformist, a shy child, always done as she was told, she loved her mother and always carried out her mum's wishes without argument. This is most likely due to wanting her mother's attention as my nan had her son, her golden boy, he got most of the attention, instead of fighting for attention she followed my nan and always done as she was told without question. My mum never really thought or lived for herself, she was conditioned from a young age to carry out behaviours that would please others, learning that it gives her positive attention. She never said boo to a ghost, did not like any sort of confrontation and this continued into her adult life. Until, just like me, she had realised her conditioned patterns, learnt her own valuable life lessons, and started her own journey of self-reflection, learning and growth.

My dad grew up in a family orientated household, with an overprotective mother, she had separation anxiety, she worried, you could say she over-worried about him all the time which I think it influenced his psyche. The consensus of the household was very much Victorian England, the boys are superior compared to the girls, having three older brothers, I felt the difference growing up. My dad was smart and bright, but he had his struggles, I believe it to be due to the era he was born into, maybe if he were born into my era he would have stood more of a chance. As an adolescent he suppressed his thoughts and emotions and found his escape from society, reality, and himself, in alcohol, which continued into his adult life.

Before I was born, I had a family all set up for me, but it was not always roses and sunshine for them. My mum and dad already had two sons prior to my birth and my mum also had another son prior to her relationship with my dad, but as far as I am aware my brother was basically a baby when they met. Most of this information I had learnt later in life, unfortunately the environment of which I was to be born into was not very productive. My dad was an alcoholic, he worked as a black cab driver in London, we lived in Holloway N7, he drank too much. He was an abusive husband, psychologically and physically, he was controlling and cruel towards my mother, especially when under the influence of alcohol. My mum did not really know how to show love to us, her mum did not really show it to her with hugs or words and maybe towards the end all her love got beaten out of her. I had no clue my dad was like this, my parents divorced when I was 3, I only remember one fight they had.

I remember many good times with my dad, only when I was little and at that point in time, he made me feel like he really did love me. I used to love him so much, you could have called me a daddy's girl, I think that is why it hurt more. My dad continuously broke my heart with every broken promise, with every time he did not show, until eventually he stopped bothering all together. I was a child and at the time I was confused, I felt as if it were my fault, but I did not know why. I didn't know how he could stop loving me, especially as my love was still as strong as ever. I felt abandoned and it was the start of an unconscious fear of love, or to better put it, someone falling out of love with me. My love for my father had been shattered by the man himself, it made me feel sad, angry, and unwanted.

I can remember one time when I was about nine years old, I was staying at my dad's for the weekend in London, he was in a pub one night and I was playing outside on the AstroTurf, I liked playing football. It was time for us to go home and my dad was drunk, I can't remember for what reason, but he hit me in the face with the back of his hand, I remember falling to the floor, and him screaming at me. "Ring your fucking mother to come get you, I don't want you here! I've got eighty pound here; she

4

can have it all!" I rang my mum crying and shaking, I was confused, I told her what my dad said, and she replied saying. "He has said that before Frankie, he won't give me the money, I haven't got any petrol, I can't come." I woke up the next morning confused with my dad sitting next to my bed smiling, asking if I want to go shopping. I did not realise how it had affected me at the time, but I felt like my dad was not protecting me, and my mum did not have my back either, I slowly stopped caring as much about everything.

The feeling of a parent not loving you, can mess with any individual let alone a child, it can create a lot of internal issues, so if anyone is feeling like this or has ever felt unloved by family and friends, all I can say is do not worry. What is important is not the love they can give to you, but the love you can give to yourself and if you do not, then that is your first step to take on your internal journey. If you do love yourself then you are on the right path and keep your chin up, keep pushing forward. Whenever you feel a lack of love just remember, the love you hold for yourself inside is more powerful than anything, or any love anyone can give you, and know that you are good, even when you are not good, you are good. Once you love yourself you can incorporate self-respect, set limits of acceptable treatment, do not let anyone treat you less than you deserve. You do not have to come across as rude or horrible when setting your own standards of treatment. You can be assertive, which is getting your point across but saying it in a calm polite manner. Do not ever feel like you must keep someone in your life because they are close family or friends, especially if it brings negative experiences which create negative emotions within you.

Sometimes distance is a blessing and ultimately no matter how strong the hold someone can have over you, it is still your choice whether you let them stay, you could be swayed by fear or corrupted love, but if you take this internal journey of which I speak of, then these will not be a barrier for you. The same applies for holding grudges, the situation replays itself in your mind and you are constantly feeding yourself the negative emotion and emotional state, to be free of it you must let it go and move on. Forgiving a person, situation, or yourself, does not mean that you think what they, or you, have done is right, but it allows you to let go of the hate and baggage and to move on, to do better. After this you will be able to look at the person or situation from an objective point of view, you will see all the factors that contributed to the end result. Seeing the bigger picture will allow you to understand better and find the lessons within the situation, which in turn can help you learn and develop in your life.

Life lessons

My life experiences have taught me some vital life lessons, when learnt I became a better me, I am sharing them in hopes that you will discover the lessons in your life, to become a better you. I remember the first time I had to forgive somebody who was not sorry, I forgave them for myself, not for them. I realised I had to do this after years of following a self-destructive pattern, instead of recognising and healing from the actual situation. Taking responsibility and realising it was me following a self-destructive pattern, had made me aware of the impact that person had on my life, or should I say the impact I had allowed him to have over my life.

I was twelve years old, I was playing out with my friends, I stayed out an hour past the time my mum had asked me to be home, a boy we were with tried to bully me, saying things like my period is gravy, calling me fat. Me and my friend Maggie chased him into a block of flats, I punched him in the face, he started crying for his mum, a woman we both knew came out of her door and drove him to his house.

Me and Maggie went towards Eastwood park, we were standing by the alley when he came back on the phone to his mum, she was threatening us and our parent's, so we cursed her back. She said she was making her way to the alley, so me and my friend started running through the park, we were only twelve, it is not like we were grown or was conscious of the world. While I was running through the park from his mum, my mum kept on ringing me, due to me being late coming home, I kept cutting the calls as I was running. The one time I answered I said in a rush, "mum I can't talk right now I'll ring you back." Then I got another call from my mum's number but this time it was a different family member, I said the same thing to him. When I had stopped running, another call came through, of which I answered but without being able to say anything, he said, "how dare you hang up the phone on me, I am coming to get you now!" The way he said it, it sounded so aggressive, so as soon as I got off the phone I turned to my friend and said to her. "Maggie, we need to go and hide, Benny rang and is saying he's coming to get me, and it did not sound good."

We went and crossed the road, it was a big dual carriageway on Kent Elms corner, we walked towards the shops, I was behind Maggie, she went around the corner then quickly started walking back towards me. She had a worried look on her face but at the time I could not work out why, she suggested that we climb over a fence on the corner to try and hide. We were climbing the fence and the next thing I heard were tires screeching heavily behind us. I felt a sudden pull, someone grabbing the back of me, smacking my body off the fence, I felt blows to my face and my body, I remember screaming to Maggie to run because I did not want her to get hurt. I can remember being bent over, my jumper covering my face, feeling blows from his knees, and getting smacked off the van, he finally opened the door and chucked me across the front seats. It was Benny, with a rage unlike any other, I could see it in his eyes. The van had two passenger seats in the front, I sat on the one furthest away from him and closest to the window.

The drive home was the worst, every ten seconds or less, all I could feel was the side of my face shattering from the impact of his fist. With every punch he would yell at me "You fucking cunt, none of this fucking family love you, you cunt!" This was the pattern for the whole drive home, we pulled up past my house, I was shaking unable to stop crying. He opened the door, he made me stand and wait next to the van, whilst he went and knocked on the front door, I was well out of sight from anyone. When the door was open and nobody was around, he came and got me and sent me straight upstairs to the bathroom. He came upstairs after me, I took off my top and then he cleaned all the blood off the back of my neck and back, then I got sent to bed and that is where I stayed. I followed a completely self-destructive path for a long time before I discovered self-healing. The self-destruction shows the impact some traumatic experiences can have, especially when we are unconscious and unaware that we ultimately control our lives.

After that experience, my life changed dramatically, I was twelve years old, my mum had never stuck up for me, never comforted me, instead she told me to stop lying as Benny told everyone that he had only pushed me into the van. My dad was never around, he did not want anything to do with me either, I felt like I had no one, no family to turn to. Just my friend Maggie who knew what had happened, but she was as unconscious to the world as I were, she did not treat me like a good friend. She put me down, put a cigarette out on me once and laughed as if it were a joke. I had no love or respect for myself, this led me to allow people that were in my life, treat me less than I deserved. The only people I had around me was older friends who done drugs and smoked, and then the younger ones, all of whom were just as messed up as me. I was confused at first, I did not understand how my family did not love me, but I let his actions and words penetrate my mind, splitting it into a complete system of self-destruction, self-detachment, depression, aggression, no self-worth, or confidence, followed by unruly, morally wrong behaviours, all while creating an incongruence between what I was thinking and what I felt, and it would all fluctuate at random. My older friends introduced me to drugs, and I would find some in my house, I used to take them off my mum's husband as he always had stashes, it became as though the only way I could be happy, was if I were high. At the time I did not realise how much it all affected me, but what Benny had said to me, had become my truth, I was convinced I was a cunt and that my family did not love me, so I acted up to the label. I did not care about myself, nor did I have any self-confidence, just a false act of confidence to protect me against people who would try to hurt me or abuse me in some way. I became intimidating, someone you would not want to mess with, I had done horrible things to others and to myself, but the sad thing is, I did not care about myself, I didn't think anyone did. I have let a lot of people do things and treat me in certain ways that I would never allow now, that's growth, that's real confidence and self-love, self-love really is the first step.

I wanted to get Benny back for what he had done, I guess it was an act of revenge, but I could not imagine how, it is not like I could go and fight him. One day I was up in the attic at my nans house because there was a tv up there, at the time Benny stayed in that room, I started nosing around and came across something. I went in his draw and inside it was a pile of little brown envelopes, all containing countless amounts of fifty-pound notes. I started taking some on various occasions and I was not the only one either. I would keep wads of fifty-pound notes in the inside of my blazer pocket when I was in my first year of high school. I would buy drugs with my older friends, cocaine, pills, weed, cigarettes, and alcohol of course, a complete mix of endorphin releasers, that would allow me to feel slight happiness in my depressed reality, my emotional pain got put on hold, at least until the drugs wore off anyway.

Slowly but surely, I was getting more detached and numb to my emotions, I was scared to allow myself to feel, since all feeling ever done was cause me pain. This destructive cycle continued for some months but sooner or later, everything had to come to an end.

We were at my nans house and Benny offered to pay for my mum's wedding car, but I had taken some money, so I wanted to get out of there. We went home, I was in bed and my bedroom door suddenly flew right across my room, Benny in a furious rage kicked my door across my room, he was screaming saying he will cut my fingers off when he finds it. He trashed my room, smashed it up, looking for his money, I was in a terrified state, frozen in fear, crying and screaming as I thought he would kill me. My mum ran into my room and jumped on top of me and told him to leave me alone, screaming. "CAN'T YOU SEE SHES TER-RIFIED," the only reason I was so scared was because I knew what he was capable of, I had already seen and felt it before, and I knew I had been caught. Luckily, he did not find anything that night, I cannot even imagine how it would have ended if he did. I did think, it does go to show that he knows I was the only person who could have a motive for taking his money, especially since he came to me first without any doubt in his mind, to me that was a silent confession of what he had done to me.

My family must have thought the worst about me, in denial with what had happened to me, thinking I was just a little shit for no reason. Sometime after, I was in the park with my friend, my nan and grandad approached me and warned me to give Benny his money back. If I did not have it back by that night, he will be coming after me, they said there would not be anything they could do to protect me. I loved my nan so much, she used to always be there for me whenever my dad would let me down, she would take me places when I was little and give me hugs, I used to feel so safe around her. I did not know why she never believed me, maybe if she did, none of this would have turned out the way it did.

I had no way of giving Benny his money back, I had spent it all on useless things and drugs, I had around 30 pills and a half oz of weed on me in a little bag I bought. I went home that evening; everyone was panicking telling me Benny is coming over to get me. I remember my nan coming into my room crying, screaming, continuously punching me, saying she will kill me if he goes to jail for killing me. I stood there and took the punches, I could never hit her, she broke my heart, it seemed that my family liked to do that to me.

Everyone left me except my cousin Damion, he was living at my nans at the time. He said he could not just stand by and let Benny beat me up, he took me out in his car and drove around, after he dropped me off near my house. I was thinking about taking all the pills I had on me, I was so sad, I did not know how much longer I could take the pain. Little did I know, this was the start of many situations of suffering, pain, and trauma, at this point I was only thirteen. My brother's friend had come to meet me, we sat in her car and talked, she convinced me to give her the pills and asked to take me home. When we pulled up to my house, I never went inside, as I was trying to hide from Benny. I remember walking the empty dark streets, sat crouched in a dark corner and cried all the pain out that I could, I was a child, I was alone, I never had no one try and make me feel better at the time, I did not know I could do it for myself, to learn that it was going to take the journey of my life.

Self-love is vital for the first step of an internal journey we must all take, it is not easy to accomplish but it is vital, the environments around us can make it harder to love ourselves especially if no one has shown us pure love, but you have the power to do exactly that and more, that is the first step for each of us. Benny did not find me that night, it all calmed down because my grandad gave him some money, I guess Benny would not quit until he got some sort of result for himself. I did not get better though, everyone was looking down on me even more than before, still not one conversation to see why, or how I was feeling, I was left to myself, I got worse.

Trauma can facilitate stupid decisions

I would run away a lot, I could not stand to be at home, the emotional pain hurt so much. I was sleeping in an alley one night and a man came over acting really concerned, he offered me to come back to his place, I guess I believed him as I was young and naive. I went back to his place; I will never forget that children in need was playing on the telly all night. I was on the couch laying down, he had made me a tea and had given me some tobacco roll ups, I remember him sitting on the armchair opposite me in his boxers staring at me. I could see his penis hanging out the side of his boxers, it made me feel sick, so I jumped up, grabbed the tobacco, said thanks for having me and ran out of the front door.

I was always naughty at school, I saw everything as a joke, how could I take anything seriously after what had happened to me, no one took me seriously, so I never took the world seriously. My teachers would say I am throwing my life away, I am wasting my life, I was so bright. I used to have such a zest for life, a natural intelligence and would excel in what I applied myself to. This was before a dark shadow got cast over me, I would learn later in life that I had the power all along, to evaporate any cloud, to control, live, love, and learn, from any storm. I had no respect for myself, I had no respect for society, I started getting in trouble with the police continuously, usually for theft from shops. My mum never had no money after bills, food, and whatever else was paid for, and my dad would never give us money in fear it would go to my mum, so I decided to get it myself. Especially because I felt a big urge to buy emotionally numbing substances like weed, alcohol, and whatever drugs my friends would introduce me to.

From the age of thirteen I was trapped in youth offending, always at court, always doing new programmes. I would never open myself up to my youth worker Sam, I did not think there was anything to say, because my family did not react to what had happened to me as a bad thing, so I thought it was normal. I did not think anyone would think that there was anything wrong with what happened. It took me about three years before I said anything, but I am glad I did. It opened a window of opportunity and growth, expressing and facing my pain, it enabled me to learn that I did not deserve what happened, and that I should never have been treated in that way.

Me and a couple of my friends who also had their own trauma to deal with, started self-harming, we would sit there and watch the Stanley blade penetrate our skin, while the blood slid down our arm. That moment of physical pain felt so much like a pleasure, it did not hurt, it was more of a relief. The moments of physical pain took away any emotional pain, which in turn made the whole situation seem pleasurable and good, like taking drugs and drinking, except that numbs it for the period your high, self-harming is more of a short-term relief. It got to a point in later years when I started to slowly love myself, that the thought of wanting to penetrate my own skin made me feel sick, to cause myself some sort of pain, these are points I look back on and can see the change, the growth, all from an internal journey developing from my life lessons. That is why I am sharing this information, so you can read my story and put factors together to help you learn and grow within your own life. Anybody that has ever had it hard, you deserve to discover your light just as much as I do, you deserve a happy life just as much as I do, and you can only live a happy life if you tune your perception and mind into a positive frequency.

When cocaine takes over

The next life changing event for me, was an unforgettable experience. I went into my brother's room one day before school and could smell weed, so I sniffed it out and discovered a dictionary in his draw. The dictionary when opened was a metal container with a lock on it. I could smell weed and really wanted a joint, but I could not unlock it. I used to rob weed off my mums' husband and brother, my brother had robbed it off me and him as well, it was not a good habit to be in, but I guess we were all kind of messed up. That day I went to my new school called Belfairs, I had been there for a few months now, I had Information Technology class that day. All I did during that lesson was go on google and look up how to break the lock I saw. It turns out there are tiny cylinders inside locks that move, but each lock has a unique pattern that matches the key made for it. I had to get all those cylinders down at once and it should open. I got home after school that day and wanted to test what I had learned. I went up to my mum's room, because her husband builds models, he had perfect tiny sized tools. I took what I needed and went to the dictionary and tried my luck with the cylinders. I was shocked that it worked.

I opened the dictionary but there was no weed in there, just a big bag of white rocks with a lot of powder at the bottom. I had tried cocaine once before but was not sure about it, I took a little bit and sniffed it off my window ledge. That night I was up for hours on the computer writing paragraphs to my friends. I started taking little bits as no one would notice and would share it with my two friends. After some time, I was constantly sniffing lines, it was the only thing that made me happy, the only thing at the time worth living for. I got greedy and addicted to the buzz, I took more and more, I was hallucinating, I was never sleeping, I was destroying myself. One day I had taken too much, the dealers were outside my house. In a panic I grabbed the rest of the coke and ran with my two friends out of my back garden, we jumped the fence and started running through the alleyways as fast as we could. They had my brother, but wanted me, I was scared and stupid, I told them I was in Leigh when really, I was on my way to Southend. We stopped in public toilets and done a line off a card each, making our way to our friend's house by the seafront.

When we got to my friend's house, my brother had rung me crying, asking me to come back home, he was screaming that if I did not hand myself over, they would cut his eyes out, he said he will not die, because of me. I did not know what to do, I was Thirteen, I had loads of shit happen to me, I ended up doing a lot of shit to other people. I was numb and in pain at the same time, I was depressed and in way over my head. I was sitting on my friend's bathroom floor alone crying, I had just done the last line. I knew I had to hand myself over, but I thought it would be better if I died, I would not be in pain anymore and my brother and family would be free of me. So, I picked up my Stanley blade, ready to slice open the big vein in my arm, then suddenly my friend burst into the bathroom, she jumped on me crying, telling me not to do it, and I didn't. I guess no one really wants to die, they just do not know how they can live.

I vowed to myself after this that I will not lie anymore, I will try and tell the truth no matter what, even if it hurts me or others around me, it makes life more real. I always owned up in the end, but prolonging the truth always got me and others in more trouble than needed, so I decided to stop. It was not easy, any time I could feel myself begin to lie, I would literally have to talk to myself inside my head or out loud and say, no it is not worth it, do not fall back into your old patterns. If I do not want to lie but cannot say the truth, I will stay silent, its hard and sometimes I fail, but never for long.

It seems that life shows how time can help a situation fade out, different productive or corruptive solutions arise but it is always subject to change. Time can help situations work themselves out, but when decisions are made in the moment, in the mist of the situation with all the emotions at play, making hasty decisions instead of letting things play out, can make things go in a direction you would not want them to. Taking time for yourself or for a situation is golden, it allows your emotions to pass, it allows you to think about everything and to see everyone's perspective. Practicing this will serve you well and it is something I am still practicing myself.

We all deserve to take time to ourselves, to think, to reflect, to tear away our conditioned layers, to learn to love ourselves and to do things that make us feel happy. The beach is my happy place, so I go as much as possible. What makes you happy? Why don't you do it? Now or later, or in ten minutes? Why not go to that place you have always wanted to go? Go alone, why not save and go? Enjoy your own company, you are the best, I hope you know that!

Developing an illness

The next eye-opening life lesson taught me to surrender to myself. I developed epilepsy after taking the cocaine; out of the blue I started having seizures. I had a consultation with a neurologist at the hospital and got tested, they found epilepsy, a mis-firing and over-firing of electrical current in my brain. They say lack of sleep or brain trauma, or certain substances can trigger it in people, well I could tick two off the list. At first, I refused to accept the illness, it made me feel like something was wrong with me, like I was broken. I could not face it, I denied it, and never told anyone, I was embarrassed to tell people. I never took my medication the doctors gave me, when I would have a seizure, I would pass out, so I never knew it happened until I woke up. Sometimes I would wake up and realise I had wet myself, or the insides of my mouth and my tongue would be bitten up. Most times I woke up aggressive and would lash out at whoever was around me, telling them to fuck off and that I don't need their help, I felt humiliated. It happened in front of my friends, my family, everyone got really worried about my wellbeing, so I felt like I had to give in and take the medication. Soon after I started taking these pharmaceutical drugs the neurologist gave me. I developed an extra two different types of epilepsy, before I would pass out and have a seizure. After I would have seizures whilst I was conscious, jolt aggressively whilst I was awake, as well as passing out and having a seizure. I have many seizure stories, but the main point was that I had to find a way to learn how to cope with developing a life-long condition. When I had not dealt with any of my other issues yet. I managed to take my ego out of it and began to accept what was happening, I learnt to look after myself internally and externally, now I do not take any medication and I am seizure free. This was a long process and took years to attain, it will not be the same for everyone, but self-love and acceptance is vital, it enables you to put more goodness into your body, mind, and soul.

Self-destruction

The truth is, even when my epilepsy was bad, I still carried out the same destructive behaviour as before. I was still doing drugs, until I began associating cocaine and seizures together; any time I took cocaine I would have a bad seizure, so I decided to stop. I developed a fear for taking it. I was stealing from shops and selling it on for money. I was always in trouble; I would be doing my probation hours with grown men, whilst other kids my age were at school. I remember wearing big overalls, cutting church gardens, or painting, or fixing street poles. A lot of the time I used my epilepsy to get out of doing the work, I would say that I need sleep to prevent a seizure, and the officer would let me sleep in the van.

Being reckless committing crimes, was the only way I could think to make money, within my environment people were committing crimes for money, I thought it was normal growing up. I was too young for a job and my mum did not have any money, so I thought I had to get it myself, one way or another. I was so numb to any emotion, any bad thing I did, I would justify it somehow, it would not make the action right. It is the mechanics of a corrupted mind trying to maintain itself. I used to go out with my best friend's mum when I was young, we would go to big supermarkets and fill trollies up with loads of expensive food and alcohol, then walk out with it and sell it for half the price. It got to a point where I got caught with £1000 worth of stuff on me, I ended up having to go to court for this. I had so many other offences on my record, all from thieving from shops, I used to see it as, taking from big companies does not matter as much, considering the way they exploit us, that is how I used to justify it to myself.

On this arrest, I was already doing community service and having probation meetings. They decided to give me four months inside a youth correctional centre, basically baby jail, but I only had to do two months inside. I was kind of happy because I thought after these four months, I would have an opportunity to start over, no longer owned by the system having to complete probation and meetings. Life can sometimes be weird and confusing, especially how you end up meeting people and how you learn your life lessons. I learnt a few things in jail, the first thing was to be careful of who you trust and believe, the second was learning the importance of listening and I mean actively listening, to understand not just to reply. The last lesson was to be confident in my own voice and to never let anyone speak for me.

I was sent to Medway Detention Centre and put on a unit with four other girls, Bailey, Ishna, Jessy, and Kellise. Ishna arrived at the same time as me and asked if I would write to her at night. I did and I gave her a pair of new bed clothes because she said her mum would not send her any. I remember one day I was writing at the table; Kellise was sitting on the pool table playing with her belly fat, I got this gut feeling, I do not know why or how but I liked her. One day the girls approached me and asked if I was writing to Ishna at night, Ishna was standing behind them shaking her head in a no gesture. Confused and stupid I said no and went on with the day. The whole time Ishna was talking about me behind my back, saying I was talking about the girls; I had no clue what she was saying. I only found out because one day all the girls tried to attack me on the unit, to be fair they did not do any damage because the guards were on the situation, so they moved me to another unit. After a couple of weeks, the girls turned on Ishna, probably because I was not around, they could see what she was doing. I only knew because the guards pulled me out of class to talk to her, to see if I would mind if they moved her onto my new unit. This experience taught me not to follow what people say, to trust myself more, to have confidence in my own voice instead of following other people.

The next lesson was on Listening. It was quite a simple but powerful realisation; it came from a booklet the counsellor had shown me. I will never forget it, her explaining the importance of listening and that so many people have not acquired that skill. The booklet explained that most human beings tend to interrupt and jump in as soon as they have a counter thought process, I could apply this to my own life and admitted to myself the amount of times I would interrupt people. It takes a lot of power and self-control to hold in your thoughts and opinions, to truly listen to understand, not to automatically respond, to wait and then to put your input in. Listening without interrupting, shows the individual that you value what they say and will hopefully lay out the framework for them to listen more attentively to you. It is not an easy skill to acquire, I incorporated it into my own life after I received this information and actively practiced it until it came a natural process to listen fully. Even now I sometimes interrupt automatically but I stop myself, apologise and ask them to please carry on. If this makes sense to you and you try to incorporate it into your own life, I promise you will see the fruits of this practice throughout time.

Life is always a re-lesson, a re-attempt within the present moment to act through the life lessons you have learnt, or to fall back into an unconscious negative pattern. The good thing is no matter how powerless you feel, you are the only one that can flip the switch at any given moment.

I felt like I had changed a little, but when I was released and back out on the road, it was too easy to fall back into some old destructive patterns. After a while I started making money for myself again, always smoking weed, I was unconscious still, but somehow could feel that I had levelled up. My thinking was gradually changing, I started caring and started wanting my life to improve, whereas before I did not care. Unless you take responsibility and tell yourself that you want to be better than your last mistake, you will not be, you are likely to repeat them.

A quote that I love from Maya Angelo sums it up beautifully. "You do your best until you know better, and when you know better, you can do better." This does not punish you for what you are born into, or your mistakes, or your negative thinking, but it gives you a chance to grow, to develop to become the best you can be. It takes a great deal of motivation and determination to change your life around, for me I got to a point where I had finally had enough, I surrendered to the pain. The pain from my life and lives of people I have loved gave me the motivation I needed to change.

Environmental influences can feel so intense, sometimes it feels as if it is the only option we have, especially when you have an intense internal influence like an attachment, or self-worth issues. Luckily for us, once we become conscious of our internal conditioning and our external influences, when we become awake. Our way of thinking and perception of people and the world will less likely become unconscious again. If it does, it only will for a short period of time before you realise yourself again, it just takes you to make that internal journey.

The years between the ages of eleven and eighteen were very intense and negative with a lot of emotional turbulences. I followed people, I let people talk me into things that split my soul that even now it is hard to admit to myself. I let someone I thought was my friend, someone I thought I could trust, set it up and convince me to sell myself for sex when I was thirteen, which is one of my biggest regrets and horror. All because I had no love for myself, or confidence and I felt no one had any love for me either. I was extremely low, I felt incredibly sad all the time, I was lonely even if people were around, I stole off my family, I hurt my family purposely, I stole from society, I hurt myself. I completely let loose and a lot of times I thought everything would be easier for everybody and myself if I were dead. I tried to overdose a few times, I caused pain, all these behaviours were really me crying out for help, help I never received, until I decided to help myself.

In my worst years I was always running away, sleeping outside, I had a machete held at my throat, whilst my house was getting robbed. I had my mum's boyfriend's son expose his genitals to me when I was eight years old, whilst he was laying in my bed. I had old, perverted men try to target me. Drugs were everywhere, I was offered to sell crack at thirteen, I was selling crack and heroin when I was seventeen, to make some quick money. I was addicted to cocaine at thirteen, then I got epilepsy. I was always smoking weed, I smoked crack about four times when I was fourteen, I smoked heroin twice and injected it once. I did not care about what happened to me, following friends who had their own problems. The time I injected heroin I was with someone I thought to be a friend, who put it in for me, I must have been fourteen or fifteen. I injected it and got a big lump stuck in my arm; I remember laying in my bed for two days straight, feeling like I was going to die. Any slight movement would feel like the whole world was spinning at the speed of light around me. I remember I kept rubbing the lump down and it must have worn off, luckily for me being addicted to those drugs was not meant to be, I never felt anything good from crack and heroin, it was disgusting, I hated it. I was always feeling so deeply depressed, I was sad most of the time when I was not high from weed, feeling like my heart was constantly ripping apart or sinking into my stomach. Convinced that I was unlovable and that my family did not love me, I could not help but feel this way when I was young. I did not know I could control my emotions by controlling my thoughts.

21

I learnt and began to think better about myself, about life, love, and other people, I became more understanding about the world and about external influences. Which can corrupt a person with so much internal conflict and pain, it will cause them to act in ways that are reflecting their inner life. An individual's negative behaviour towards you or others, says more about their internal conflict, than it ever will about who you are as a person. You have ultimate power over your own life, no matter how low you have got, or feel, or the things you have done, or what you have been through. You can always get yourself out of it, you must believe you can, be determined, and keep up with a psychologically, active, positive, internal journey. After time I was realising if I did not want to be sad or in pain, then it is up to me to be happy, no one was going to make me happy except myself. I started finding my strength in little things, like stating my opinion in an assertive non-aggressive way, making sure that I would not allow myself to be silenced by anyone.

Forgiveness

In my time of self-healing and change, I was given a book about forgiveness, when reading, it helped me understand my own situations. Around the age of sixteen, I finally found the courage to go and forgive Benny, for what he had done to me all of them years ago. I approached Benny while he was sitting in the conservatory, I did not know what to expect. All I knew is that I was ready to set myself free of the pain, the burden, and the grief. I took a deep breath and stated, "Benny I am here to say I'm sorry, I'm sorry for what I had done to you. I want you to know that I forgive you for what you have done to me, and I'm here asking for your forgiveness." He saw red, anger got the better of him, he probably did not know how to process what I had said, I am sure it was the last thing he expected me to do. So, he went to his safety net, aggression, what he may view as some sort of strength, but I believe it is a flaw we all need to work on. He grabbed the back of my neck, man handling me, screaming, "you are a thieving cunt," my brother Billy was there, he got between us. In shock, he could not believe what was happening, of course I got the blame, because if I did not say anything Benny would not have reacted. Healing is talking, letting it out, so no matter how scary, intimidating, or unnecessary it may feel, do not let anyone silence you, let it out for yourself, and move on.

If your family makes you feel crazy for saying anything, if they try to physically hurt you and if they try to blame you, do not listen! You know yourself best, if you feel like something needs to be said then something needs to be said. I got chucked out of the house in a muddle between Benny having hold of me and my brother between us. I walked away, crying my eyes out, constantly repeating, "I forgive him, I forgive him, I forgive him, I forgive him," I believed myself, I did forgive him, and it did not matter if he forgave me, because I forgave myself. If I could forgive him for what he had done to me, I could forgive myself for what I had done to others. That is the most important thing with forgiveness is that you forgive yourself, for whatever bad things you may have done, or for falling for manipulation, or allowing someone to violate you, forgive yourself, forgive others, move on and do better. While I was walking up my nans road my mind would replay a quote, I read in the forgiveness book stating. "Forgiving someone does not mean you condone their act; it means your setting yourself free." That's exactly how I felt after, free, free from his hold in my mind, telling me I'm worthless and unlovable.

After that moment, anything he ever said, to try and belittle me, put me down, or make me feel less than I am, had no power, it affected me in no way whatsoever. I found it quite pathetic that a grown man would want to treat someone in such a way, he obviously was not happy within himself. I had finally freed myself from the umbrella of emotional pain he had inflicted onto me. Now I had to dive deep and face all the other conditioning that stemmed from it, I was glad that I had finally got to the root cause. The good thing was that after this, I started to choose happiness and kindness no matter what, I was satisfied I did not feel the need to fight or argue with people anymore. Something changed in me, I could not hurt people anymore, not now I was healing myself. The thought of inflicting pain physical or emotional, onto someone else after all the pain I had felt in my life, even just the thought made me feel sick. How could I hurt another, especially as I know how it feels to be hurt, no one deserves to be put down, walked over, beaten, abused, or hurt, I never deserved it and neither does anyone else. I started to realise that most times it is the people who have never experienced love or, are so unhappy and in pain on the inside, a way to express themselves is to deliver that pain onto others, maybe subconsciously thinking it passes it onto the recipient.

<u>Changes</u>

I began to change my behaviours by observing any anger or negative thoughts that would automatically arise. I would observe it and then change them by trying to find the positive in the situation. This was all with the aim of changing my thought process into a more positive automatic response to situations. This is hard to achieve and takes constant re-evaluation and reflection. I failed a lot, but I never let any fails or loss get me down for long. Instead, I would consciously decide to learn from them, to do better in the future. When you repeat pattern's, you will recognise growth by how quickly you can identify something not being good for you, compared to before. Real growth is recognising things more prematurely and adjusting your life situation, using the tools and lessons you have learnt in the past. I was trying to improve myself and my life situation, but there were many more lessons until I would reach my better self. I was still poor, making money the only way I knew how, thieving from shops and selling it on, or selling drugs. Having a low economic status can make things a lot harder, I wanted to be better, but my environment seemed to hinder my progress.

My well-being, confidence and emotional state had significantly improved, I would not let others walk over me, I stopped talking to anyone I thought brought anything negative into my life, I had a power I had never felt before. When I was 17, I was still getting into trouble, facing court with a possible sentence of 18months. I was given the option to either do 8 months inside, or, to take part in a final attempt of rehabilitation and conform to a 18month ISSP order, (intense supervision surveillance programme). This consisted of 3 months on tag, (house arrest), concurrent with 6 months of daily meetings and community service. At first, my thoughts were to go to jail, to get it over and done with. Then in the last second before entering the court room I asked my solicitor to try for ISSP, and that is what I received. I do not know why I asked her to keep me out of jail, it was a feeling I had inside, I guess it was not meant to be at this time.

Starting this process and journey of self-healing and empowerment, I became determined, I was still sad at times, it was on and off. The difference for me was that I would consciously try to overcome the negativity, were as before I would let it consume me. It was normal for me to feel sad and negative; I had been let down continuously and negatively emotionally influenced by family, friends, and societal institutions from a young age.

First love given - A love hidden

After getting sentenced I met a girl whilst doing community service and we developed a platonic and sexual friendship. I met a girl through her who after time I considered a friend, she introduced me to her friend who was Kellise, the girl from my unit in the young offender's centre. I was not sure if she was okay with me, considering what had happened before when they jumped me. I explained what had happened to my friend, but she said that Kellise said that it did not matter, it was all in the past. We all started hanging out and developed a close bond. I remember one-night Kellise told me she had a crush on me, she was subtle and guarded but wanted me to know. I could not believe it, she was stunning, I thought she was attractive of course, she was beautiful and so was her soul. It was unexpected for me and at that point I did not know how to show emotion well. I tried to act cool, made it look like I did not care too much, but on the inside my belly was doing backflips. My life up to this point had taught me not to show too much love, kindness, affection, or emotion because it will only get me hurt, so I never told her how I felt.

One night, Kell asked me to come to London, me, Kell's boyfriend Dan, Alfie, a guy she classed as her brother, and Kell was up the flat in Woolwich. We were having a drink, doing some MDMA, and smoking weed. Me and Kell were in the bedroom sitting on the bed, she was by the wall, and I was sitting on the edge. I knew I wanted to kiss her, but I felt shy, regardless I said to myself. 'Frankie, she has already said she is crushing on you, she obviously likes you, just do it.' I leant over the bed went up to her face and started kissing her, I guess we both really wanted it because we did not stop, the next thing I knew she had pulled her trousers off. I chuckled, we started kissing again and I was playing with her, then suddenly the door swung open, it was Alfie, we jumped up and stopped.

That was the beginning of me and Kellise, our situationship got deeper as time went on. I kissed her, made love to her, we were together. She

27

would put in the effort and travel miles to spend time with me, when we made love, it was the best thing ever, she was never selfish, always wanting to satisfy me completely. It breaks my heart thinking about it, it was a time in my life where for the first time, someone was showing me pure love, affection, support. Somebody wanting me, wanting my time, my company, and my love.

We had various bumps on our path that we overcame together, but Kellise had my back until the end and she, exactly as she was, managed to light up my heart. With every smile, every joke, every kiss, it was complicated, but she loved me in her own way, and I loved her in mine. I still do, I will always have her back no matter what, I just wish I were more open with her and told her how much I cared. I feared love; I feared her love. I thought that if I let myself feel too deeply, or for her to know how I felt, then it would hurt ten times more if anything happened.

My love lost

The next life experience I endured, shook me up, broke my soul completely, internally killed me, and changed me in ways I never thought previously possible. It was a Saturday and Kellise had text me asking me to come down to London, as it was her friend Tyrell's birthday. I bought two ecstasy pills off my brother and some weed, then got my clothes together and went for a meal with my family before I would take the journey to London; it was also a family members birthday. I will never forget that there was a problem with the train, I do not know why, but I started getting hysterical. I had this feeling inside that I had to get to London no matter what, I felt anxious and in a panic. I had an argument with my mum and convinced her to drop me off at Upminster, so I could get a train from there to Kell's. I arrived in London and met up with Kell at King George the fifth station, I felt at peace when things started to fall into place. When I saw Kell we hugged, I showed her the pills and she laughed, I went to the shop and bought a 49p tropical juice and we took a pill each. We were both eighteen, feeling as adult as you like but also reckless and carefree like a child.

That evening I remember Kell telling me that she feels low sometimes and wonders about life. I knew exactly how she felt but I never wanted her to feel it, I gave her a kiss and hug and told her everything is going to work out and be ok. Back then I was not good at talking about personal things, I could not open myself up and talk deeply about situations or feelings, I did not know how. My whole life my family had told me to keep quiet, to sweep all my emotions and experiences under the carpet, so that is what I had learnt to do. Mine and Kell's relationship was somewhat complicated, it was not a normal set up. We were both 18, I was confused about being attracted to women, we knew and accepted it, but I was extremely shy and cautious of who I would let know. We were overshadowed by society, me on my order and she was running from hers. I was too embarrassed to live my truth, back then I cared too much of what people thought. When I met Kell she had a boyfriend, which is why I was shocked when she approached me and expressed that she had a crush on me, but ever since we kissed, we couldn't stop it. During this time, I had got into a relationship with a guy called Alfie, one night me and Kell spoke, we decided that we can both have boyfriends if we want, but we will be the only girls for each other. I knew she loved her boyfriend, he was a cool guy, I really liked him, I was so young and caught up that I never thought of how others may feel, and I am sorry for that. Even though I am grateful for all the times I spent with her, and the experiences we had together, how close we got, the love and affection shared.

It was Tyrell's birthday, Kellise's friend, that night we went over to his house, we were all drinking and smoking, at one point I remember being in the room alone with Kell, naked, laying on top of each other, kissing. I had not seen her for a couple of weeks, she looked up at me and asked me if I had missed her, I was honest and said of course I did. I will never forget her smile after, her face lit up, she was happy that I had missed her, it made my heart melt. In my mind I love her so much and I always missed her company, but I never felt brave enough to express it to her. The fact that she did not know, or should I say, that I never made sure she knew from my words and actions, breaks my heart. Especially as she was the one person who treated me in ways, where she deserved all the love I held inside. My strongest excuse was that my life experiences had taught me to not express feelings too much, this excuse would not last long.

The following day, we went back to the flat in Woolwich, Kell borrowed me some clothes, then cooked for me and Dan. We all smoked and chilled until her friend Rosie came. Rosie had bought a bottle of Jack Daniels whiskey with the intention of catching a wave. Since me and Kell took pills and drank the night before last, we were not fussed, but Kell did not want to let her friend down. Rosie wanted to do some cocaine, Kell and Dan asked around to try and get her some. Kell finally found one boy called Debo who could get it, we knew him through a mutual friend. When we got it, Rosie and Kell took the coke and I stuck to the drink and weed. I was convinced that if I sniffed coke then I would have a seizure, and I did not want that to happen, I could have a seizure without taking cocaine, so why would I take something that would more likely bring it on. We messed around that night, walking the streets, drinking, laughing together. We ended up at a chicken shop, Rosie offered to buy us chicken and chips, we all ate it, then went to a bus stop where we waited for Rosie's bus for her. Me and Kell jumped on our bus, she turned to me whilst we were sitting down and asked, "where shall we go, Tyrell's or Dan's?" I replied saying, "it's up to you I don't mind." I think she could see I was tired since I was not buzzing, she said let's go back to the flat. Everything in life is always one decision from being this or being that. You cannot burden yourself worrying about making the wrong choice. This will cause anxiety, you must make a choice and have faith that what is meant to be, will be.

We arrived at Dan's flat, Kell made up the sofa for me, made me a cup of tea and put the film Beauty Shop 2 on. She knew I could not fall asleep without a film playing, she then went into the bedroom and went to sleep. I fell asleep shortly after, then suddenly I got woken out of my sleep by a loud noise, "BANG, BANG, BANG!!! Kellise Indigo Todd, we know you are in there." I got up off the sofa to go and have a look, but the lack of sleep must have affected my epilepsy because my legs kept giving way and I was falling over. The people banging on the door was the police, when Dan saw me falling over, he told me to go and sit down. I got myself together, woke up properly, took my medication, so I calmed down, then stood up and asked what was going on. I got greeted with silence, the police would hardly look at me, let alone talk to me, they were talking at us, being intimidating with their mannerisms. They were talking in an aggressive belittling manner towards Dan, they were not acting how they should under oath, you could see the power had gone to their heads. They would look in stupid places, in cupboards, under the sofa, out back, even I did not know where Kell could have been at this point.

Dan knows how to deal with the police, as do I, if you become rude or aggressive back, no matter how they are acting towards you, it will be you who is getting arrested. Dan was talking to them in a calm and respectful way so they could not arrest him, as they would have no reason to. Dan politely asked them, "I have allowed you to check my house, now will you please leave?" As they were finished and about to leave, one officer started tugging on this door that was inside the flat by the entrance. It would not open, the officers started asking Dan for the key that opens it. Dan continued to tell them that he does not have the key, the landlord does, and that the door is locked from the inside. The officer persisted and kept on tugging at the door, harder and harder, it would

31

move a little until the last tug, then Kellise fell out of the cupboard. The two officers grabbed Kell as quick as they could, even though she never tried to run, I guess they did not give her the chance. I could hear them shout at her, that they are going to lock her up for the longest time.

Dan insisted that the officers let her get herself together, she went into the bathroom, so I followed straight away. She sat on the toilet and peed, I grabbed her face and told her not to worry, that we will get her address and write to her, that everything will be okay. I remember her eyes could not look at me, she looked worried and scared, it looked like a million thoughts were rushing through her mind at once. She left the bathroom and took about three steps until she was in the bedroom. We were in a flat on the seventeenth floor of a tower block, I thought Kell was going to go and get dressed. When she left the toilet the two officers were on each side of the bedroom door, Dan was standing in the hall next to the door. After Kell went in the room, I stopped for a second next to Dan and looked at the officer and asked. "So, what do you actually want her for?" He did not answer me, he just chuckled under his breath. Straight after I had asked him, Dan ran into the bedroom, and I followed. Me and Dan were looking out of the window, we could see Kell on the ground, looking up at us.

Dan screamed in pain and started punching the officers, I ran out of the flat into the lift. It had not processed in my mind, except when I was inside the lift, it was taking so long. That is when I started to feel it, I pressed the ground floor button continuously, erratically. I finally reached the ground floor and ran for the emergency exit, but when I reached it, it was locked, I ran to the next one but that was also locked. I ran to the main entrance, out of the door, jumped up a metre-high wall, I do not even know how. I ran straight over to Kell. I started to slap her in the face, shouting her name, saying "Kell its Frankie, come on, wake up, please Kell wake up! You're okay, Kell, please!" I started to do CPR, I would do compressions on her chest, then breathe into her mouth. When I did, I could feel my breath bounce off her chest, back into my mouth. Her lungs could not receive any oxygen from me, I do not know if they were punctured. I looked down at her eyes, they were open, but you could see she was empty, she had gone.

My tears fell like raindrops of a thunderstorm, my heart felt like it had stopped beating just like hers. It felt ripped apart, all I could do was lay there with her, crying, hugging her, and kissing her forehead. Before I knew it about six police officers had picked me up and chucked me down onto the floor, I was screaming and crying, they were all using their strength to pin me down. I do not know what happened, but something switched in my brain, I stopped struggling, I laid still, I stated that I am calm, and acted so, I sat there and pleaded in a calm way. I told them that I am okay, I will not fight, I wanted to stay with Kellise. The ambulance had arrived, so I pleaded for them to let me sit there and watch the paramedics do their job, I did not want to leave her. The police agreed to let me stay, within five minutes I had two female officers who kept trying to get into my space, putting blankets on me, and kept telling me I was in shock. I had to tell them, "Leave me alone, you guys just killed her, stop telling me how I feel, I just want to be here for her, I want you to leave me alone," they insisted that they could not do that.

I watched the paramedics when they announced her dead, I asked if I could go and give her one last kiss, to say goodbye, the officers said that it would be too traumatising for me. I had to make them know again, "this is my life, I can decide what I can handle, I understand your concern but please let me say goodbye," I was not rude, I was assertive, I knew that if I were rude, they would not let me. I had convinced them to let me go and say goodbye. I laid beside her, crying continuously, I stroked her face and kissed her forehead, I closed her eyes, I covered her with the blanket and walked away crying.

Dan had been taken away by the police, I rang Rosie as she was the only friend of Kell's that I knew well at the time, and we had just left her hours before. On the phone I was crying, I told her that Kell was dead, she could not believe it, she was on her way. I sat in the doorway with my head in my hands, I could not stop crying, I had no thoughts in my mind, all I could feel was pure pain and confusion, my whole being had been torn apart, I did not even know myself at that moment. Rosie arrived crying as much as me, the police wanted to tell Kellise's mother what had happened, but I said I did not want them too. Especially since it was the actions of their own that led to this outcome, that led to Kell's death. I rang her mum, I did not want to say what had happened over the phone, it was too delicate. I wanted to tell her face to face, I just stated that I needed to talk to her and that I will be coming over shortly. All I wanted to do was tell her mum what had happened, I had no money, no phone, and the police would not let me back into the flat to get my belongings. I had nothing but one sock on, ripped pyjama bottoms and a top on. The police kept telling me that I had to make a statement, they made it seem like I had no choice, but I did not care. I told them no many times, I did not want to in that moment, they kept insisting, then they said if I make a statement, they will drive me to Kell's mums house, using the one thing I wanted against me.

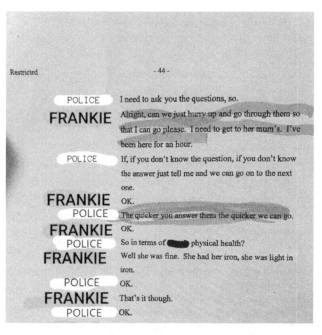

Restricted   - 44 -

POLICE   I need to ask you the questions, so.

FRANKIE   Alright, can we just hurry up and go through them so that I can go please. I need to get to her mum's. I've been here for an hour.

POLICE   If, if you don't know the question, if you don't know the answer just tell me and we can go on to the next one.

FRANKIE   OK.

POLICE   The quicker you answer them the quicker we can go.

FRANKIE   OK.

POLICE   So in terms of ▓▓▓ physical health?

FRANKIE   Well she was fine. She had her iron, she was light in iron.

POLICE   OK.

FRANKIE   That's it though.

POLICE   OK.

    I decided to make a statement as they agreed to take me to Kell's mums house straight after, they did not offer me a solicitor or any support. I was in shock, all I wanted was to get to Kell's mum, I had no access to my money or phone. I gave the police my account on what happened. They tried to question me more about little details, even when I said I just wanted to go, they pressured me by saying the quicker you answer the questions the quicker you can leave.

    When I got out of the station, they finally gave me a ride to her mother's house, I went up to the front door with my clothes still ripped, wearing one sock, I had no shoes. As soon as me and Kell's mum saw each other, we burst into tears, the police had already told her what had happened, she invited me and Rosie inside. After this day, I was shattered, but I never once thought about myself. I done what in my mind, I thought Kell would have wanted to do if she was there. I stayed and comforted her mum anyway I knew how; it broke my heart the pain she was feeling, I wish I could have taken it away. I tried to be there for her sister even when she and her mum argued, I tried to make her know she was not alone. I done my best to be a support for her friends and family, I do not

34

know how they perceived it, but I hope at times they appreciated it and knew my intentions were good. The time I would get to myself, I would go to the park, drink desperados, smoke weed and cry. I was not good at showing my emotions to other people.

Home but not healed

Being back at my mums, it felt like the whole experience was a world away. My brain forced amnesia onto itself, I could not remember anything, my past was mentally wiped out. Usually, I have a very photographic, imaginative mind, I can see memories as movies playing in my head, but after this incident that ability got wiped out. I think it was too painful to face, so my mind protected itself by blocking everything. At times I thought I was going crazy, I would have dreams that I was chasing Kell and that she would die, when I would wake up, I would think it was all a dream and that she was still alive. Until someone would remind me that it did happen in real life, and then I would have to deal with it over and over again. It was a very confusing time for me, I could not remember anything, things that were not even related to the incident. I did not know what was real and what was not, I had to keep being reminded of what I went through. I remember our mutual friend Nina was coming out of jail, she was locked up when Kell died. I intended to be there for her, it took her a while to see me when she came out. I understood though, it was a hard thing to face. When we did meet up, I brought her up to Southend where I lived with my mum. We went to chill at a girl's house called Roxy, this is when my memory came flooding back.

I asked Nina to tell me, how me and Kell met, as she was there. When she was telling me, I was trying my hardest to get the images in my mind, but all I could retrieve were flicks of images. That night I had a dream about Kell, I cannot remember what, but I do remember the next day all my memories came back. They filled my mind like a flood, it was intense. I remember sitting on top of a building, crying, until a lady saw me and told me to get down off her property. I could have faced the memories in a better way, but the pain was so intense, I was only eighteen. I turned to what I knew best, alcohol and drugs, to numb the pain, partying with people that I would never now consider true friends. I would get triggers from songs, people on the street, random things. Eyes filling up, whilst

I would try and blink the tears away, heart extremely heavy, drowning. I had panic attacks often, where my breathing would go funny, I would get dizzy, feeling like my whole world was crushing around me. I cannot tell you, how many times a day my heart would sink into the pit of my stomach, only I knew. I was a master at hiding my emotions, I thought it to be the safest thing, oh how I was wrong. I would tell people that I was okay, but really, I was breaking a little more inside.

Hugs were non-existent, never to be seen or felt, maybe because I acted like I did not need it, I guess I just wanted someone to force me to surrender and accept help or a hug. It never happened, no one offered me support or emotional support. The police had lied in their report saying they told me to enter the room with Kellise, to take some of the blame away from themselves. After this I started to get some backlash and blame from some of Kell's friends and family, saying it was my fault that she had died. I never felt any guilt because I knew that Kell knew the truth. I did everything in that situation that I could have, I had her back when nobody else could, and I know she would forever be grateful. It was an extremely long journey of healing since this incident, I remember I started talking to a guy, one day I went to his house to chill, after some months of getting to know each other. I remember bursting into tears on his bed, saying that it is going to take someone special to love me, to save me. It was not until later in life that I realised, the person to love and save me, was me.

I still have not fully recovered from what happened and sometimes I still cry. I feel Kell here in spirit, achieving the impossible together, every change I make, I make it through motivation of not wanting individuals, especially children, feeling the internal pain we have both once felt. Every breath I take, we take together, every change I make, we make together, with purpose, with intention of positive change.

At first, I blocked what happened, then I tried to cover and numb it by smoking weed, doing drugs, drinking, and partying with toxic people. When I stopped chilling with Roxy and people from Southend, and tried to stick with myself, I still felt broken. I gained friendships from Kell's close ones and love was felt from her nearest, but the way the friendship started maybe it was never meant to last. If people are already negative about you, they will just wait for you to fail. Instead of being understanding because they love you, friendships based on rocky grounds will always crumble.

A try for a change

As years passed, I still felt broken but tried to keep pushing forward, actively being more positive, being kinder to others and to myself, trying to think of solutions instead of concentrating on problems. I wanted to be happy, I wanted others to be happy, the thought of hurting someone made me feel sick. Hurting someone else felt like I was hurting myself, it was time for the pain to stop. The pain still creeps through sometimes, but because of the work I have done on my inner self, I am too powerful for it to last or to have major effects on my life, like fear and pain once had. I wanted to help people, relieve themselves of their negative state of mind, I know we can get out of it, because I have.

I had an urge to learn more about psychology, so that I could get a better understanding of the tools that are out there, to help me understand my mind, train it to be more positive, to be in control of it. Rather than the mind controlling me, and how to address the experiences that had created internal issues. There are so many theories to explore, not just the internal journey I think we all should take. Maybe different approaches would help others as well. My plan was to gain knowledge, to travel the world, to help and spread the word.

My friends mum suggested that I study social studies as it has some psychology within it, I looked online, I found that south Essex college had an available funded social studies course, so I applied for an interview. The day of my college interview I was feeling a bit low, allowing old emotions in, maybe because I was nervous, it began to feel like everything was going against me. I could not find my buss pass anywhere, I was getting stressed out, crying, I picked up my mums Yankee candle and smashed it on the table, obviously not a good outlet of anger. I ended up slicing my finger, blood pouring out, tears on my face, then I looked at myself in the mirror and thought 'what the fuck, you need to sort it out.' I put plasters on my hand, I had an argument with my mum about driving me to the college as she did not want too. I felt like not going, thinking maybe it is not meant to be, or maybe I am not ready. We started driving to the college, we were passing my friend's house, so I asked my mum to stop. I knocked but no answer, I got in the car and said, "fuck it, I'll just go to the interview." I got myself together as we pulled up, I apologised to my mum, I felt like an idiot now. I used to lash out at my mum from pain of feeling like she did not love me, I had to stop as I would learn the most important love is the love you have for yourself. Her love never got shown in the way I expected it to be, or the way I show love, that is why it is good to not expect things as everyone has their own issues, baggage, and ways of doing things. It does not mean they do not love you, maybe they do not know how, but in the same breath it is not easy to not expect, especially if you give out so much. If they are your parents but they are not willing to accept responsibility and consciously put effort in to change and give back your bare minimum. You do not have to give them your space and time, it can be hard but sometimes necessary.

As I walked up to the entrance, I could see myself in my mind walking out smiling, waving my ID badge in my hand, with a cheeky grin on my face. I am a dreamer, I did not have the correct qualifications to even get on the course, I only had a D in English and Maths GCSE, which is a high school qualification, but I still went to the interview. The interviewer asked me why I wanted to be on the course, I remember explaining that I wanted to gain more knowledge in psychology, sociology, and then travel. Another teacher joined him, and they insisted that they did not think that it was the course for me, as it was an access to Higher Education course, they explained that it meant it would prepare me for going to university the following year.

I sat back and remembered a dream before my nan and Kell died. Studying GCSE psychology, then working my way up to get a university degree, I remembered I would speak about it with Jane, my teacher I met through youth offending programmes. My nan and Kell died halfway through my GCSE psychology course, I dropped out as I was not in the right state of mind to complete it, it was a dream that I thought had been lost. In that moment, I insisted right back to them that the course was perfect for me and that I knew I was exactly where I was supposed to be. I explained how I wanted to go to university and then I told them about my nan and Kell dying. I expressed to them that I was there for a reason, I knew that this was the path I had to follow, I knew I was

39

supposed to move forward within this. They said at first that they will let me do a test, to see if I was smart enough, they both went into a room then came out smiling. They stated that because of my determination and willingness to get on the course, they had decided to enrol me without having to take a test, they told me to go and sort out the paperwork, get my ID and that they will see me when term starts. I walked away and filed the paperwork, went to get my ID, with this smile that would not budge, this feeling of wholeness inside, of accomplishment. I was ready, I was ready to change to develop into my future, being more every day. Learning from every prior mistake, always pushing forward no matter how many times I might slip, or trip, I will always move forward. I urge this courage in everyone, I urge you to be warriors of your own soul, of your own actions, within your own lives.

Education

The Higher Education course introduced me to new friendships that would offer me laughter, support, and happy memories. I felt like I had faced something, like I had learnt from my past mistakes, it was time to move into the next stage of my life. I was educating myself, developing thinking strategies, that were helping me progress within my life. Most importantly I was believing in myself, gradually getting more and more confident. Situations kept fitting into place, I was motivated, everything that had happened previously in my life, made me unbreakable. I now know, undoubtably that I will never push away or ruin any good thing that comes into my life. I feel worthy now, if at times I think I am not, I know that is not true, I know it is negativity trying to hold me down. Within the access to higher education social studies course, we learnt about sociology and psychology and research methods. We also were preparing for university. I was not too bothered if I did not make it into uni, I would have still used the knowledge I had learned to travel and help people. My tutor told me if I ever want to make real change, it would be better for me to have the credentials behind me. To give individuals a real incentive to listen and understand the information I will be expressing. To allow myself to add worldly knowledge above my own experiences.

I decided to pick the University of Westminster in London, it is near parliament and across the world Westminster is known, the University holds its own credits, and I knew I wanted to hold mine. I had to write a personal statement, I did not want to follow a template, I wanted it to be completely unique, written in a way where the reader would not want to say no. It was proving hard until one night, it all spilled out of my mind, I kept on writing, it would not stop. We prepared for interviews and carried on with our usual classes at college.

Whilst at college one day my dad rang me, I went into the hall to speak to him. He had explained that the doctor said to him, if he did not stop drinking alcohol and does not go on a special diet, the alcohol could kill him. He told me since then he had been four months sober. I told him how proud I was, how hard I knew it must have been, considering he had been drinking from a young age. He was happy I had said this, he felt good within himself, it made me want to share my good news too. I told him that I was at college and working towards going to university. He told me to not bother, that I was not bright enough for university, saying a degree does not mean shit anyway, he told me that I might as well wipe my arse with it after.

I did not retaliate out of anger, like I would have when I was younger, I healed myself to the point that I could deal with it like this. I simply said, "dad can I say something to you please?" To which he replied, "of course." I reminded him that when he was telling me about his achievements, I told him I was proud and tried to motivate him to do better. He said, "yes," then I said, "as a parent you should have done that to me, but instead you say I'm not bright enough, even if you didn't think I could, you should have at least supported me." I think he learnt something from that conversation even though he never said, as every time from then on, he would say he was proud, and that he hopes my studying is going well.

I asked my mum to come to the university open day with me, I wanted her to experience it as much as me. We looked around, went to the lectures that explained about the course, it looked real posh compared to what we were used too. We went to student halls in Wembley, I remember smiling and saying, "take a good look mum, I'm gonna be living here next year." She told me to not get my hopes up as I still needed to be accepted. My family can be so doubtful, but I knew you can only succeed if you believe in yourself. I stopped her and insisted that I cannot have that negative energy, I asked her to say that I will be going to Westminster university and living here in Wembley, I asked her to believe it, she laughed but she said it.

Months had passed, me and my class did not know when, or if, we would get acceptance letters. I remember it was my 20th birthday, 17/12/2013, my friend Rumi and I were in my room, she was doing my hair for me, I had my laptop in front of me and opened my emails. I started screaming, "mum, mum, mum!!!" I screamed so loud, continuously, I could not believe it, she ran in my room with a worried look saying, "what's wrong?" I replied saying, "I've been accepted at Westminster, I've actually been accepted, no interview, I just have to get 35 at merit or distinction since it was a conditional offer!" I was beaming with pride, I was so happy, I felt like my life was starting to take off into a more positive direction.

I finished college with 42 merits, 9 distinctions and 9 passes, I surpassed every expectation and had more than enough qualifications to enter Westminster, I felt so proud of myself. I had come from someone who constantly got in trouble with the police, society and always bunked off school. I was locked in a police cell for one of my GCSE exams, I had been youth-jail. I had a lot of traumas to deal with and yet I still became a student at the University of Westminster, I felt like I could achieve anything. I defeated all odds, any circumstance that in the beginning went against me, ended up being the thing that was strengthening me. I broke through my environment and my conditioning, I had found my power, myself, and now in my mind the possibilities for me are limitless. Of course, negativity can seep through, you must keep reminding yourself that you deserve better, that you are better.

You should never let another person, situation, society, or yourself, convince you that you cannot achieve. Believe in yourself, you and your thinking are your only limit. If you let external circumstances get into your mind and convince you it is impossible, it will be. Their impossible is your possibility, so dream big, dream limitless. Follow your passions, what drives you, the things you love, life is too short not to, and why shouldn't you, why should you only do what others want of you? Once you know where you want to be, and that you believe you can get there, even if you do not know how, your motivation and determination will make it happen, one way or another, just do not give up. The following years were filled with ups and downs, but my mentality was constantly growing, so the downs did not seem so bad, more like lessons and progression. I had to attend court for Kellise's death in my first year of uni, there ended up being an investigation into the police because of the nature of her death. I delivered some justice, she would have been proud, I stood there as a strong woman who got herself out of the pit, not a broken, young, easily manipulated, eighteen-year-old girl anymore.

The most important thing with situations in life either sad or happy, is that we ultimately choose how we react, consciously or unconsciously, we decide our happiness. The best way is to allow it to be, try to stay positive. Allow and understand the emotion, be sad, what happened was a sad thing, it is okay to feel that, but do not let it consume you, and effect your life. Let the feeling pass and then carry on moving forward. Doing this, the pain slowly gets weaker and weaker, while your understanding and acceptance gets stronger and stronger. If you refuse to allow yourself to try, you will always be stuck in the same position, continuously living similar situations, with different people and circumstances.

Even at times, if you feel like you have failed, you can see the positive within. As it has given you the chance to find a different or better opportunity, until you no longer feel like things fail. Instead seeing them as signs and lessons, directing you to becoming more conscious, more aware, and more prepared to fulfil your dreams. All the experiences that happen in your life, bring vital lessons with them, no matter how painful they may be, they can allow room for internal wisdom and growth. If you take your ego out of the equation, you can reflect and learn from your mistakes and behaviours, this will enable you to do better in the future. If you continue this journey of growth and try to do better quicker, or right away every time, then you are on the right path, no one is perfect but taking responsibility is key to progress.

Even after learning so much and transcending for the better, I still had hard experiences to overcome. The difference was I had learnt not to be consumed by it. Instead, I developed more understanding, empathetic perspectives, which enabled me to not only help myself, but also help others.

I accepted a long time ago that I will have to lead by example, that I cannot expect the same treatment back, if I do, I will set myself up to be disappointed. I want to lead by example and let my light shine, for me, because I belong there, I want to be surrounded by a pure energy. When you do not expect things, if it happens it's a bonus, if it doesn't your good regardless. I learnt that sometimes we need to be strong, strong in our understanding and kindness. I learnt this from hard lessons.

I was at a family members house one day, making enchiladas for dinner. His fiancé was upstairs, we were downstairs in the kitchen. Harry thought he heard his fiancé kick his dog; they were having an argument of sorts. He shouted up "don't you dare kick my fucking dog." I said to Harry, "you need to calm down Lilly is getting scared, you really scared her the other day when you got angry." He saw red, started strangling me, saying he wishes I was dead; he was roughing me up punching me, we were wrestling through the house. I managed to shut him out of the front door. I could hear the door thumping like it was going to come off its hinges. I knew I had to open it, it was his house, I flicked the switch to open the door. He bulldozed in like a bull in a china shop, I remember him grabbing me up, he dashed me and my bike out of the house onto the ground. His fiancé was begging me not to ring the police because she didn't want them taking her child. I was on the floor of the street crying my eyes out, I got myself up and jumped on my bike, I made my way to the train station to go to my friend's house. I arrived at my friend's house, but she wasn't in, my mum was ringing me. The first thing she said was, "what did you do to make him do that?" Like anything I could have done would have warranted that attack.

I could have walked away from my family then, after all these years, I was trying to better myself and they still treated me like that. I didn't, I decided to help, I had a different perspective, maybe because I know what pain can do to people. I said to my mum one day soon after, we need to talk to Harry, he has too much pain inside, that is why he can do that to me. I said, "you should never have chosen your husband over your sixteen-year-old son, you should never have made Harry leave his house and let the husband who beat the shit out of him stay." That's why he has internal pain, I told my mum that she needed to say sorry. I set up a meal with my mum and my brother, and we went and spoke. She apologised to Harry and said she was wrong, she took responsibility for her actions and tried to make amends. This big strong boy sat there and cried, he shed his tears and got a hug off the woman he loved the most, the woman who just helped heal him of his pain. I told him how it feels that he puts his hands on me, and said he cannot do that to me, it is not right. He apologised and we hugged.

After that day Harry became a changed man, no longer painful, no longer in pain. Compassion and understanding can go a long way, sometimes we need to be brave, sometimes we need to lead by example!

Achievements

Aged 21 and ready to start a new year, ready to do everything I had ever wanted to. I made new friends at university who I still talk to now, I went on four holidays. I went to Mexico by myself, I was finished with waiting around for people, I was ready to do what I wanted to do. I was enjoying my own company, I found love and strength in being alone. I would always meet people regardless; in Mexico I was not even there for two hours, and I had met people and had been invited to dinner. I made friends from Canada, from England and from Paris. I was invited to Paris, the woman let me stay at her place and showed me around, it was welcoming, humbling, and amazing. I went to four festivals, the first time I had ever experienced them, met life-long friends, I met people everywhere and we shared great moments together. I continued this path of traveling, even if alone, I decided to empower myself. I cut off friends who I felt treated me less than the bare minimum I give out, with regards to respect and effort and even quality of friendship. I got invited to Italy, by my friend that I met at uni, she is from Italy. I met her family and spent a week in the south of Italy with her sister, cousin, and friends. Even though we did not speak the same language it was not a barrier, we all got on well and enjoyed each-others company. I studied hard and finally graduated university in 2017, with a second-class Honours Degree in Psychology. I honestly believe that if I can do it, anyone can, and a big part of my achievements, was a result from the internal journey I took on bettering myself, believing in myself, loving myself, self-empowerment, and growth. This internal journey healed the parts of myself that were broken, working on my flaws and the automatic negativity, it allowed me to find my strength, my power. Positivity is key!

Beliefs

I have certain beliefs that I stand by due to my experiences and learnt lessons, some would seem obvious but somehow have been lost to many. I believe this as I had lost them myself, but once regained the fruits can be so sweet. I hope and have faith that these can benefit you in some way, within your own lives, if you decide to live with these beliefs.

Honesty

Firstly, it is my belief that we should live in truth, this can make life clearer for yourself and for others. I know lying is a hard habit to unlearn but if you do not want someone to know something, you are completely entitled to stay quiet. You do not have to tell anyone anything if you do not want to, but you also do not have to lie. What if a lie can save a life? Yes, sometimes a lie could save a life, is being honest more important than someone's life? I do not believe so, I believe we must be aware when responding to situations and if we are in one like this then yes, a conscious decision to lie will not be a bad thing. Although this is true, I believe we must live in honesty as much as possible. We must be honest with ourselves, with our wants, our likes, our dislikes, and we must be honest with others. Once you get into the habit of lying, your life turns into a lie itself, how can you live your truth if you cannot be honest with yourself? Not living your truth can create an incongruence, an emotional and psychological disturbance that can form itself as depression or anxiety and elevated stress with defensive behaviours. Being honest with yourself and with others will not solve all your problems, but it will mean you have one less problem to worry about.

Being honest with others can only work if you are honest with yourself, you must look at yourself and really ask and answer, some deep truths, about actions, reactions, you must take responsibility for all the bad parts of yourself as well as the good. Many people do not like to admit when they do bad things, or treat people badly, they would rather portray themselves as someone better than that. No one is perfect, if you make a mistake or do something wrong, own it, try to learn from it and make amends. If you are honest with yourself and others, learn from all your mistakes and consciously try to do better. Then you will continuously grow, and you will truly be able to create the life you dream about.

Stripping yourself of your negative aspects and allowing emotions and experiences in, letting yourself feel them fully but at the same time allowing it to pass, this will create a content peace within, where you know that even when you are not good, you are good! I know it is hard admitting some mistakes, there are things you may be ashamed to admit, trust me I know. No matter how much you want to deny or resist it, the only way to heal is to face it, to be honest with it, to forgive the situation, forgive yourself, and move on. Be strong, face whatever it is and allow yourself to move on into a better future without negative patterns repeating themselves, break the chain!

Taking Responsibility

I t is important to take responsibility for your actions in any given situation. You may have felt that something caused you to react in a certain way. But in reality, you still allowed yourself to react in that way, it does not make it right, own it, forgive yourself, do better. My dad died never taking responsibility for his actions, he always said that it was my mum's fault that things turned out the way they did, because she took us out of London. The funny thing is that, if he did not drink so much alcohol, psychologically abuse her, beat her and my brother, then we could have all stayed as a family, but he never owned it and he died, lonely and sad. It is sad that all of this could have been resolved a long time ago, if people were not so stubborn and took responsibility for their actions, try to make amends and do better. People find it hard to truly take responsibility, individuals are more likely to say, yes, they behaved in a certain way, but it was because something or someone made them react in that way. We are not responsible for what happens to us, we are only responsible for how we respond. If you always put the blame on things that make you react, you will never be able to learn or do better, because you will never think that you are in the wrong. Even if you did not do anything wrong for something to happen, you are still in control of how you respond. You must take responsibility for your actions, regardless of how they come about. When you take responsibility, you can genuinely learn and grow to do differently or not allow whatever bothers you, to bother you anymore. We all must remember; we have no control over what happens to us or how people act. We only have control over our response and perception.

When you start to take responsibility for your own actions, you take hold of your power over your life. Instead of letting the behaviours, words and actions of others dominate your life. Letting things push doubt, intimidation, fear, anger, lack of confidence and a low self-esteem into your life. Take control over your own thinking, watch what your mind is saying, you do not have to agree, if mostly negative, then interrupt with a positive alternative. Try not to look at your thoughts through a conditioned mind, thoughts are influenced by many factors, do not let your mind control you. Anger for example, try not to give a person or a situation the satisfaction of reacting with aggression, see it, recognise it, and move on.

Look at nature for example, grass will not say to itself, "oh I am not good enough to grow today," it grows, effortlessly, it is purely being, that is what we can achieve, allow things and yourself to be. Think positive things about yourself like you are worthy, strong, kind, lovable, a smart human being and that your opinion is just as valid as any other person. Take responsibility of your own actions, your own thinking, the good and the bad, learn from it, do better, grow, and watch your life transform. Then watch yourself become strong enough to help others transform and move forward into a better life together. Strong people lift others up, they do not put them down.

Trust

My third belief is to trust. To not let any experience convince you to be untrusting, trust until they give you a reason not to, this could be as simple as the vibes you feel. I like to use this analogy; imagine your phone battery, you can see it fully charged on 100%, imagine this being the trust you have for anyone who enters your life or who is there, it should always start at 100%. Then their actions and behaviours determine whether it stays at 100, if they lie, disrespect you, hurt you physically or psychologically. If they ignore you or treat you less than you deserve, and less than the bare minimum you give out, then let that percentage fall. If it falls below, for me its 70%, then cut them out of your life and know you were true, you done your best and you cannot help everyone, when you are a good person, you do not lose people, they lose you.

I refuse to be disrespected and treated with negative behaviours. I consciously make sure I do not treat people as such, I refuse to settle for anything less than I deserve. I understand that it is hard to trust people, when you have had so many experiences where people have broken your trust, even parents can be the culprits. Negative conditioning from life experiences can feel strong, your mind can create automatic negative thoughts. Try to over-ride this and turn it into a positive instead, having power over your thoughts is how you have power over your life. You should try to analyse your mind and ask, is this person or situation negative or is it more so the way I am looking at it. If there is no real reason to dis-trust someone or a situation, then don't. Do not let your past or social conditioning take control over your present moment and stop you from trusting people. By not trusting you could potentially miss out on some amazing people and experiences. All because you are scared to trust, obviously be smart and assess everything, and go with your gut instinct, but do not let your mind be overrun by negative thoughts that hinder your life progress. Be strong, know your worth, know you can handle any hurt or betrayal and that you deserve happiness, trust, and loyalty.

Listening

My fourth belief is the immense importance of listening, I mean truly listening and trying to fully understand. Not to listen to respond but understand deeper, from their perspective as well as your own. Understanding the bigger picture as well as the tiny details, listening that requires your full attention and put's effort into one another, making everyone feel like they want to be heard. Listening is something most of us take for granted, a lot of people cannot help but interrupt someone whilst their talking, including myself, I slip up at times, it is a bad habit we have picked up but also one we can work on and eradicate. Anytime I interrupt someone when I should be listening to them, I apologise and ask them to carry on, this is how we grow, to be better. You have the right to state your opinion, but you should also allow others to get theirs out. Sometimes you will be first, sometimes it will be others, we all need to respect, understand, and listen to one another equally. We all live here together; we should see it as a good thing and lift each other up.

Truly listening can give you a deeper understanding of an individual's life, adapting and using this skill within your own life, can create others to want to listen and be more attentive to what you are saying. If individuals do not have this skill, then educate and lead by example, do not be a hypocrite.

All of these beliefs and behaviours, I feel to be beneficial to us as human beings. They may not be easy to carry out, but we must try to remind ourselves to be positive, to stay strong, to trust, believe, listen, and love. Sometimes we may forget, or the pressure and circumstances of our environment will take over, but once you are aware, even if you trip and fall back, you will always be able to pick yourself up again!

Everything has happened, and everything was to come

Kellise died in the beginning of 2012, at first all I had done was put negative toxic distractions, in front of the incident instead of facing it. It was too painful to face, but all of this was a part of my growth, even if I could not see it at the time. I started to replace toxic distractions with positive ones, these were helping me grow, helping me progress within my life and be happier, but the underlying pain was still there, I had not faced what had happened. I knew university was coming to an end, I knew I would have so much free time, it would be inevitable for me to finally, fully, face my past, whether I felt ready or not. I guess any time is the perfect time when you realise you want change. Before I had finished university, I had decided that when I graduate, I will go away by myself for three months. I wanted to heal myself and face my past fully, so I could move into the next stage of my life. I felt like I had progressed from being wrapped up in broken turmoil, to studying being hopeful and motivated. I felt it to be due to my realisation of worthiness and intent to help the world and myself. Now in my eyes, after gaining all the knowledge I had, it was time to heal, to retreat. I was ready to heal myself fully, to enable me to help others heal effectively, I want to be a founder of institutions, to educate and put systems in place that give people a better chance to become conscious, aware, and ready to live their lives abundantly. I did not know where I wanted to go, I had the opportunity to go anywhere in the world. My dad died and I had £6000 that he left me, plus some money from my student finance loan, so I had enough to go anywhere.

I knew that I wanted to go somewhere hot with beautiful, clear, turquoise water, waterfalls, beautiful nature, somewhere tropical, being in that kind of environment automatically makes me happy. Looking up at the blue sky, feeling the warm sun on my skin warming me up like a heater. To see the turquoise ocean fills me with so much joy, I would find myself randomly smiling or laughing, feeling so grateful that I am on that point of earth in that moment, in the middle of nature's finest. I believe self-healing is important, taking time out for yourself in an open space where you can think, reflect, forgive, move on, and learn. You must create a safe, open space for yourself, so you can dive within and face all the people, situations and experiences that have ever caused you pain. Things that make you feel weak, and experiences you cannot seem to shake out of your mind. Nature has natural healing abilities; you may be surprised how freeing and healing spending time in and with nature can be. When you take the time to think and self-reflect deeply, about each aspect, you find yourself getting to the root cause, all while gaining a fuller understanding from numerous perspectives involved.

The more you understand the less blame and anger you give to people or things, because you know their actions are governed by their own histories and biases. When you have found the root cause, accepted responsibility for all your actions against yourself and others, your consciousness gets raised and you become more aware of the situation. After this you begin operating from a higher more aware level of consciousness. You, yourself, will be able to offer multiple solutions to all past problems, and any future problems that may arise in your life, that is if you still view them as problems at that point. Self-healing is an active behaviour which will need continuous recognition, re-evaluation and daily motivation, every moment, especially when you can notice the negative thought patterns entering. After time it will become natural to be more positive, daily active self-healing and positive thinking will re-wire your brain.

When your brain runs mostly on automatic negative thoughts, if you are in the habit of thinking negatively, then the brain has created neural pathways of negative thinking that are extremely strong. When you inhibit these pathways by thinking of a positive before, or straight after the negative thoughts come, you begin to re-wire your brain. The more you think positive, the more power you give to the neural pathways associated with positive thinking. The neural pathways associated with negative thinking slowly but surely fizzle out. Whatever you give your energy and attention to, gets stronger, you decide if your life is positive or negative by what and how you think!

Try to never discredit yourself for how far you may have come on your journey, try not to compare yourself to others and their journey, you are special as so is your own path. You have no reason to feel lack or like you are not where you are supposed to be, embrace the process, embrace the moment you are in now, let it give you motivation and determination to get wherever you want to be. If you are on the path of self-reflection, healing, growth, and love, then you are winning. Self-healing is not for the weak of mind and of heart, you must be strong and brave, you must face your inner demons who are everything but good and nice.

You must be brutally honest with yourself, admit that something has gone wrong, with your thinking and behaviour or that someone or something has corrupted it. Maybe due to your environment from birth, from peer pressure and societal influences, but all of which you must face along with your fears, it is not easy to admit that you are wrong. When you do take responsibility, self-heal, reflect, learn, and grow. You end up becoming a better version of yourself, one of which you may not yet feel would be possible to exist. As you take your power back over yourself, you also take power back over your life and the possibilities become endless. Each of us are born with the power to do, not just to think, with capabilities to reach our full potential. The worldly environment of which each of us are born into, plus our society, family history, culture, religion, race, gender, class, economic status and any other stereotypes or oppressions we are born into, can affect our development psychologically and materialistically. It will either make it harder or easier, you do not choose what you are born into, so try not to internalise these preconceived ideals, learn to shine through them and be you.

You cannot blame individuals that seem to be born into better circumstances than you, just as you cannot blame people or look down on people who have it worse than you. We do not choose what we are born into, but as we grow, we can choose what we deserve and what kind of life we want. Instead of judging or feeling jealous, you could offer help and understanding, you can change yourself at any given time, we all have free will, you must believe that the power is in your hands. Many individuals give up and never take the time to look within, due to it being hard to take an internal journey, as external influences can feel so strong. Negative experiences can be hard to face, and even harder to take responsibility for one's actions. Individuals can end up living their lives as the conditions, stereotypes, and all the other influences society gives them, with brief moments of their true self shining through. Those who soldier on, take the internal journey, and gain their higher consciousness, can see when you are self-aware, there is nothing to stop us changing society for the better, because changing ourselves changes the world. Improving our knowledge, mental health, physical health, habits of prejudice, discriminations, and judgement, all of these come from mental constructs. So, if we all tackle them within our own minds and improve, then the world can only get better. Considering we materialise our thoughts through action, the more we think positively and with kindness, the more we will have in our environments. Individuals can live their truth, their authentic self, what they say and what they do should be in harmony with each other. You can find and develop your purpose in life, then die with learnt lessons and no regrets, if you choose too.

Part 2

<u>Building up to go</u>

I was scared to face my past because of how painful it was, I was scared to accept it, and letting go of that part of me felt like, if I did that, then I was letting go of Kell and I did not want too. I did not know how to let my pain go, until I realised. You must focus on the present, focus on feeling happy, doing things that bring you joy, focusing on positivity. It slowly makes things feel better; always thinking in the past will have you trapped there. That is why the love you have for yourself, and your growth is so important.

My happy place is the beach, many times I would feel the need to run to the beach and smoke some marijuana. Looking out onto the ocean, empty space for miles, gives me such a freeing feeling, hearing the wave's crash on the shore, fills me with a peace inside. If I am sad or stressed, it feels as if the waves carry all the negative feelings away. I love nature, it has unimaginable healing properties, I knew I wanted to spend three months in the best nature has to offer, from my perspective anyway. I believe in following my own path and going with the flow, although it can be difficult, as sometimes I let my mind interrupt the moment, however I always try my hardest to get back on track. When it was time to decide where to go, I did not want to choose with my mind. I wanted the answer to come to me, I wanted to feel it within myself, that this is the place I was supposed to go.

Luckily for me I had the means to be able to go anywhere, the options were endless. Instead of using my logic, the destination came to my mind like an internal magnet attracting the answer. Subtle signs would enter my consciousness, of which I would flow with until one day, the destination Jamaica, came into my mind. I never thought of this place before, and out of every other country in the world, this is the only one that came to me, once I saw it, it got more visible and louder, until I had no doubt it was the place for me. I felt as if it were my destiny. I started to research Jamaica and travelling alone, everything I came across was negative, telling me not to go, trying to install fear into me. My mum was uneasy about my choice, as our government website said it is a high-risk country. I felt like it was a sign, either the universe is telling me not to go, or I am supposed to face my fears to achieve something great, I was not sure what the answer was, so I looked more. I finally came across a blog of a Swedish woman who travelled alone, she explained that it is as safe as anywhere, if you are street smart you will be fine and most of the locals are kind and welcoming. Reading that blog made me remember that there is good and bad wherever you go, I thought to myself that everything happens for a reason, there are signs everywhere. Jamaica is the place that came to me, and the place I was going to go. I would not let the fear, that the negative information was trying to put out, stop me from following my path.

It was the start of a new journey, I was entering the next stage of my life, I had now obtained certain tools that would help me within my life journey and any ventures I undergo. I am brave, smart, kind, caring, strong, understanding, and willing to accept and love everyone. I do not let fear live within me, if it knocks on my door, I face it, and shine my light onto it. I had regained power back over my life after many years living through fear and past conditioning, now I was ready to fully heal and live. Everything in life there is a risk, things turning out good or bad, this does not mean you should not take the risk. If it becomes a good thing, you get to enjoy the fruits of your action, if it turns out to be a bad thing, you can receive a lesson of what not to do in the future.

I had stumbled upon a private roomed accommodation, for an affordable price, near town and walking distance from the beach. I looked thoroughly on the profile, the host was classed as a super host and had over 100 reviews from happy previous guests. The wording used was extremely inviting using language such as, 'welcome to our family home, ` it felt like everything was starting to fit into place. I decided to message the host to find out more about the accommodation, we had a lengthy discussion about my trip. Everything looked great, he had answered every question in detail, he seemed nice, safe, and a decent guy. I was sure that the accommodation was secure, safe, clean, the room was private and had locks on the door, plus I had an En-suite bathroom, I was happy to book. The only thing he mentioned was having to share the kitchen but that was fine for me, the accommodation was right near downtown MoBay, it is out of the way but also near everything.

A woman called Pauline invited me for dinner before I went to Jamaica. Me, and Pauline had kept in contact for years since Kellise passed away. We would talk over WhatsApp, offering support for each other. I was excited to go and see her, while I was there, we ate, spoke, chilled. I was explaining about my plans to go to Jamaica for three months and that I had booked the accommodation. Pauline expressed how much she could do with a holiday especially after all she had been through in the past few years. As with all my friends I offered for her to come and visit me while I was in Jamaica, it would be nice to have some company and I thought it would be nice for her to get away. Pauline explained how she had not flown alone before, and she felt a little uneasy about it, so we concluded that she was going to fly out with me and fly back home alone. I finalised the details and spoke to Edward the host about Pauline coming to stay. I got a deal for her to stay for 3 weeks for the price of two, so it was planned for her to come and stay for the first 3 weeks of me being in Jamaica.

Even though most things online were negative I still had a confident feeling, me, more than most, understands that there is good and bad anywhere you go. I knew I was street smart, polite and real enough to be fine on the streets. I am good at reading situations and the more intense, the better I am at keeping my composure, I guess practice made perfect. I do not feel scared, especially about dying, I refuse to let fear stop me from doing what I set out to do. I allowed it to have that power over me when I was younger and I was living in hell, I learnt how to get out and I will never go back. I live in confidence, in faith, in positivity, in love. I respect the bad and embrace the good, I understand it all has its purpose and are both here to teach us necessary understandings. I want what is meant for me, the good, the bad, everything! It is the only way we could ever grow to the development of continuous productive evolution within our consciousness.

Jah will be waiting there

Before I left, I was happy, confident, and excited, I felt like I was on the right path, and I was ready to experience what was to happen. I was ready to learn what I needed to learn, I thought I needed to heal myself, I guess the universe knows best. Even if you feel that you have learnt a lot in life, you must stay humble, there is always more to learn and more growing to do. The day had come for me to fly out, it was the 15th of September 2017, I was meeting Pauline at 9am at London Gatwick airport. Luckily, the drive to the airport ran smoothly, we left in plenty of time and managed to avoid any traffic. Even if I missed the flight, I was so content in life, I fully believed what is meant to be, will be. We arrived at the airport, I said my goodbyes to my mum and grandad, I gave my mum a hug, I could not believe she cried a little. I reassured her that I would be fine, I said, "come on mum, you know I can take care of myself." I said goodbye to my grandad and went to look for Pauline, when we found each other, it was all smiles and hugs, we went up the escalator to the departures floor. Pauline stopped to smoke a roll up and offered me one, I could not finish it; I was hoping I could get some marijuana in Jamaica. We were standing at the entrance of the departures as Pauline was finishing her cigarette, we were chatting about how excited we were to be in the warmth and to go to the beach, we both just wanted to get there. Pauline mentioned she had a couple of friends already there, so she thought it would be nice if we saw them.

In my mind, my intentions, I wanted Pauline to have a relaxing holiday, to do whatever she wanted to do. The plans I had for myself were, I wanted to spend time alone, doing things that make me feel happy. Giving myself space to think and reflect. I had decided to put my plans on hold, considering I had two and a half months to myself after Pauline goes. We were walking through duty free, Pauline asked me if I would pay half for a big bottle of pineapple Cîroc vodka, and we would share it. I thought I could drink it now and again, thinking it would save me in the long run. We bought the bottle then made our way to board the plane, we got on a Virgin 747 jet. During the flight I was braiding and cornrowing my hair, I thought I might as well since it was a nine-hour flight. The air hostess said it looks good on me and that I do them well, it was a hard skill to learn but once you have got it, it will stay forever. The flight overall was fine, we had a little drink and watched films, we finally arrived at Montego Bay airport in Jamaica, it was time to collect our luggage and go through customs.

We made our way through arrivals to go outside to the Groovy Grooper bar where the host had asked us to meet him. As we walked up to the bar, Pauline had bumped into her two friends who were waiting for an available flight while having a drink. Pauline was chatting to her friend while I had spotted Edward the host holding a JUJU sign, we all introduced ourselves. Pauline's friends explained that they may need a room for the night, so they spoke with Eddie to see if he had an available room. All seemed well, he was polite and kind towards us on our first encounter, I asked him if I could smoke marijuana at the property. He replied, "sure, there's a spliff waiting for you, I smoke marijuana myself, but I don't allow cigarettes on the property." It felt like I had hit the jackpot, not only does he not mind, but he also smokes it himself! I looked at him and see a short older man, I thought it would be like living with my grandad, maybe he might have some wisdom to share. We said our goodbyes to Pauline's friend's, they were assured, if they need it then there is a room available for them and we made our way to the car with our luggage.

Upon arriving at the car, we could see that Eddie already had two guests with him. Clara was an American woman who had brought her mum to Jamaica for a break. Eddie drove us to the supermarket, we spoke to the women, they were polite, I got quite a warm feeling from them. Knowing I was going to meet all kinds of new people from around the world, made me feel so happy, I love learning new things and meeting new people. I was excited to indulge in conversation, to learn and grow through communication with others. Expanding my knowledge of the world through stories of their experiences and perceptions. I quickly discovered that Clara smoked marijuana as well, so I was happy about that. In Jamaica, the money that is accepted is Jamaican or US dollar, the only problem was that we had neither, we expressed our concerns to Eddie. He kindly resolved our issue, by lending us some money until we could change up our pounds at the Cambio on Monday morning. Then we could pay him back for the airport pick up and the loan. We all done some shopping, got some coffee, bits we felt may last us, we grabbed some dinner from a place called ole Joes, they serve tasty Jamaican food. I obviously got my favourite, curry goat with rice and peas. When we were all finished, we met at the car and made our way to the house.

My new home

Upon arriving, it looked just like it did in the pictures. A beautiful big garden space with big trees and flowers planted, the driveway went up a big hill, with the house situated up top. I could see another separate little house, next to the main house, as I walked to the front entrance, I could see a beautiful veranda. It had a roof and walls but no windows, just the metal décor grills. Hammocks were on each end where you could lay and chill and enjoy the beauty of nature in front of you. In the middle of the veranda there was a massive round glass table, perfect for people to relax and talk around. The rest of the veranda had two comfy chairs, and a big rectangular wooden table at the back wall. A skateboard was underneath the table and three little toddler chairs, with the names of his sons engraved on them, he praised his family. When you walked through the entrance on the veranda, there was a round wooden table with books. There was information books and a guest review book. To your right there was a bedroom, as you walked past the round table you then enter the living room.

You could see beautiful paintings on the wall in front of you, we found out that his wife painted all the art that was in the house. To the right was a large bookcase filled with all kinds of curious books from physics to physiology, to the left were sofas, a coffee table, and a television. As you walk through, you could see the dining room, it had some draws by the left wall, in the middle a great big rectangular wooden table, stretched through the room with his wife's paintings hanging on the walls. To your right was a long hall with a bedroom on its left side, another bedroom at the end and another to your right at the end, the room at the end was mine. To the left of the dining room was the kitchen, it was filled with all the utensils you could need. The kitchen wall was covered with pictures of his wife and family. When I first met Eddie, he seemed like the kind, family man he portrayed himself to be, his behaviour showed me no different, not in the slightest way. The first vibes I got from him, or maybe it was a projection of what I had expected, but I felt as if he may be someone I could learn from. I thought this would be through conversation, not experience.

Me and Pauline went to our room at the end of the hall, it had a nice double bed in the centre, a good-sized clothes space to the left of the bed, a sofa-bed, an en-suite shower room and toilet, with a big mirror and sink. Eddie had told us the room sleeps two, which it does, just not very comfortably. The bed would have been fine for two I think, but Pauline knows herself better than me, we both decided to take turns on the sofa-bed anyway to resolve the issue. It was our first night staying there, I was ready for the spliff Eddie said had my name on it, we went out on the veranda and met another guest called Karl. He was from England also, an older man around fifty, he smoked marijuana, was skinny with a grey beard, he wanted to buy a house in Jamaica and live there for good, I cannot say I blame him, it is beautiful. He reminded me of a hippie type and of my older brother Liam, Liam is a lot younger than Karl, but it did make me smirk, thinking that is what my brother may end up like. It gave me a feeling almost like a sign, that I was on the right path. We all drank, smoked, shared stories, it was nice being able to share your opinions and philosophies of life, some parts of the conversation would get deep, I enjoyed every moment of it and was ready to dive right in. It was a nice and refreshing change, compared to dipping your mind into the shallow conversational topics, that dance around a consumer-obsessed illusory system of slavery, within the likes and dis-likes of nearly every aspect of the man-made world. Whether that be beauty, reality shows, politics, sports, or any other matrix fuelled distractions.

The next morning Eddie drove us to the fishing village as he said he would help me get some weed. The next stop was the beach, I was more than happy with the weed I got, it must have been over a half oz for only six pounds which is an amazing deal. The beach we went to is a local private beach called Doctors Cave, which meant we had to pay admission of six US dollars. We went down the steps and walked onto a white sandy beach, the water looked so tranquil, it was picturesque. We made our way to the far end under the trees because you can smoke weed there, and that is exactly what I wanted to do, wind down, soak up the sun and smoke my weed. It was lovely I could not have dreamt for more, warm clear turquoise water, blue sky, a bright sun. Feeling the sun on my skin soaking up the sun's energy, feeling the rays going through my body.

It is the best feeling, with beautiful views of nature, it feels like a higher vibration, pure joy.

Later that afternoon the sun went and the cloud's turned grey and purple. We made our way to the entrance of doctor's cave beach; we met a taxi driver called Kube. He spoke to us in a nice comforting way, even though when we were in the taxi he enjoyed shouting, "Battyman to Bludklarrrt" to a young gay Jamaican boy. Pauline laughed her socks off, it made me weary of who to tell about my sexuality. I did not want to be treated differently because I am attracted to girls, I guess this is just one of thousands of things everyone with an oppression goes through.

Oppressions are socially constructed, they exist because some individuals benefit and feel superior, which can give them an ego boost by holding prejudiced ideas about certain individuals. Some oppressions are a lot more insidious than others for example, my privilege is that I can hide being queer, so I do not get treated negatively or receive violence. But racism you cannot hide being black, and because of your complexion you have individuals who do want to be violent and rude to you. It can inhibit people getting jobs, respect or education, the feeling of entitlement needs to be changed. Not one human being on this earth is more entitled than the other, no matter who we are! If you let pre-constructed systems, things, people, or theories convince you that some people are worth less than you, then you should be ashamed of yourself, know your worth, we are all one, we are all human!

Kube wanted to sell me some pineapple express weed, it smelt so nice I could not resist. He kindly took us to get some food in town, then took us back to the guesthouse. We arrived and ate our food, we were chilling with everyone, Clara and her mum were thinking about going to Mayfield falls, Eddie was to drive them. They explained that if more people go then, it is a lot cheaper. Eddie was charging, one hundred and eighty US dollars, that was way out of my price range I wanted that to last me over a week, not just one trip somewhere. I knew there were cheaper ways to accomplish this, maybe a little more difficult being a tourist but there were ways. It was too expensive for me and Pauline, plus I did not think she was bothered much about going, so we declined. I rolled a fat spliff of the stinky pineapple express I just bought. I had sunk into the hammock on the veranda, sparking up, not needing a blanket because it was already warm, looking at the stars in the dark, black, night sky, it was a dream come true, no stress, just peace. I underestimated the weed he had sold me, it smelt so nice like a sweet smell, I was smoking it, enjoying every puff until boom! I got halfway down the spliff, and I was gone, I fell asleep on the hammock, snoring without a care to the outside world. I must have woken up around 1:00am dazed and confused, I went to my bed and fell back asleep. The next morning when I awoke properly, all I could feel were loads of mosquito bites on my legs, it gave everyone a good laugh.

In the morning, I was sitting on the veranda drinking a coffee, Eddie said to me, "I've been thinking about how I am going to manage you, to host you" with a smirk on his face. He expressed that it was rare for him to have guests stay so long, that I am essentially living with him. I did think, he did tell me prior to me booking that he has had guests stay for long periods of time before, boys and girls and even Karl had been there for two months. He asked me to look in the booklet that was in my room that he had prepared for all the guests. In the booklet it says to use the kitchen, you are required to pay seven fifty USD a day. I was annoyed when I saw this because when I had messaged him prior to booking, he told me I can use the kitchen and that I will have to be responsible for cooking my own meals. He did not say anything about a kitchen charge which he should have, considering I was staying for a long time. I went out on the veranda and spoke to him about the situation. I expressed that I do not have that kind of money to be paying out every day, and I explained that he gave me no prior notice. I felt that it was very unfair of him to spring it on me now that I had arrived. I tried to understand where he was coming from, by putting myself in his shoes, yes, he hosts people, essentially it is a business, and he would like a bit of private space considering the rest of his house is open for guests.

When I looked back, I could see no warning of a kitchen fee, the only thing online I could find was it said there were kitchen rules to follow. I felt this to be deceiving but I had to stay there for 3 months as I had already paid through the company he is registered with, so I had to come up with a solution that pleased both of us. I was always polite, kind, and assertive, I did not want to be stranded in Jamaica. We spoke some more and came up with an agreement. Instead of him paying the cleaner to clean my room on a Friday I will do it myself, he stressed that it must be done to his standard of cleaning, then I can use the kitchen at no charge, but only in the allocated times. It was ridiculous really, an hour in the morning and in the evening but not when he is using it. When you would go in the kitchen because of the rules he made, it would make you feel uncomfortable. I asked what if I wanted to make a drink and he said you must ask first. I wanted to be respectful as it was his home and business, I was grateful he bargained a deal with me, so I did not have to pay for the kitchen. I did have to stay for another three months so I had to be smart and respectful. I could not act out of anger and create arguments as that would not help me.

I was happy with the resolution, since I had no problem with cleaning my own room, I expected that to be the case before I had arrived anyway. He also had other rules, he explained that he would like to be kept in the know if anyone plans to stay out past a certain time, so he does not shut the gate. No parties and no people back unless you have cleared it with him. He is a very particular man, likes things done the way he wants them done, there is no room to do things differently. Sometimes it is not good if these kinds of individuals have too much authority. It can inflate their ego and can make them act out control over other people, so individuals do things the way they want them done. There are millions of ways to do things, we should never let anyone convince us one way is superior. I didn't see it as a control issue at the time, I was ignorant to the situation but how do you really know someone's `true self,' if all they show you is a certain side to them, you will never know the other faces they hold inside, unless they show them and if they don't? You will be living with a stranger, feeling like you know them like family, you can only know what a person wants you to know about them. Some people are honest in their self and actions, you need to have faith that you can pick up on these vibes. If you get gut feelings, try not to shrug them off as nothing, no matter how minor they are, you feel it for a reason.

Everyone except Pauline liked Eddie, when Pauline would say things about him, the things she did not like, I would stick up for him. I would try and get her to see things from his perspective, I thought of him like a grandad figure, we got on well as people, someone I could talk to and learn from. He seemed knowledgeable, he did hold a big issue with religion, he did not follow religion, he was extremely discontent with believing that God may exist. He told me this was due to his sister, he labelled her as a God fanatic and stated most people in Jamaica follow religion in the same way, irrational as he would say. He did not believe in God, I tried to explain that God in other terms is just energy, the energy of everything, of pure love and positivity. He disagreed and insisted there is no such thing as God, just energy, no repercussions. It is easy to live by this mantra, it is easy to do wrong, but there are repercussions, maybe not for you, but actions create reactions within others. You do not know what you are doing to another's life, all because you think you will not get punished, that is selfish.

I tried to explain my belief that we have positive energy, like motivation, love, compassion, empathy, inspiration, this can be termed as God. Then you have negative energy, hate, anger, jealousy, murder, this could be termed as evil, the devil's work, in religious terms. What energy we feed and emanate, governs our lives, we will either create a living hell for ourselves or a living heaven by how we think, what we do and the energy we give out and give ourselves. We can do this because we all have the essence of God inside us, no matter what you look like, no matter your skin colour, where you are born, or what the systems of the world may say about you, we are all able to reach a higher consciousness. We all have God inside of us, we are all creators of not just life itself but of feelings, systems, we create the world we live in, let us stop being selfish and create a better world for everyone. I believe God is not a 'him', it is not a man, human or masculine, it is energy, an essence, genderless, the original source of the highest purest energy, the positive, the light, within us all.

When I said all of this to Eddie, he listened but stuck to his original beliefs, if he did not, he would have had to face and take responsibility for the things he had done in his life, and that is not for the weak of mind.

Me and Clara, the American woman, really clicked, our thinking was in sync, it is like she could see where I was on my path and had no problem motivating me to carry on. I remember one night we were all chilling, smoking, talking and then Pauline started talking about Kellise and what had happened. Telling everyone I was there, I stayed silent which was weird considering it was usually me who could not keep it in. I slowly began to realise that the more I replayed it within my mind, the more I inhibited myself from healing. I did not feel as though I could share with Pauline my true relationship with Kellise, I did not feel like I could tell her I like girls in general. I do not think she would have treated me differently, but I do think she would have thought of me differently. I explained to Clara that what had happened to Kellise was mostly the reason why I came to Jamaica, so I could spend time to heal myself, I wanted to spend time alone in nature.

Clara stressed to me to do what I need to do for myself, to not worry about what Pauline wants to do, she explained that she is a grown woman, she does not need to follow me around. That is not how I saw the situation though, it is not me to leave her, she was my guest, and I was willing to put off my own plans until she went home and for her to try and have a good holiday. I did appreciate Clara's concerns; I do think she missed my point; she was insistent that I should do what I want regardless, being selfless for 3 weeks was not an issue for me. Unless I feel that its unappreciated, then I will begin to do less and less and let them get on with what they want to do. I do understand where she was coming from because many individuals in this world always put others first, especially above themselves and although it is nice to be caring, you do need to find a balance and make sure you put yourself first as well. I was happy with my decision regardless and I felt it to be the right one. I did feel as if I developed a connection with Clara, she understood about life and was a figure who was willing and trying to offer me some productive advice which would help me within my journey, so I was grateful.

Eddie seemed to be trying to make our lives easier but the things he would say could be quite undermining and negative towards at least one person involved. Sometimes it felt like the things he said were to benefit him, instead of benefitting us like he made out. For example, one day I had asked him about the market where I can buy food so I can cook for me and Pauline. He said it is unsafe for me to go, that I should stick to the supermarkets, so I did not get attacked or robbed. He stated that it was cheaper to buy take out every night than to cook for myself. This was false, after spending three months in Jamaica, I had been to the local markets alone. I went to all the places he told me not to go and I was perfectly safe, I never felt in danger. It shows subtle intentions, when he was explaining things to me originally, I felt as if he had my best interests at heart. When he would say these things about Pauline, I thought he was trying to look out for me, but looking back on everything, I can see that my vision was clouded. I was only in Jamaica for roughly five days when all of this came out. I did not know the area like he did, so I took what he said as the truth.

The seed

Clara mentioned that Eddie goes exercising in the early morning on the beach. I asked him, he told me that he walks on the sand for some time, then swims for about an hour. It sounded great, so I asked if I could go, so did Clara and her mum, I asked Pauline too, but she was not sure because she said her leg hurts. Clara and her mum left Jamaica, we all said our goodbyes, it was a pleasure meeting them. After they left, I still went and exercised with Eddie in the mornings, I wanted to get fit and thought what better way. It was beautiful, getting your heart pumping walking across the smooth sand and swimming in the crystal-clear sea, the water was so warm, with the sun rising and the world waking up around you.

One day we went exercising, everything was as it usually was, until we were coming to the end of walking on the sand. On approaching the concrete ledge, before I had a chance to say anything, Eddie turned around with a smirk on his face and said, "strip then," he chuckled a little and said, "it's time to go swimming." I replied with a chuckle and a sarcastic "funny one." It threw me off balance, but I shrugged it off as nothing and carried on. I guess I wanted it to be nothing, but it was like a seed had been planted and no one could stop it from growing. The way he had presented himself up to this point, a man coming up to his seventies with a wife and kids he loves. Like butter wouldn't melt, kind and harmless, you would not have thought there was anything sinister within what he had said. I did not personally, I thought surely not, he was just trying to be funny, so I ignored it, at least I thought I did.

After that morning I felt like my thoughts kept deceiving me, it is a weird feeling being in denial, especially when the person who creates them thoughts inside of you is conflicting in their behaviour. It is like deep down you know the truth but because of their behaviour you will put numerous excuses in front of whatever happened, but underneath in your gut, you always knew. Some people wear beautifully woven masks of deceit, lies, manipulation, betrayal, and coldness. This master was so well disguised that everyone would not think to question or doubt his character. I was convinced that he was the man in the mask, until he peaked through his mask at the beach. I briefly saw what was underneath, it is true you cannot unsee what you already have seen. My sub-conscious knew it, even if my conscious mind denied and rejected it, due to being over-riddled by conflicting thoughts, seeing conflicting behaviours like him also being kind, seeming honest and helpful, acting genuine. Seeing everyone's positive opinions, others who only saw the man in the mask, like I did. I think Eddie had a tension towards Pauline because from the beginning she could see him for who he was, the man underneath the mask.

Pauline did not like Eddie and could most likely feel the vibes he was giving off; she would express to me how she finds him weird and controlling. Especially since we pay for our accommodation, she felt as if there were too many aspects, he had complete control over. No one would listen to her, even me, because we all liked him and could understand why he has certain rules. Since it did not bother us, it began to feel like Pauline would pick at everything because she did not like him. I felt stuck in the middle, I did not know what to think. I had Pauline saying things to me about Eddie, and at the same time I knew everything he had been saying about her, I could not be bothered with it all.

His 'Friend' Becky

I was sitting on the veranda smoking a joint, Eddie came out there as well, he sat down and started smoking. We were sitting there enjoying the view, chilling, when he started to tell me about a girl called Becky. She was from America and was 23 like me, he said she was due to stay for a few days. He explained to me that she was less of a guest and more of a friend to him, as she had stayed there previously. He expressed that he thought we would really get on because we have a lot in common, he kept saying he could not wait for me to meet her. He looked at me with a smirk on his face and told me that she is also bi, and that I might even like her. I doubted that I would have hooked up with her, though at that point It had been two years since I had sex, I still did not want to give up myself to just anybody. When he mentioned Becky, I did think maybe it could be a possibility that I would find her attractive, I guessed I would have had to wait and see. He went on to speak about her, saying she is very much like me, in the sense that she smokes weed, is nice and like's going on adventures. He told me that he thought it would be good for me to spend time with someone my own age. I was thinking, since he was telling me about her, I thought he must be telling her about me and the dynamics around the house. Why wouldn't he, he did express to me that they are friends. When he would talk about us meeting and spending time together, he would seem so enthusiastic, at the time I gave him the benefit of the doubt. I thought he wanted me to relax and have fun with someone.

Before Becky arrived, Eddie took me aside and asked me in secret, his tone was a whisper. He wondered if I would like to come for a road trip to Negril with him and Becky, he explained that there is a bar we can go to, called Floyd's pelican bar, which is situated in the water. He also suggested a nudist beach that he and his wife frequently visit. I replied saying "I am not sure, how much would it cost because I need to watch my money." He quickly replied saying, "oh, it's not like that with me and Becky, we are friends, we just do shit together, so I wouldn't charge you either." I was shocked, especially considering that he charged Clara and her mum one hundred and eighty US dollars to go to Mayfield falls, which is even closer than Negril. At the same time, I thought this might be a good opportunity to see places, without having to pay. I asked him whether Pauline could come, he replied saying, "I'm sorry I would offer, but I can't spend over 2 hours with her in the car, she would do my head in." I told him that I appreciated the offer and that I would think about it and let him know. I was tempted since I would not have to pay any money to go, it is not like I would have to do everything they would be doing, but I also was not sure. I could see him and Becky being platonic friends, well maybe that is what I wanted to believe, and at the time I did believe it, he portrayed himself as the type to be like that. I imagined him getting bored, so if he liked a person instead of charging them, he would offer to do something together, which in turn would keep him busy and build a better rapport on the accommodation site for future guests.

The day before Becky had come, Eddie told me Becky said she wants to go out clubbing with me at Pier one. He specifically said that she only wanted me to come and not Pauline, I felt awkward. I did not understand because it is not like she had met her before. I went and told Pauline what Eddie had told me, I asked her if she would mind if I went, but she shrugged it off as nothing. She said it did not bother her at all, and to be honest she is grown, why would it? I did feel like I was put in a certain position, which I did not like.

Becky's here

Becky arrived, Eddie went and picked her up from Montego Bay airport. They pulled up to the driveway in his mini-van, Pauline was smoking on the porch, and I was smoking my joint on the veranda. Becky came straight up to me, greeted me with a hug, said hello and sat down. I offered her some of my joint since I already knew she smoked marijuana. She looked around 5'4" or 5'5" in height, a little bit taller than me, she was skinny built with a very fair white skin complexion. She had short messy hair and small random tattoos all over her body. She was wearing a tank top and denim jeaned short shorts.

Me and Becky were sitting on the veranda talking, Pauline came through after smoking her cigarette, she came to say hello and introduce herself to Becky. Becky treated Pauline very dismissive, distant, and uninterested like she did not want to talk to her. It was unsettling, I did not understand why she was acting like that, it was rude, it was the first time she had ever met Pauline. She did not know her, but she thought it was okay to blow her off. Becky seemed like the type of person that would treat someone according to what she may think she knows, from information given by others, not actual lived personal experience. We finished smoking and ended our conversation, I went into the room with Pauline so I could shower, I began to get ready to go out, Pauline noticed that Becky acted a bit funny with her. The way Becky completely dismissed Pauline on the first time of them meeting made me think, why?

Our night out was about to start, I was dressed and ready, Pauline was now in bed, when I went to the veranda, I saw Nieve, a Jamaican woman who cleans Eddie's house, his friend too. She was around the same age as Pauline, so when I found out she was coming, it made me question even more as to why Becky specifically said for Pauline not to come. Becky did express that her and Nieve are good friends but even so, she had never met Pauline before, so how did she know that she would not like her company? It was not until days later when I was reflecting on the situation that I thought Becky had contradicted herself. Well, I did not know if it was Becky, as Eddie was the one who told me Becky said she wanted to go out with me alone! He said to me that a grown woman should not be wanting to go out with a couple of young girls, yet his friend Nieve who is also around Pauline's age came. I do not know why I went along with it; I did not agree, I have friends twice my age, even more so, age does not matter, the connection does, I believe with platonic friendships anyway.

Eddie offered to take us there in the mini-van and to pick us up if he was awake, I was completely shocked as he was usually tight. I would normally have to pay or wait until he wants to go shop or beach to get a lift, but here he is jumping at any opportunity he gets to help, when Becky was around. I did not question what was happening, I was going along with it, I knew he was only doing it because Becky was there, I figured they must be good friends, I did not know how long he had known her for, so I could not judge. Me, Becky, and Nieve got into Eddie's car, we drove down to Pier one, it is a restaurant and a club in the evenings, it was the first time I went there. I had been out to Margaritaville down the hip strip with Pauline once before, but I do not usually go out, it does not interest me as much as it used to. I would rather sit on a beach at night with someone, talking about life, their opinions, the universe, society, their fears, hopes, experiences, ambitions, and dreams, I view it to be much more worth my time, forming deep connections rather than shallow ones. Eddie dropped us off at Pier One, we said goodbye and he told us to let him know when we want to come back to the house.

As we were walking towards the entrance, I could see a car park on my left. To my right I could see the ocean, it was beautiful, calm, and still. We approached the main doors and walked through, the lay-out was stylish, to my right was the DJ booth and past that was the toilets. Opposite the toilets was the Bay with loads of yacht's parked up. In front of me was a massive rectangular shaped bar with stools around it, the dance floor space filled the rest of the club up, it was all around with the bar being the main attraction. The club was open plan so we could enjoy the tranquil view of the water. During the day you can have meals in this spot as it turns back into a restaurant. We walked past the bar to a little rectangle booth, it was just at the beginning of the pier that joined onto the club, at this booth they sold little quarter bottles of liquor. I bought a bottle of liquor and two mixers for two thousand Jamaican dollars, that comes to about twelve pounds fifty. Considering how much drinks were, I was happy with this deal.

We got our drinks and walked onto the pier, it was long and nearly two metres wide. Standing on the pier feels magical, hearing the calm waves of the ocean under a dark black twilight sky. It was warm at the same time with a cool breeze, it was the perfect time to reach into my bag and pull out my pre-rolled spliff. We walked right to the end of the pier deeper into the ocean and sat to smoke it there. I love finding beautiful spots in every country I visit and smoking a joint there. Some do not agree with marijuana and to be honest it does effect people differently, but so does penicillin and alcohol, but I guess that is none of my business. I think individuals should do what is good for them and not what they are told is good for them. The joke is that when cigarettes were established, a board and panel of scientists and doctors stated they were good for people. Now look all these years later, having an alarming rate of increased deaths linked to smoking cigarettes. They are forced to admit the truth, just because it comes from a place of authority or power does not make it the honest factual truth! Never use someone else's truth as your own, the only thing you can ever know to be true is your personal experience. Even then our perception is influenced because we have been raised and developed in a way of generational conditioning from birth. We need to work on ourselves by stripping each layer away, and look within to find our truth, truth not governed by fear, hate, pain, manipulation, and corruption. The truth that sets our souls alight, fuelled with bravery, honesty, reflection, love and positive thinking, this truth, this light, it is your power. No one can silence you except yourself, you are strong! Never allow another or an experience manipulate you into thinking you are not, be your strength, know your worth, know your power!

After we had smoked, we made our way back into the club, we all started catching a vibe dancing, chatting, drinking, we saw all parts of the club as we moved around throughout the night. I went back to the pier and smoked my other joint on the steps, I went alone this time, I like time alone, sitting, smoking, thinking, I had a nice chat with a Rasta. Throughout the night I caught a wave and could feel the alcohol, but the more time went on, the more it wore off. A few hours in, Becky had met some guy, she took me and Nieve to where she was dancing. It was a cluster of tables, the guy she was dancing with looked middle aged, black hair, standard looking I guess, Becky said he was a pilot. He looked as if he had taken drugs and so did Becky. I could tell they had taken cocaine; they were buzzing. We danced with them for a bit, but I was sobering up more and more and began to look around. I felt a bit anti-social being surrounded by people; I was ready to go home.

When it gets to that point when you look around, everyone is partying on drugs, still drinking, music blaring and you are sobering up. Feeling like you wish you could shut your eyes and when you open them, your alone, in a space that you love. For me it would be on top of a cliff in nature, in silence or at the edge of the water on a sandy beach listening to the waves, not surrounded by drunk people and noise. I had enough, I could not force myself to feel the vibes anymore. I pulled Becky to the side and explained that I wanted to go back to the house, and I asked if she is ready to leave. She told me to go back whenever as she had decided to stay at the guy's house. I cannot say I was surprised; she had been snogging his face off most of the night. Me and Nieve left and went to chill in the car park to sort out how we were going to get home. She rang and spoke to Eddie but when she got off the phone with him, she told me that she is going to get a taxi up with me. We jumped into a taxi and went back up to the house. I walked in, as we saw Eddie, we told him that Becky had met someone and decided to stay out, but she should be back tomorrow. He chuckled and said, "yea she does that sometimes." I was so tired I went straight to my room to sleep. I did not even know if Nieve stayed or went home.

IM SO WITHIN IM NEVER WITHOUT

The truth will always be revealed

The next morning, I woke up and made my way to the kitchen to make some coffee for me and Pauline as I usually did. I went and sat at the top end of the long wooden table by the fridge, to wait until it was ready. Eddie walked into the kitchen, so I asked if I could use a bit of his sugar. I questioned him if Becky had come back yet, he said "yes, she came back this morning." He suddenly stood in front of me, he is a medium sized man around 5ft6, he looks short but not tiny, he has short grey hair. His face looks somewhat innocent, wearing glasses, looking like butter would not melt. His persona changes from time to time, he tried to act cool and a lot younger than he is. He stood there in front of me, a big seventy-year-old man in his three-quarter length shorts, with the shirt and vest top he usually wears. He was look-ing at the floor, then took a deep breath, he looked up with a nervous expression on his face and said this.

"I know you're not stupid, so you have probably guessed by now that me and Becky are more than just friends, we are friends with benefits." I do not know how he thought I would have guessed that, when she only came last night? I was shocked, it was unexpected, before I got any chance to reply he looked at me and said, "I want you to also be my friend with benefits."

I was frozen in shock, I just sat there and looked at the floor for a bit, I did not know what to say. My younger self would have kicked off and told him what a pervert he is, and that he makes me feel sick, how could he even imagine I would entertain him, he was brave. But I am older now, more consciously aware of any situation I enter. I knew I had spent my money on this place to live for the next three months. If I left, I would not have been able to afford a new place because I would not get all my money back. When he put this on me, I felt like I had been trapped in this situation, I was stuck and felt powerless. I looked up, he was there waiting for my reply, I said to him "okay I think I understand what you are asking, I will need some time to think about this and then I will let you know." This way he is not angry, but I suppose I put him in a sort of void, not knowing what direction I would go in, this would make him still want what he wants, keeping me out of any danger, for now.

I got up and took the coffee and cups out onto the veranda for mine and Pauline's morning drink, I was still in shock, I did not want to think about what had happened. I rolled up a spliff and drank my coffee, that is it, no usual chatting away, stuck frozen in my mind. When Becky came out of her bedroom, she sat down on the veranda, lit up a cigarette and drank the drink Eddie brought out to her. Eddie went back inside, and we all decided to go to the beach together. Pauline got in a taxi with Karl, me and Becky decided to walk down to the beach together. I wanted to ask her what has been going on with her and Eddie, but I knew I had to come across non-judgmental, because she would obviously run back and tell him everything. I knew I had to keep him in a state of comfortability, so I would not put myself in any danger.

It takes about twenty-five minutes to walk to the beach from the guest house, we stopped at a place called Floyd's pelican grill, Becky had told me about it because we wanted to eat some breakfast. Situated on the hip strip, it is a nice restaurant, kind of fancy. The local Jamaican restaurants are in Bay, where you can get Jamaican food for a great price, there was one place I discovered months into my stay in Jamaica, near my friend's little girl's school. I bought food from there quite a few times, big size, great food and only four hundred Jamaican dollars, which is about three pounds Sterling, it was off Barnet Street down River Bay Road, it is called Yaady's Jerk, a place to go.

Me and Becky walked inside Floyds Pelican Grill and they seated us at a round table booth, it had reddish leather seats, the interior inside was nice and clean. I was hoping it was not too expensive as I needed to stretch out my money as much as possible, but it turned out to be decent. I ordered Ackee and Saltfish with veg and a big fried dumpling. I also ordered their special cocktail, the strongest one, with Wray & Nephew inside it. I think I needed it to settle my mind after what had happened that morning, I had a few questions to ask Becky. We were sitting there eating our breakfast, I was demolishing my food as per usual, drinking my cocktail trying to shake the morning from my mind. I could not believe they were having sex; I could not believe he wanted to have sex with me, I kept thinking surely not. I decided to ask her, I had to know her perspective on the situation, I knew I had to be careful with what and how I was to say anything, especially as her and Eddie seem to be close, well really close apparently.

I could not go and speak my mind and say what a filthy old pervert I think he is, especially as he is deceiving everyone including his own wife and kids, acting perverted, preying on young vulnerable girl's. Coercing young girls into a sexual situation, using his accommodation and the area to his advantage. He must have thought I was vulnerable, he knew about my past, not having much of a home life or positive support from family and friends. He knew I grew up poor and that I had been through some traumatising experiences growing up, he knew this due to our deep chats about life. He made me feel like I could open up to him and now he is trying to use it to his advantage. He underestimated me but little did he know, although I went through all that pain, it made me find my light and turned me into a warrior. So, no matter what may happen in my life now, no matter how low it may make me feel, I will never stay down for long because I have my love. I have my light and I have my power, all of which I had to realise and recognise on my own, no one can give it to you, you must take it and own it for yourself. I honestly believe I can look after myself anywhere in the world and I believe we all have the right to travel anywhere we so desire, all land is our land to share. I know this is not the case, but it is an ideology I believe we all should follow, considering none of us get to choose where we are born. If people want to offer genuine help, I am not scared to accept but I do not need it, if anything fails or falls through, I will find another way.

I knew I could use Becky to my advantage especially as she is Eddie's ears as well, if he thought there was a possibility I could say yes, I was in control. I had to use this time I had given myself wisely, I had to be smart and figure out what I was going to do. I explained to Becky whilst having breakfast, what Eddie had said to me that morning, that they are friends with benefits, and he wanted the same with me. We were sitting at the table, she looked at me and confirmed that she is in that kind of situation with him, and shrugged it off like it is nothing, she told me that I should as well, that he is nice and will look after me. I was in shock, I could not believe what I was hearing, I wanted to know more information, so I could be completely clear on what was going on. I asked her what they do together, how does he look after her. She says they go places together and hang out, he would never charge her for a ride, they drink together, he would take her anywhere she wants to go, share his weed with her and lets her smoke her cigarettes anywhere. I asked if they have sex with each other, she laughed and said, "of course! That's the whole point of being friends with benefits." Obviously, I knew, but I just wanted to be crystal clear with what I was hearing, she asked me if I was going to say yes to him. I told her "I'm not sure at the moment, I need to think about it and talk to him and find out his perspective on it all."

I was sure that I did not want to do it and I knew I could not trust her, so I told her what I wanted Eddie to hear. When we were finished, we made our way to the beach, we made our way to the far end under the trees where Pauline was with Karl. I sat down next to Pauline about a metre away and Becky sat the other side of me the same distance. I did feel a little stuck in the middle, I would have preferred to have sat with Pauline, but I did not want to give Becky any reason to think I am off with her or Eddie.

As I had this situation to deal with, my mind kept repeating endless amounts of commentary of which I could not pause. My thoughts were all over the place, I was thinking of everything and anything, all at varying degrees. Since he had asked, I was still in shock, I felt that deep down my gut instinct knew this was going to happen, but I ignored it and pushed it to the side due to his persona. The way he was with me and the other guests, how he would talk about his family, I thought he was being platonic towards me, just a caring guy. When he asked me that question, that morning, he stepped over a line and there was no turning back. Neither did I think he wanted to, he asked me with strength and certainty. I was still in disbelief and now all I could think of was all the pornographic visualisations he could have of me and him. My mind is too imaginative and every time I would see it, it would make me feel physically and psychologically sick. All these visualisations must of gave him the motivation to finally ask, especially as Becky was there, his little 'friend,' he must have thought she could help sway my decision.

Thinking about the visuals he could have been having of us disgusted me, on the outside I made sure I stayed composed, tried to seem as normal as I was before, I did not want him to have any reason to think I was not good. On the inside my mind was travelling at the speed of light, I was anxious, powerless, nervous, worried, confused. I felt like I did not have a clue who he was, he could be anyone, for all I knew he could be a mass murderer ready to chop me up and put me under the floorboards. Therefore, I knew I had to make out I was as normal as before, to treat him nicely like I was, and to not make him hostile, I was not about to underestimate anyone.

One morning in the kitchen when I was making coffee, Eddie came over to me, leaned in and whispered, "when Pauline leaves, one day we can spend the whole day fucking all over the house!" When he said this, my jaw dropped in shock, my nervous giggle came out since I did not know what to do. I jokingly and softly said, "I can't believe you just said that" he chuckled at me. I could not believe my ears, but I had to take it, if I shouted and screamed and told him what I was really thinking, he could have easily kicked me out and left me with nothing, no money and nowhere to go. I couldn't believe this was happening, all because some men cannot control their impulses. I had come away to heal myself on a tropical island, and this gross old man was trying to get me into bed.

I felt as if I were all on my own with this, with no one to tell, all my family and friends were back home. It is not like they could help me; they did not have any money to send me to get a new place or a plane ticket and I did not want to go back home, I am not going to roll over at the first sign of an obstacle. It was annoying feeling like I could not turn to anyone, but I had learnt by now how to look after myself, so it did not really matter. I did not know who he knew in Jamaica, so I was weary telling any local friends I had made. I was worried about telling Pauline because I knew they both disliked each other. If I had told her there could have been a chance that she would have gone off on him. I did not know if she would, but I knew there was a fifty percent chance, and I was not willing to take that risk. My return flight was in 3 months, I needed somewhere to stay so in my mind, if I told her and they did have an argument before she left, I could be stuck in shit, and it could have made life a lot harder for me. I started to look online at the booking site I had used and how they handle cases of sexual harassment. I thought since it was him who was making the moves and stepping over the host to guest borderline, they could make him refund me all my money back instead of a smaller portion of it.

Eddie had a strict cancellation policy, so if the booking site could not help me then I would only get a percentage of my money back, which also could take up to a week to be refunded if not longer. I would have needed it immediately so I could book a different accommodation, otherwise I would be waiting with nothing, with no money and nowhere to stay. Them making him refund me my money in total would have been the easy, positive, happy outcome. Unfortunately, that was not the answer that I had found. When I was doing my digging, I could not find anything, no secret contact, no help offered, and no refund help offered.

All I came across were many blogs from women and some men, speaking out about the sexual harassment they endured whilst staying at a property booked through this booking site. They all expressed that this booking site is useless when it comes to dealing with sexual harassment, apparently, they sweep it under the carpet and act like nothing has happened. I do understand why, if this got out it could ruin their entire business, if you think about it, if they were to admit that there is a problem with some hosts with no way to tell if they are sexual predators, it could completely blacklist the company. What they need to do is offer a point of help if this does happen, ask for proof from the victim like recordings, or a letter of misconduct, let them book a different accommodation with the same booking site, paying like a noninterest loan. Then take the money from the host due to misconduct and unprofessionalism, this way everything can happen straight away especially concerning safety reasons and no one loses out on any money.

What makes this situation worse is that on this booking site, anyone can be a host if they have a spare room. Eddie was labelled as a super host, a verified user, with over 100 reviews. I thought I was completely safe, but this showed me that you can never really know who you are staying with regardless. Knowing that the booking site was not going to help, I knew I was going to have to deal with this myself. All this information led me into a despair within my mind, I was confused, I felt violated and trapped, I felt like he had all the balls in his court. I started questioning myself, since I had arrived in Jamaica, everybody kept telling me how I needed a Jamaican man while I am here, an island boyfriend who can show me around and look after me, so no one will take advantage. At first, I thought no way, I do not need anyone, I can look after myself just like any Jamaican woman that has not got a man. I felt confident and safe that I know what is good with myself and the world. Then after all of this happened, I started thinking and wondering if I should get with a man, maybe I could deal with it, I can find the rare man attractive. I thought that my only other option, would be to get a Jamaican boyfriend, in hopes that Eddie would get bored, scared, or feel like he cannot ask me anymore. Even though I knew that deep down that is not really what I want, I did consider it, which shows the impact of his actions on my psyche. What I find attractive, that ignites passion in me, is a beautiful face and nice smile, a smooth woman's body on top of mine, the shape of her waist and breasts running through my fingers, kissing her soft neck while rubbing my hands across her back, grabbing a nice batty.

When I sit and look back, I was putting my truth and feelings aside, I was giving Eddie my power and looking through his lens, he wanted me to be with him, a man, then I started thinking about getting with a man, not him, but a man. It was like the options he put in front of me, were the only ones I could see exist, and this would carry on unless I could figure out how to take my power back.

Education is key

Becky became ill and stayed in her room most of the time, that is what Eddie said to me and Pauline. One night I was smoking, and everyone was sleeping. I went into the kitchen to get a drink; Eddie was already in there, topping his up. Then and there I decided, this is the perfect time to talk to him, so I can figure out what my next move will be. I wanted to listen to his mind, to see if I could find anything that could possibly help me get myself out of this situation, I knew I would have to make him feel like he was not being judged. We sat down at the long wooden kitchen table. I knew to get as much information out of him as possible, I needed to make him feel like his opinions are safe with me. So, I conducted myself in a calm manner, to produce a level of comfortability within the atmosphere. I knew if I were speaking in a curious way, he would be more willing to answer my questions truthfully, if I showed no sign of judgement. If he thought that he made me feel sick and disgusted, then I did not know what he would do, or how he would treat me. For all I knew he could have tried to make my life hell, some men do, a rejection is a bruised ego for some, I had to make sure I had a stable foundation before I blew the lid.

We sat there at the table, he asked me what I thought with regards to his question. I told him that I had spoken with Becky about it at the Pelican grill. He wanted to know what she said, so I told him, "She explained to me how you look after her, take her places, hang out together and have sex." He chuckled and asked what I think of that. I told him that I feel like I want to know more about the dynamics of the situation before I decide. I was trying to delay deciding, so I could get the best possible outcome for myself, and to stay out of harm's way. I rolled another joint and he rolled one too, I said to him to make it completely clear for myself. "So, friends with benefits, where you hang out, do things together and have sex, that's what you want?" Eddie replied saying, "well yea, but it is more relaxed, we have a stronger friendship. I wouldn't charge you for anything especially the kitchen or car rides, you could have whatever you want." I replied and said, "Yea I get that we're friends, but I told you I am gay, so why would you even ask?" He explained to me that he believes no one can be completely gay, they have not had good sex with the gender they do not find attractive. In my case he believed sex is different with different people and, if I had good sex with a man then I would like it. Saying some are pleasurable and some are not, it is that simple. I was thinking but even so, why would I have sex with you? Some seventy-year-old man in front of me convinced he may have a chance. For all I knew he has manipulated situations to have sex with young girls many times before.

I explained to him about my ex and how she lied convincing me she loved me when the whole time it was lust, he knew I wanted something more than sex. I want someone who matches my love, now they do not have to be perfect, no one is, I am not, I am always learning and growing, like I would like my partner to aspire to do. I want to feel like I am the only one in their eyes, no one else, I will wait for the person who knows without a doubt I am the one for them. If we are meant to be together, we will feel this and an attraction mutually, I want passion, I want depth and I will not settle for anything less. When your happy within, you do not need anyone to satisfy any needs. What is the point in settling in a relationship if they cannot vibrate on your frequency, bringing each other to our highest selves? I am not saying you cannot experiment or date people, but you should be extremely mindful about who you get into a relationship with, as you are sharing the most intimate side of your life with them. We spoke and spoke, I told him that it had been over two years since I had sex, since I split with my ex, I did not want to give myself to just anybody, I wanted to give it to the right person for me. Someone I am attracted to, who is not afraid to say they want me and put the time and effort into knowing me past my physical body.

He told me, that is exactly what my problem is, I connect sex and emotion together, he explained that for me to not be attached in my mind, I need to separate the two and allow myself to experience sex as purely pleasure. I had to disagree with him, it may be like that for some, but I get more pleasure, more power, more passion, more of a connection when my emotions are involved. When I am happy, loving, attracted and comfortable with the person, sex is so much more passionate, something beyond just pleasure. It is exhilarating especially when you know that person is completely attracted to you and holds enormous amounts of importance of you within their mind, when they know and treat you how special you are, that's magic.

I did not want him to think that I was judging him, so I curiously asked him how someone could detach themselves from their emotions, as I do not understand because I feel so strongly tied to mine. He explained that it is quite simple, you must concentrate on the pleasure aspect, I still could not understand. I asked him about his wife, did she know? For all I knew, she was in on it all. He told me that she does not know and that he would not want her to find out, he expressed that when he makes love to his wife, he is emotionally connected but when he has sex with others it is purely pleasure. I asked what she would say if she found out, he told me that she would probably want a divorce. He expressed greatly that he is his own person and no woman including his wife could ever own him, he is ultimately free to do whatever he wanted.

Then I asked about his sons, as soon as I mentioned them, he switched to be defensive, he said his sons could never find out, he would want to kill the person who would tell them. If they were to find out what he was doing with these young girls, completely undeniably betraying his wife, it would contradict the way he has raised them and would shatter the image he has created for himself as husband and father. The only reason he cared so deeply about his sons finding out was because they came from him, they are a part of him, he bred them, he could not bear the thought of them finding out all the disgusting and deceiving things he is doing to others. Do the people closest to him even know the real him? I replied, "oh okay fair enough," and moved on, I did not want to make a big deal out of it. He began bragging that he is also friends with benefits with his cleaner Nieve, I was like, "no way, you had sex with Nieve too, okay." I wanted him to feel like I was being light-hearted, so I chuckled at his bragging. It was getting late and my spliff was gone. I told him that I was still not sure about what I wanted to do, that I needed to think about everything. I told him this so I still had him in a void, not knowing what direction I would go in; I was trying to protect myself.

The next morning, I went into the kitchen to make coffee for me and Pauline as I usually did. Eddie had come in, he must have been thinking about me, as I am standing by the cooker, he leans over and whispers, "I just wanna fuck you." I said, "yea, but I am gay," I wanted him to think it was me, why I cannot sleep with him, so he does not get hostile or defensive. He replied saying, "no penetration then, I'll just eat your pussy." I couldn't help but laugh, I tend to do that automatically in certain situations, but I switched it up quickly, and said, "I'm sorry for laughing, it was funny you sounded like some road man in England, no penetration, that's jokes." I wanted to make the atmosphere a little lighter but to be honest I was in shock, I could not believe his confidence, did he really think that I would open my legs to him. He did have an advantage in the sense that he had power over my accommodation and money, I was in a foreign country which he knows better than me, since he lives there. All the pictures of his wife and kids over the kitchen wall, and he is there saying things like that to me, the betrayal and deception is a joke.

At this point I did not know what to do, I knew where I was lacking and what he had over me, but I could not think of any solutions to get everything back. Luckily, Pauline was there, so I was not going through this completely alone, even though I felt like I could not tell her, it was nice to have the company. I was glad she was there, even though some tension got created between us, I am glad it did not get too deep. We had decided to go to the beach, Eddie was at home with Becky. It was nice as it was just us, but even when we were alone, I was the only one that knew what was going on and I could not escape my thoughts. All I could think about was what was going on with Eddie and everything it entails; I had invited my friend Brandy to come and stay with me for a week. She had booked her flight, so she had a ticket to fly out the second week before I was due to fly back. We planned for her to stay with me in my room at the guesthouse like Pauline. I did not know what to do, I felt so guilty she had already booked her flight and I could not have her staying there with me, knowing what goes through his mind.

What kind of person would that make me? Knowingly letting my friend stay in some old pervert's house, it made me feel sick thinking about what he might think of her, especially now I know what he thinks of me! Just the thought of letting her stay there filled my whole being with guilt and it had not even happened yet, I knew I had to do something to get myself out of this situation. It was how and what, I did not know who he was and what he was capable of, I had to be very smart. All I knew is that I could not have Brandy stay there, so I needed to sort out accommodation for when she stays. I needed to take the power back over my accommodation and money, I did not know how. I thought maybe it would be okay if I stayed there by myself, if I was not rude or argumentative, but at the same time make it clear that I am not interested. I thought that he would not do anything if other guests were also staying there, and when there is no one else around, I could use that time to travel to other places on the island and explore like I wanted to.

I needed back up, to protect myself from him going sour when I say no, I decided to download a voice recorder app after he said those filthy things to me. I started having my phone on record when I was around him in hopes I caught some of the dirty things he had been saying on file. I could use it as protection if anything went south. Then I thought I should record Becky if I get the chance, maybe get her speaking about the two of them for more evidence. I was not sure about my plan, but it was the best I had.

I left the beach and went across the road to a discount shop, I had befriended a local Jamaican woman that worked there, she was my age. When we first met, I was trying to hustle the shop keeper to get some money off my rizla and juice, it made her laugh. I did not know the shop-keeper was her boyfriend, we instantly got along and from then every time I would see her, we would have a chat. Her name is Lauryn, she is medium build around five foot five, she has a pretty face with freckles over it like me. I could feel a warm nature about her but also someone you do not want to get on the bad side of, like most people, I guess. She had invited me to come to her house one day and see where she lives, her kids and her family. We were standing outside the shop and by this time I was bursting to tell someone, I turned to her and asked, "Loz can I trust you? I've got something going on and I need to know you will not tell anyone, until I sort it, to keep me out of any kind of danger." She said of course I can trust her and that I best start talking now I have got her worried. I was standing there all indecisive with anxiety building up and it just spewed out. "Well, you know where I am staying in the guest house, the old man that runs it, has asked me to be his friend with benefits, it's disgusting, and he's been saying sexual things to me."

I explained everything that had happened from the first sign at the beach up until now, all the things he had said, and I told her about him and Becky. I explained that I am going to keep my phone on record around him. I wanted to have some evidence, I explained that I will sort something out for when my friend comes to stay, and to make sure that I am not in the house alone with him. Loz did not agree with me, she thought that I should get out of that house as soon as possible. That would have been the best thing to do, but at the time I did not know how to achieve it, I could not just ask for my money so I could leave. I would have exposed myself and my displeasure of his behaviour and then he could say no to refunding me and I would be left with nothing. I understood where Loz was coming from and ultimately, she was right, but it was not that easy, I had to think of the next steps I was going to take. I felt better after talking to Loz, a weight had been lifted off my shoulders.

I went back to the beach and chilled with Pauline, but in my own little world, plotting. I knew that Eddie did not want his family finding out about him and I still had not given him a definite no. If I got him on recording, I could use that somehow, as leverage or protection. I needed his wife and sons contact details in case he tried anything I could bribe him, for my safety. With regards to Brandy, I saw it as Eddies fault as to why she could not stay there, none of this should have happened and it has all happened because of his uncontrollable perverted desires for younger women. Its primitive, living off instinctual drives and desire, forces of predatory instincts, he should be using his consciousness to shift his energy into more important things like his family, it is not like he has no one to sleep with. I decided since it was all his fault, he will be the one to rectify it by paying for a hotel for us, as I was not letting her stay at his. This would have been, with or without, his consent, I was not playing he had completely violated me, this was the least he deserved.

I needed a way out, I did not know what way this situation would go, all I knew is that I was not going to have sex with him, no matter how he would like to label it. Emotionless, or friends with benefits, it would always and forever be a no, I felt disgusted he overstepped way to many boundaries. Some old man I thought was being a genuine host, a grandad like figure, wanted to penetrate me, no thanks, I felt sorry for his wife. All I could think was how he could turn nasty and try to make my life difficult if I say no to him, that is why I had put off answering him for so long.

I needed to step up, it was time to put my plan in action. That night I sat on the veranda with Becky smoking a joint, I put my phone on record whilst talking to her, and I asked her about her and Eddie. It turned out she was a prostitute back in America, she told me some stories of what she had been through. When we spoke about Eddie, she explained that he did not know that she was a prostitute when she first came, but it soon came out through talking and then they were both happy to start their friends with benefits relationship. Becky was not paying to stay at the guest house, not this time anyway. I shared some of my own life stories to make her feel more comfortable, she told me how Eddie performs during sex, saying he is good, that it is nice and that I should try it. All I wanted recorded was confirmation that she has a sexual relationship with him, I did not expect other stories too, but the more evidence the better.

The next morning, I saw Nieve come through the kitchen, Eddie and Becky were elsewhere, I asked her curiously as she walked past me. "Nieve, can I ask you something?" She nodded, so I said, "have you fucked Eddie?" She replied saying "why, you on him?" I shook my head as if to say no, then she told me that she has not fucked him. Why would Eddie say he is her friend with benefits but when I ask her, she says no. I wonder if they team up or Nieve gets paid to help hook him up with young girls, it would not have surprised me. Nieve has five kids, maybe if I were in her situation, in a country where you have to break your back just to get a dollar, maybe I would too, for us to judge before experiencing the same thing first is pure ignorance. We do not know what it is like or what options people choose from, not everyone has the same options. Some must pick from a pool of shit, while some get to pick from a pool of gold, this is oppression, exploitation, and corruption. Therefore, you must never judge or try to inflict more suffering on others, help if you can, even a listening caring ear, some advice, or a hug, can help beyond understanding. Help is not always down to money sometimes compassion and empathy is worth more than any money or gold.

This with Nieve did not make me judge her but it did show me she is not someone I can personally trust, as her loyalties are already tied to Eddie. Now I knew I would have to keep up pretences around her as well as Becky and Eddie, I could not spill the truth to her impulsively. If I said anything negative about Eddie, I could imagine them both running back to him to let him know what had been said. That afternoon I went into the kitchen to get a drink and saw Becky and Eddie in the laundry room together. I quickly started recording my phone and got them on tape. It was nothing explicit, but they are in the same room together, so if anything did happen, they cannot say they have never met. My body of evidence was growing, I was feeling a little happier but still very much on edge, living in the moment doing the best I could, each second, to get the best possible outcome for myself. I had finally decided in my mind to tell him no, I knew I had to record it but also, I had to be clever in what I said. I did not want to make him defensive or hostile, or feel like he is lacking anything, I did not want my life to become difficult because of this. I knew I had to say it in a way to make him feel comfortable, to not bruise his ego, I thought it would be best if I put the blame onto myself. What was going through my mind and what I said was contradicting, I only said it in the nicest way possible because I did not know him. I was considering my own safety, if I did not care I would have told him exactly what was on my mind.

Tell him NO!

I t was morning time and I had gone into the kitchen, Eddie was there, I sat at the table and put my phone on record without him noticing, I was nervous but knew it had to happen, it was time. I spoke to him about me speaking to Becky about their situation, I said that I have also been thinking about my situation, him wanting to be my friend with benefits. He confirms this, then I go on to say that I would not be able to do it, if I did, I would be going against my true self. I went on to say, "I am too gay," in hopes it would lighten his mood, but he replied saying, "we can get drunk and fuck." I anxiously laughed and changed the topic asking how Nieve is, he said she is sick as well like Becky. He mentioned he noticed Pauline is sick too and asked if I was going to be a nurse for her, I said nope I am going beach alone I will bring her some food back. There was no way I was staying there, I did not want to get sick, he told me he would have to look after me if I got sick, when it is only me and him there. It made me cringe when he said that. I told him "I'm probably gonna go to a Rasta village for a week to stay," then left the kitchen.

In my mind all I could think, was to scream, 'no, of course I would not want to have sex with you, you are a perverted old prick and furthermore I feel sorry for your wife and kids, the deception is a joke!' I did not underestimate him at all, I knew I had to be smart to get the best out-come for myself. I got myself ready and started walking towards the beach, inside I felt confused and that I was not living as my truest self. I was being nice to him, pretending nothing had affected me or that I do not think what he has done is wrong. I felt that I needed to act like this, until I had put myself in a position where I was able to leave. I did not want him turning on me for the worse.

I felt disgusted at how he had used his position as a host to coerce me into a sexual relationship, it was disturbing seeing pictures of his wife and kids everywhere. Hearing him on the phone to his wife whilst knowing he is here having sex with Becky and having perverse thoughts about me. I assume not a lot of people know about his secret sexual life with young women. I would not have, if he did not want to have sex with me, he completely portrays himself differently around other guests. When he revealed himself to me, I was shocked just wishing that it weren't true.

When I was younger, I did not care about myself, I had no sense of self-worth or self-confidence, I used to do whatever people would ask of me. Due to this I got myself into some disgusting situations, of which I wish now never happened, but I faced it, forgave myself and moved on. Now I would never do anything I am not completely whole heartedly comfortable doing. I had no sense of justice for myself, I did not think anyone loved me including my family, but I learnt to love myself. I found my power and respect, now I could never let another individual violate me, no matter what. I have put up with a lot of physical and emotional abuse in my life, I am now at a stage where I refuse it. I will do everything within my power, to learn as quick as possible and to never let anyone's negative actions have a hold on me and my life for too long. I feel as if I would rather choose death than give in to the darkness of the world. Although I do not really believe in death as such, as we are all energy and energy can never die; it continuously emanates when it has nothing to enclose it.

A battle kept reoccurring in my mind that day, I knew deep down I had to do something and leave like Loz had said, but I had no clue of how to achieve this. I would only leave if I could get all my money back, so I could use it to book a different accommodation. I knew I had the recordings which made me feel a little safer incase anything turned nasty, I knew I did not want my friend staying there, so I still had to sort something out for that. I had all these thoughts running around my mind, sitting alone at the beach.

I had finally decided to tell someone from back home, now I had all the recordings. I went onto the WIFI and sent all the recordings to my friend Anna. I told her to keep them safe and that I might need them if something happens. I saw it as my insurance, if anything were to happen to me, she had them recordings and could put them out there if needs be, at least she would know and have copies. When we were talking, she could not believe what had been happening, she said something like this would only happen to me, because shit always seems to happen to me. It is funny really, I do not even mind anymore because it teaches me and gives me room to grow. She was wondering what I was going to do about it all, I told her that I was not completely sure. I knew I would not have sex with him, I was sure I would be fine, I had to see how it played out. She knows me, she knew I would be okay one way or another, we spoke for a while on the phone about my situation. She was making me laugh, we were making jokes together cringing about my situation, laughing at Eddies expense.

Everything happens for a reason

The next morning was the first day after I had finally told him no. I did not know what to expect, in my mind I still had to be nice and respectful, since I was still needing to live there. I thought the best thing to do was to keep it clear that I did not want to have sex with him, I was hoping that he did not decide to turn malicious or nasty towards me. All I knew is that I thought I knew him, he proved me wrong, then I felt like I did not know him at all, or what he is capable of.

I woke up early and went to make coffee in the kitchen as usual, I did not bother taking my phone around recording anymore as I felt that I had enough evidence to back myself. I have him admitting he has sex with Becky, admitting on recording that he wants to have sex with me, and when I tell him no, he says 'we can get drunk and fuck then.' I have Becky on recording talking about their sexual relationship and them both on recording together in the same room, so I have proof they know each other.

As I walked into the kitchen Eddie was there making a coffee, I walked over, and he asked how long I have had my braids in. I explained that I had done them myself on the plane and have been re-doing the cornrows when they have loosened out. He took out his phone from his trouser pocket and got a picture up on the screen. It was of me with straight hair, he then swiped it to the left and another picture of me with straight hair appeared. Just after he swiped to the next picture, he stated to me, how better I look with straight hair. I muttered a thanks, I was getting tired of keeping up pretences, I cannot be something I am not. It was making me feel like I was split in two, I had told him no, what more could I do?

Me and Pauline got ready and went to the beach. My introvert side had taken over again, and I was very much into myself. Maybe because of what he said that morning, it was a possibility that he would keep prying on my physical appearances and that it would never stop. I still felt off balance, even though I had accumulated some recordings, I did not know how I could use them and get a favourable result. I felt like my control and power had evaporated, I felt trapped into the situation.

That day at the beach with all these thoughts swimming around my mind, they suddenly came to a halt when I looked up, my mind was silenced. All I could see was the magnificent wonder of the natural beauty in front of me, the turquoise waters, fine sand, the strong, tall mountains in the distance with the ocean continuing for miles. The beauty, the magnificent awe, had silenced my mind. Even with all the negative toxic energy that was consuming my thoughts and life situation. In that moment it did not exist anymore, because I was not thinking about it. Nature, the natural beauty of nature pulled me into a calm stillness, which allowed me to experience a break from my disease-ridden thoughts.

In this moment of silence, a quote that I have never seen nor uttered, entered my consciousness. "The most powerful person in your life is you, you just have to let yourself be!" The significance of these words did not sink in, until I allowed myself to dive into the realm of thought. Whilst I was there, I could see my light, my power, within my being shining brighter than the sun. I saw how I had willingly handed it over to Eddie, due to the fear he had embedded within me, because of the external circumstances he created around me. When you face your fear, you no longer become governed by it, there is always a way to triumph. I had realised that I had willingly given my power over my life, to this situation and to Eddie, this was the same precise moment I was able to take it back. My light had returned, all because I had let it, because I became aware, present, and faced the obstacle that was within me, the fear.

We all have our own power within, we are creators of life, emotions, abstract to physical materials. We ultimately decide how our lives will be by the way we allow ourselves to think, remember everything starts from within the mind. It is easy to give our power over to others within our lives, usually through fear, they may intimidate, manipulate, be violent, bribe or abuse us into thinking of submission. Convincing us we are optionless, that their option is our only one. They can make us feel less powerful than we are, but again this can only happen if you let them convince your mind, that you are less than what you are. Some individuals manipulate love, by having conditioned love, so when you do not meet these conditions, it gives them a false sense of justice for their mistreatment. You give them your power by believing, by allowing yourself to be convinced that this is the type of love you deserve, instead of unconditional. It is easy to fall into this trap because we grow up in a society where everything is conditioned. We only get praise for socially accepted good behaviour; we do not get recognised for being our natural authentic selves. When you fully embrace self-love, it will be extremely harder for you to be manipulated by love. You set your own standard of love you want to receive, by giving it to yourself. This will allow you to no longer stay in situations that are less than you deserve and will give you the confidence to not settle.

This also goes for societal structures; they take our power away by making us feel less than who we are. You can develop a low self-esteem, low self-worth, low self-respect, low confidence, low courage, and low power. They do this by constantly telling you that you are not good enough how you are naturally. Giving you standards to reach and celebrities to idolise instead of being your own hero. Love and embrace your own likes and dislikes. The media set beauty standards, corporations then provide you with make-up, making you feel like you need it to be beautiful, creating trends, so you feel cool if you fit in. They have divided us and created levels of living, so you will constantly strive to get to the top and constantly consume.

You must realise that if you take an internal journey there is nothing you could want, because you will realise your own divinity. You will realise you are as amazing as anyone else in this world, and we all can be the best we can be internally. We must remember external is temporary, our internal journey is what lasts. Only you can find your strength, you must believe that you have the power within. Constantly believe that no matter what anyone says or how hard life may get, you have all the strength and power you will ever need inside of you. Only you can ignite your light, no-one can give it to you, you must take it for yourself. Become more and more positive and keep the faith that you are light, you are power and nothing dark or negative, can interfere with your journey. Accept your past, forgive yourself for all the bad things you have done, forgive others for all the bad things they have done to you. Recognise your strength, your power.

Be active, learn, become aware of your thoughts and emotions, become aware of the world and the structures and its impact on you. Become aware of your family's impact on you, if it produces negative feelings, face it, learn from it, and change. If it produces positive feelings embrace it, love it, and magnify it! Start with an internal journey, facing your demons, finding your love, doing things that bring you joy, you are your biggest hero, you must let yourself be. If you wait for someone to come along and save you, you could be waiting forever, only you can save yourself. You need to be attentive whilst also being still, dive inside yourself, take your internal journey. Take back your power that is inside you, this journey will give you the universes most blessed treasures. When we all have found our pot of gold, the earth will shine bright and we will live in light, pure greatness.

Before my realisation, I was scared to tell Pauline everything that had happened. When I had taken my power back and faced my fears, I effortlessly walked over to her, now being governed by my light, instead of my fear. I was acting through a heightened consciousness, I guess deep down I always knew what should have been done but I let fear halt my progress. Fear of loss, fear of danger, of sexual abuse, a fear of the unknown, these negative ideas consumed my mind. The realisation, that I ultimately choose what to think and what to do, cleared all the negative thoughts out. I was now living through positive thoughts, I was confident, brave, happy, I knew I was going to be fine.

I sat down next to Pauline at the beach, she turned and asked me, "Frankie what's wrong, you haven't been yourself lately?" I explained to her that something had happened, that I would have liked to tell her straight away, but I was worried. I told her I was worried that she may kick off at the person, and I did not want that to happen as I still had two and a half months left to live there. I asserted that if I tell her she cannot tell anyone, to keep acting completely normal, like she had not been told a thing, not to create any arguments.

She insisted that she would not argue with anyone, I told her about the morning after I went out with Becky, that Eddie said he wanted to be my friend with benefits. I told her about all the filthy things he had said to me. Her facial expression changed in disgust, she explained that she felt she had known for ages, she looked at me like it is shocking that he said something. She told me about a time that I rode a skateboard and was showing her and Eddie, she said she saw him staring at my boobs whilst it was happening. I was horrified when she said this because I could remember my thought process at that moment in time. My thoughts were purely innocent, thinking that I was doing good, even showing off a little. To realise the whole time, he was perving over my boobs felt disturbing, I saw him like I did my grandad, it is disgusting. I told Pauline all about him and Becky, how there are friends with benefits, and that I think Eddie tried to use Becky to warm me up to the idea, Pauline said she knew. She had heard Becky and Eddie having sex when she went out for a cigarette once, she knew something was going on, as Eddie would let Becky smoke cigarettes anywhere, on the veranda and in the room. I explained that I recorded Becky talking about her sexual relationship with Eddie, that I recorded him when I told him no and even on recording, he says 'we can get drunk and fuck then.'

She knew something was going on between them, she had suspicions and now I had confirmed it, it made me feel sick, I let her listen to the recordings. I played them right there on the beach but only we could hear them, my phone was not that loud. She was shocked and disgusted, I think she could not believe I had the recordings, she asked me what I was going to do. I told her that I had sent the recordings to my friend in England, so if anything goes south there is an insurance that has already been sent out. I explained about the conversation I had with Eddie and what he said about his wife and sons. I told her that I knew his son's names as there were engraved on the little wooden chairs that were on the veranda, but I did not know his wife's. I needed her name so I could try and find all their contact details. If need be, I would have to use what I have, to get what I need. Pauline stated straight away that she knows where his wife's name is, she remembered someone pointing it out whilst reading the comment she had left in the guesthouse review book. I told Pauline I was thinking to still stay at the guesthouse and to make sure that if there are no other guests there, then to stay at other places, like hostels or go to different parts of the island that I wanted to explore.

I explained to Pauline that I felt as if I needed to sort something out for when my other friend stays as well, Pauline did not feel like I should stay there. I was thinking that I knew what was best for myself at that moment, so I carried on doing what I was doing. I was happy when I had told her, it felt like a big weight had been lifted, she expressed that she thought to say something sooner, when he was looking at my boobs. She considered how Eddie and I got on, and at how he would manipulate anything she tried to say. She felt as if there was no point, it would have all been twisted. I agreed with her, I could see that everything happened for a reason and in perfect timing. If she would have told me earlier, I would have been filled with disbelief, instead of being oblivious I would have confronted Eddie and it would have been in a way of disgust. As soon as he would have felt that energy of confrontation, he would have denied it and manipulated it all. As I did not want to believe it, I probably would have believed him. Pauline not saying anything was perfect because it led to Eddie being the individual that said it to me, so neither of us was able to deny anything. The way it happened gave me a chance to get the best possible outcome for myself, even if I could not see any good outcome in the beginning. After hearing that quote within my head, "the most powerful person in your life is you, you just have to let yourself be." The realisation I achieved allowed me to move forward with power, everything started making sense and fitting into place. I let go of all my fear and expressed only inner strength.

Me and Pauline had previously met a couple on the beach, their names were Martha and Louie. Martha was a middle aged white Canadian woman who worked as an officer in a prison, her boyfriend Louie was a younger Jamaican guy. They were both cool, I became good friends with Louie during my stay in Jamaica, Martha went back home after a couple of months, she was paranoid when she was not with him. Me and Pauline left the beach, we saw Martha and Louie across the road by their car. We went over and I ended up telling them everything about Eddie and what was going on. They did not know Eddie personally; I think they had seen him around but that is about it. They were disgusted with what he was trying to do, abusing his authority to try to manipulate and have sex with young girls.

It made me feel good, now I had told others and received their opinions, it made me feel less crazy and putting excuses in front of the reality. When we keep things to ourselves it is just us and our own mind, when we share, it broadens our thinking and we become open to different perspectives, we may have been closed to before, or could not see.

We walked down to the shops near JRs Chicken shop, me and Pauline wanted to get some food and Martha wanted to introduce me to a woman called Sophie, as she thought she may be able to help with my situation. Whilst walking there we could see Sophie in the distance, Martha introduced us, and we began speaking about the situation I had found myself in. All she was thinking was how she could offer any help, she suggested that I may be able to go stay with her sister in country if I wanted to. I explained that I am not sure what I was going to do yet, I wanted to have enough back up plans in case it all went bad. I expressed my gratitude and said I will hold the offer close to me, and if anything was to happen, I will surely let her know. She was fuming with him preying on young girls, she even asked if I wanted her to sort out some people, to run up in his house and shake him up a bit. I said no to the offer, I did not want any other people possibly getting into trouble because of the filthy mind of Eddie, he would get his comeuppance but no one else will be hurt by it.

After I found my power, I was able to tell people about my predicament without doubts running through my mind, in return I got compassion, everyone offering help. Some Jamaicans I had not even met before, like Sophie was still willing to help me. The way the Jamaicans came together for me showed me community, something of which had been long gone from where I grew up. The reactions I got from everyone taught me how wrong Eddie really was, that his actions were disgusting and that I was going to be fine. I guess in a sense it subconsciously gave me even more motivation and confidence within myself and this situation, I knew that I would be getting the best possible outcome for myself. I was filled with positive vibes, with my power, my essence shining through. It is like I knew what to do without having to think about it, without having to go over every outcome, I knew my path.

Me and Pauline jumped into a taxi and went back up to the guest house. As soon as I got back, I went straight over to the round table that is between the veranda and the living room. I looked for the guest house review book, I wanted to see if I could find his wife's name within it. It was right there staring at me in the first few pages, this is how I knew everything happens for a reason. It was only when I faced my fears and told Pauline what was happening, that I found out where his wife's name could be, if it were not for Pauline I would still be looking. I now knew his families name's, I wrote them all down on a piece of paper with spaces between them, Allison, Ray, and Elliot. All I needed now was to write their contact details beside them. That night I was trying to come up with a plan, as to how I could acquire his family's contact details. I was happy I had recordings; I did not feel completely helpless. I felt like I needed his family's contact details, if I really wanted to protect myself, but I was stuck on, how? I contemplated various ideas but the predominant one was needing to figure out his pin for his phone and then to go down his contact list until I found their details, but how was I to do this? I thought maybe I would be able to slyly watch him enter his pin without him knowing. Once I had his combination, I could take his phone when he was sleeping, to find the information I wanted, this was proving hard to achieve. That night I fell asleep restless with many scenarios running through my mind. The next morning, I woke up just as restless, I was agitated and aware of all my surroundings, I was constantly taking in every detail.

Never under-estimate

I walked into the kitchen; I could hear Eddie around the corner pre-paring the dogs food to take outside to them. I saw Eddies wallet on the kitchen table. I knew I wanted his credit card details, so I could book somewhere for when my friend Brandy came to Jamaica, especially since I could not let her stay here anymore. I figured it was his perverted fault and we would be back in London by the time he had realised. I was anxious I did not know if he would quickly come around the corner and catch me. I opened his wallet and flicked through his cards to find his bank card, I got scared, shut it, and ran. I wondered back as he was still by the dog biscuit, just about to take it out to the dogs. I opened his wallet in a rush, took out what I recognised as a bank card and quickly took a picture. As I was about to put the wallet back, I noticed a $5000 JA note, it equates to roughly forty US. I took it out of spite and put his wallet back as I had found it. I ran as quick and silently as I could back to my bedroom, luckily all of this went undetected.

The spite I felt towards him produced me to want some sort of low-level revenge, that is why I took his money. I felt he deserved it, like he was taking a loss and I was taking a gain, I guess it made me feel better at the time. I felt like for some time, his actions influenced me into losing myself, to take revenge on him was wrong, immature, and unnecessary but I did it, I did not correct it. The reason I cared less about doing wrong to him in this case was because of how he had made me feel, I felt violated from all the things he was thinking about me. The filthy things he said to me pierced through my eardrums, like poisonous nee-dles that penetrated my mind with aggressive animalistic sexual interac-tions of me and him, all of which I could feel emanating from his mind. He had visualised me naked and him having sex with me. I knew this by all the things he had said to me, due to my pictographic imagination I could see it all, like one horror movie you cannot escape from.

As soon as I got back to my bedroom, I shut the door and turned to Pauline, I whispered to her what had just happened, I showed her the money, laughed, and I said, "well it looks like we are having a drink on Eddie today." She chuckled and said, "oh Frankie you are bad," I shrugged it off and said, "fuck it, it is the least he deserves after what he has been doing." I showed her a picture that I took of the bank card, we were both trying to make out what it said but it was so blurry, we managed to make out the name on the card. It was Albert Edward Forester, but we could not make out the numbers in the picture, so we could not use it. Now I knew his last name is Forester I knew his wife is called Allison Forester, having a last name was important, it would enable me to be able to find her contact details more efficiently. I could only take this information with a pinch of salt, instead of factual because for all I knew she may not have taken his last name, but I still saw it as a step forward. In that moment it was hard to contain myself, my adrenaline was pumping after the tense moment with his wallet, it felt unreal. Me and Pauline were getting a bit carried away with the noise. We decided to be quiet and talk at the beach, we got our things together and made our way there.

I did feel a little apprehensive and worried that he would notice the money that went from his wallet. On the other hand, I thought he probably would not notice, or he may think that he had no clue of who could take it. I did feel as though he deserved it and kept thinking, with the amount that he drinks he could easily mistake it and get confused. Me and Pauline went to the shop and bought ourselves some alcohol from the money I took off Eddie, I spent it on food and drink for us. Pauline was happy to accept especially after how he had been treating her during her stay there. We sat at the beach drinking, chatting, trying to decipher the picture of the card but we could not make out the numbers as they were too blurry. We were talking about how I could get the contact details of his wife and kids, it was necessary to have, because he had told me he did not want them knowing. At this point I did not know how I would use it; I just knew I needed it. If I had their details along with the recordings, if he tried anything with me or turned nasty, I could use them to get myself out of it.

I suggested to Pauline that I should ask the Jamaican guys we knew, Louie and Jermaine, if they can get any date rape sedative drugs. I could slip some in Eddies drink, when he drinks his alcohol at night, so he passes out. Whilst he is sleeping with no chance of waking up, I could go through his phone and get his families contact details. The only problem was that I needed to find out his pin, to get into his phone, of which I still had not managed. I could not think of a way to achieve this because every time I would look, I could not see the numbers he would put in. Pauline laughed at me, but I was being serious, I felt like my life was on the line, I had no time to mess about. Our friend Jermaine started walking over to us on the beach, his nick name is Smokey, he came over to say hello. We met him the first day we got to Jamaica and have been pals ever since, he was such a nice guy I could always feel a good, warm, energy around him. I felt safe around him, funnily enough he reminded me of my little cousin Jake, his personality was somewhat introvert, seemed to keep himself to himself but had a good, pure, kind heart.

We were all talking, I told him about what had happened to me with the old guy I was staying with, he asked me where I was staying, so I told him at a guest house at the top of union street. He said he has heard of an old man that lives at the top of Union Street on Brandon hill, who has sex with all the young girls that stay at his accommodation. He told me he heard about this a couple of years ago, I was in shock and completely adamant that there was no way I was going to stay there alone with him, or that he was going to have sex with me! Smokey offered for me to stay at his place, if I needed, but I was not sure.

Louie came over to us after Smokey had gone back to work on the beach, Louie wanted to see what was good with my situation and asked if I had made any progress. I asked him if he could get me any date rape sedative drugs, he laughed but when he realised that I was being serious, he said that he did not know, but he would ask around, he told me he could get sleeping pills. I did not think that sleeping pills would be strong enough to keep Eddie sedated, for me to complete the task of getting the contact details. If he woke up while I was going through his phone I would have been screwed. He would have caught me out and I would not have had the evidence I needed to be able to back myself up and progress forward. Getting caught, being revealed until I deemed fit, was a no go! Louie was doubtful about being able to get these sedatives for me, but he said he will try regardless and ask around for me. At this point I was more than ready for anything, I was being smart, collected, cautious, and I never underestimated anything, which put me two steps ahead of Eddie and the situation the whole time.

To be honest I did not have a clue what to do, at any point anything could have changed, I tried to make sure that I had as many options available as possible, instead of being left with nothing.

Back at our villa I rolled and smoked a joint, I still had all these thoughts running through my mind, I still needed to get his families contact details. I must of woke up around 4 – 4.30am, I opened our bedroom door, the house was still and quiet, everyone was sleeping. I felt like a spy, tiptoeing around, I started looking around the apple Mac computer for paperwork or any form of contact details for his wife and sons. I looked in the drawers in the kitchen but could not find anything, then I turned my head and saw a little green book on the table. I was automatically attracted to it, I picked it up and flicked through, it was a phonebook, I thought jackpot! I also thought, 'who keeps their details in a phone book still, maybe its old.' I silently ran back to my room with it, so I could take a better look without worrying if anyone will come out and see me. I sat down in my room and turned my phone light on, I was hoping he still had that old man mentality and wrote his information down, as well as storing it in his electronics.

I flicked through the pages and found his wife's name Allison, her phone number, also his sons, Elliot, and Ray. I found them with their family titles next to them, so it was easy to tell who was who. I wrote their numbers down next to their names on the piece of paper I had previously prepared. I still did not know if these numbers were up to date, so I checked to see if mine was in there. Considering I had only known him for a couple of months, if he put my name and number in there as well as his phone, I was sure the others were also updated. I looked and I found my details right there staring back at me, I felt accomplished, like I had taken a step forward. I now had his families phone numbers; I was lucky he still thought to write these things down, because if not I would have had to somehow get into his phone. I took the little green book back to the kitchen and placed it exactly where I picked it up. The house was still, I wanted to get up again when everyone else had awoke, so I went back to sleep, content and finally able to rest.

When I re-awoke, I made my way to the kitchen as usual to make coffee, as I walked through the doorway I noticed his wallet on the side, I thought it could be the last chance I get to do this. I could hear him out the back door, I opened his wallet and took out his bank card, shut it and then ran into the dining room, I thought it was safer in case he peeked around the corner. I placed the card on the table and took three steady pictures of the front, turned it over and took three steady pictures of the back. I creeped into the kitchen and quickly placed the card into his wallet. I carried on as normal and started making a coffee for me and Pauline, he came back into the kitchen and took up his wallet. He did not notice what I had done but I did not initiate any conversation, I had been quite distant since I had told him no. He was preoccupied with taking Becky to the airport as she was due to leave. After I had made our coffee, I took Pauline's out to her on the veranda and took mine back to the bedroom. I got my phone out and started inspecting the pictures, this time the pictures were clear, so I could make out all the words and numbers on them. I got out my piece of paper and wrote down his full name that was on the card and the card details. His name said Albert Edward Forester, but he tells everyone his name is Eddie, I wondered why he does not use his real name. I could not ask him because if I did, I would be giving myself away, he would have wondered how I knew his real name, I was suspicious though, whether he has something to hide. I thought if someone reports you and you are not using your government name, you could see it as some sort of protection, considering that you could deny it being you.

The bank card read CRB on it, but I had never seen this card before in my life, so I did not know where it belonged to, I needed to do some research. Becky had gone so Eddie was not as distracted as he was before, also Pauline would be leaving to fly back to London soon, so I was on a mission. I typed into google what it said on the bank card, and it came up with Canada Royal Bank and Caribbean Royal Bank. Without the address and post code the card is registered to it becomes unusable. I knew he had addresses in Canada and Jamaica, but I did not know what address the card was registered to, so I thought to myself I will have to find both! I felt pressured into obtaining all this information, I felt pressured by Eddie because of his perverted ways. I could never let someone I love, my friend, be subject to that, I would never intentionally do that. So, considering I did not have the money to accommodate and considering it was down to him, he was going to have to pay up, with or without his consent, it did not matter to me. I decided I was going to book somewhere for two weeks, the first week my friend would be there with me and the second week I would be alone. I did not want to spend my last week in that house, after I would be flying back to England, and by the time he finds out I would be home. I was on a mission of getting both addresses, I felt like I had obtained enough information to achieve this, that is the beauty and wonder of the internet. I knew his wife was an artist as he told us she was the one who painted all the paintings that are hanging up in the house. She is extremely talented, I loved some of her art, she deserves better than what he offers, anyone would.

I typed her full name into google, in hopes that it would give me some leads or direction, what come up was perfect, she has her own website for her art! I looked through her website, I saw it had her email address and her Jamaican home address, it did not have a post code number it just said, Sandy Beach post office. I needed the post office post code, it was easy enough to find because everyone would have the same since all mail gets delivered to the post office, not your actual address, I typed in google Sandy Beach post office post code, it gave me JNESJ18. I had the recordings, his family's names and numbers, email, home address, including post code for his Jamaica address and his credit card details, all while remaining inconspicuous to him. The last piece of information I needed to be complete, was his Canadian home address in case his bank card was registered to it, I formulated a plan that would enable me to accumulate this. I started to write a formal email on paper, addressed to his wife Allison, making out that I was CEO of a charity and that she had been chosen for a world view exhibit showing off her artwork, explaining that all the proceeds would be going to charities of the artists choice. In the letter it stated for her to confirm her acceptance, to include her name and current address, so we can send the full itinerary package.

I was running out of time to get everything sorted, Pauline was leaving tomorrow and when she was gone, he would have no distractions and no reason not to talk to me. I would be the only one there, except for Simon and Karl, whom you hardly saw, but Simon was due to leave soon anyway. Simon came last night, he was from England as well, funnily enough he was out there because he wanted some down time, whilst working on his book. Me, Pauline, and Simon decided to go to the beach together, we offered to show him where it was, he wanted to go and write.

It was Pauline's last full day in Jamaica, I tried to make it as calm as possible, we had a nice day at the beach, we had a drink, but mostly enjoyed the water. I felt like I was now two steps ahead of Eddie, he had absolutely no clue that I had him recorded, that I had his bank details, and his family's contact details. My plan of action at this point was to stay at his house, stay cool, calm, stay distant from him. To make sure that I do not stay in the house alone with him, and to book a hotel for the two weeks before I leave.

The universe always knows best, try to never resist what it has planned for you, accept the good and the bad, only that will get you where you need and want to be. Be brave, some things can be scary to face but in the long run it would be better for you than not facing it. When I had arrived in Jamaica my intentions were purely to give Pauline a great holiday, like I wanted and intended for my other friend that was due to come. There became moments where her actions were twisted, I judged and felt non caring, which is wrong, I should have never let Eddie get between us. If I did not agree with some of her actions, that is fine, but I should never have listened to him.

I do believe that we as individuals must take responsibility over our own lives. If there are things in our environments that do bring us down energetically, we have a duty to ourselves, to either remove whatever it is, or take a break from it. No one is to blame for either behaviours, it is what it is, it only gets mucky when people hold negative thoughts about it like hatred or agitation or does not bother to try to communicate effectively. I did stick up for Pauline a lot when Eddie would run his mouth about her, but I could have told him to stop talking to me about her and to keep his opinions to himself. I guess I let him speak without retaliating so I could avoid getting on his bad side, I wish I did differently now. The only reason I cared was because I was staying at his house.

Pauline was anxious and worried to leave me staying there, knowing everything that had been going on. I knew I would be okay, I had sent my friend back in England the recordings and his families contact details, so I felt safe enough. My friend Loz from the shop thought I should leave when Pauline does, but in my mind, it was not feasible, without all my money back it could not work, and I did not know how to go about getting my money back. I remember saying to Pauline that maybe I could bribe him somehow, but I had no clue how to, so until he leaves me with no other choice, I was going to stay there and keep myself to myself.

What is meant to be will always be

The next morning was Friday the sixth of October 2017, it was the day Pauline was due to leave Jamaica, we arrived on the fifteenth of September, so we had spent 3 weeks on the island. Every Friday I had agreed to clean my room, to have free access to the kitchen. Remember Eddie usually charges his guest's $7.50 a day, so I had to make this arrangement with him. That morning I woke up and went to smoke a joint on the veranda. No one was around so I decided to ring my mum, I had not spoken to her properly for a while, considering everything that had been going on. I told her what had happened, I do not know why, because usually I would not have said anything until I knew that I was safe and sorted, so she hadn't had to worry. I told her how the host had been sexually harassing me, I told her the inappropriate sexual things he had said to me and that he had asked me to be his friend with benefits. She was worried and asked me if I am coming home with Pauline. I told her that I am not, I do not have the money to pay for another flight and why should I? Because he wanted to try and make me his prey, no way. I would not bow down to this situation, because he thinks he holds more control over my circumstance. I assured my mum that I would be fine, I told her what I had done with regards to the recordings I had obtained, and his family contact details and his bank details, I had explained to her what my plan of action was. She told me to be safe and to get away from him, I told her, "Come on mum, you know I can take care of myself. I have to do what I feel is best right now, but I will keep you updated, you don't have to worry about me!"

I was sat on the veranda smoking my joint, it was a Friday, so when Eddie came out, I asked him if I could have the cleaning products. He told me a straight no, he said he was going to clean my room by himself. He went on to express that he has felt completely uncomfortable having Pauline stay there with me, considering he has not got on well with her. He went onto say that he does not want my other friend staying there with me, since the experience he has had with Pauline has been

113

unfavourable. This felt like the start of him trying to make my life harder because I said no to having sex with him. I quickly replied saying, "that's fine with me, my friend has already booked a hotel for two weeks, so I will be staying with her the last two weeks of my stay." I tried to not get agitated by the things he was saying, even though it was a joke, he felt uncomfortable, well what about how I felt! I went back to what he previously said and questioned him as to why he did not want me to clean my room, it was completely out of the ordinary, he usually would never mind. I made out that I am only asking about the cleaning because I cannot understand why he would want too, especially considering, we had made an agreement.

In my mind I was thinking, does he know what I have been doing? Why does he want to clean my room? What, does he want to sniff my knickers or put a camera in my shower? I think he could feel my agitation, so I tried to tone it down a little. I did not want him to think that I was disgusted or annoyed because I felt like I still had to stay there. We spoke about it some more, I was questioning him but trying to do it in a nice way, I was not sure if it was coming across as such. It was hard, how dare he, he had the cheek to speak to me like this after everything he had done. I quickly put my phone on record without him noticing in case the situation escalated. I told him he can clean my room if he wants, but I did not understand why he wanted too, I told him I am too high to argue, that I could not be bothered. He went on to say that he does not want any issues with me, and he can see that I do not want him to be in my room alone, he then suggested that I clean my room with him, so we will be in the room together. I said, "you can clean the room it's fine I don't mind," but he insisted "no, no," he felt he could tell that I did not want that, and insisted we clean it together.

I only needed to put the sofa bed up which was easy, so I could not understand why he was insisting so much. I could not hold my truth in anymore, he was agitating me, it had to come out, I felt like the words wanted to erupt like a volcano. I finally said it but in a sort of shaky tone to my voice, I was nervous and anxious saying it, I said to him, "to be honest Eddie I don't want to be in my bedroom alone with you, after everything you have said to me." He suddenly tried playing stupid and ignorant asking me what I meant? I told him straight, "after you said you want to be my friend with benefits, after you said you want to have sex with me." He started to deny what he had said and was twisting his words by saying he said Becky is his friend with benefits. He was denying it all, so I corrected him and started repeating all the things he had said to me before. I said to him that I do not care about what he has said, but do not lie and try to deny it, he knows he asked me to be his friend with benefits. I began to lose my temper, I reminded him about the conversations I had with Becky and him, and all the sexual things he had said to me, like when he said, "when Pauline leaves, we can spend a day fucking all over the house." Or when I told him that I am too gay and he insisted, "no penetration then, I will just eat your pussy," or being drunk in front of me grunting "ahh I wanna fuck you," even to be so bright to ask me to be his friend with benefits. He could not answer me, his manipulation tried to kick in, going on about I got it all from talking to Becky, trying to deny his involvement. I told him exactly what he had said and to stop lying to my face.

At this moment I was still trying to say things in a calm way, in my mind I was still staying there, but the more we spoke, the more patience I began to lose. Especially when he was trying to deny it and lie to my face, not knowing the whole time I have him recorded stating he wants to be my friend with benefits. He finally admitted what he had said but then tried to switch it up. He said that he could understand I would be upset if he went on about it, but as soon as I told him no it was left there, he said he believed it to be finished, so me saying this now is irrelevant. I reminded him of the first morning after I had told him no, when I went into the kitchen, and he took his phone out of his pocket and showed me two pictures of myself with straight hair. Telling me how much better I look with straight hair, pictures of me on his own phone! He kept trying to get himself out of it, he could try and be as manipulative as he wanted but I knew the truth, and I had proof, so I was good. After I had blocked his escape of denial, he began to explain to me that I was reading into things wrong, telling me that I shut it down. I had to make him know that I have come Jamaica for a solo trip, he had abused his position and authority as a host. He overstepped that line as soon as he asked me to be his friend with benefits, and he had the cheek to say to me that he has felt uncomfortable, with Pauline. I said, "and what about me, what about how I have felt?" does he not think I had felt uncomfortable with what he has said to me? I explained to him what if I wrote a review online and included everything that has happened, does he think the general population would think I have a right to feel uncomfortable? I made it noticeably clear that I have felt extremely uncomfortable, that he wants to have sex with me and tried to push that desire onto me. He asked me, "why are we revisiting this?"

I told him, "Because I have another two and a half months to live here and I do not feel comfortable with you, not after everything, and since it all has come from you, you should be giving me my fifteen hundred pound back so I can find and book another accommodation." He replied saying that it is fine that I would like my money back, but he does not have it! He tried schooling me on how the accommodation agency works, trying to tell me they are the ones who have my money, little did he know I had already done my research. The accommodation company takes all my money out in instalments, and it will go into Eddie's account regardless, unless I cancel my booking, if I did decide to cancel my booking, the accommodation company would take a portion of my money. Due to Eddies cancellation policy being set as strict, I would have only received a percentage of my money back, not the amount in full, I would not have received it back in enough time, to be able to pay for somewhere new to stay. I did not think any of this was fair, so I insisted that he gives me all my money back and let the money go into his account like it would anyway. Due to all of this being because of his perverted mind, there was no way I was going to let myself suffer or lose out. He did not mind me leaving but he did not want to give me my money, I told him to give me my money, so I can leave. I was trying to stay calm and patient, but the whole time I was boiling up inside.

All the built-up energy I had suppressed was coming to the surface, whilst he was thinking whether to give me my money or not, I blurted out in a forceful tone the result I wanted. "I am going to go pack my suitcase, I have recordings of all the filthy things you have said to me, and your wife and sons contact details! I suggest you find me my money because if you haven't got it by the time, I have finished packing, the recordings are getting sent to your family!" He tried talking to me about it, but I told him that I did not want to hear a word he has got to say, I said "you are a manipulative cunt, I don't trust or believe a word that comes out of your mouth!" I was getting angrier and angrier, I listed out what I had recorded in detail, I told him to get my fifteen hundred pounds. I shouted out, "every Bludklaart, every Pussyklaart knows what you have done," I was cursing him calling him a pervert and scumbag, allowing myself to become overrun with anger. Pauline asked frantically,

116

"what is wrong, what's happened?" I was still in a rage seeing red, I blurted out "I am leaving today, I am leaving with you!" I screamed, "PRICK!" I kicked the bedroom door and shouted, "you best give me my money," all this built-up energy was finally getting released. My adrenaline was pumping so much, I could feel the energy emanating from my being. I swear it felt as if I was floating just above the floor. I hooked my phone up to my speaker and said, "let's play them out loud shall we." I wanted to be loud and disruptive because he still had Simon the other guest there and I felt that he would rather do as I said, than be exposed to everyone.

Pauline was asking what had happened, I said "you don't need to play dumb anymore I have told him everything. You know what's happened and what he has said," she replied saying "I know, but what's happened just now." I told her what he had been saying to me that morning, I told her that it all came out, everything I was thinking. He started to talk to Pauline alone in the kitchen, arse kissing, trying to apologise, telling her that after I said no, he said no more about the situation, I could hear everything he was saying which frustrated me more. I stormed into the kitchen and told Pauline not to bother listening to a word he says because all he does is chat shit. I reminded him about the photos the morning after I said no, about all the times he slagged Pauline off, including that morning when he was telling me how uncomfortable he felt because she stayed there. I felt how dare he try and worm his way in with her, now all of this has crashed down on him, nothing and no one was going to help him out of this. He was in the wrong, he had to take responsibility and make it right, even if he did not want to. I told Pauline if I were her, I would not waste any of my time on him, he does not deserve it, he is a manipulating scumbag. He asked me if we could sit down and talk about this, but I could not bear the sight of him. I told him no and that I do not want to hear anything he has to say because he manipulates everything, I told him to get me my money, that is all he needs to know.

I went to the bedroom and started packing my suitcase, I was buzzing with energy and awareness, I must have come across quite intimidating, but I am sure it was necessary. I went up to him and told him again to get my money together by time I have packed my suitcase, otherwise I will be sending the recordings to his family. I went back into the bedroom, Pauline was telling me to calm down, she said she thinks he might have a heart attack and that he looks terrified. I thought, yeah only because all of this has come as a complete shock and I have not given him enough time to think of any type of solution, except for my solution. I did not even give him enough time to properly process it all, he must have been scared that all his secrets could come out, all he could do was what I asked, he did not have enough time to think of a counterattack. It was so hard to calm down, I had held so much in for what felt to be so long. I was relieved when it all poured out of me, as if I were finally living my truth again, not in anyone's shadow. I got back to packing my suitcase and took some deep breaths, my mind was running wild, I would never underestimate someone, so for my own sake I took a deep breath and made my way back out there to him. He was sitting at the veranda with his head in his hands, I walked over to him with no intention in listening to anything he had to say, but I needed to make a statement, so he knows not to try and mess with me.

I stated to him, "I am only saying this because I do not know you, I don't have a clue who you are or who you know. Yes, I have recordings of you, and your wife and sons' names and contact details, I have sent all this information to a friend that is back in England. If she does not hear from me via voice note every ten minutes with me stating I am okay, she has clear instruction to send these recordings to your family. If you try anything, if anything is to happen to me, your world will crumble and everything you have done in the last 3 weeks will be out there in the world for everyone to see." He tried to say that he is not like that and that he is not going to do anything, but I shrugged it off and said, "I do not care what you have to say, I don't believe a word that comes out of your mouth, you know my stance and that's all that matters to me, I suggest you hurry along and get me my money as I have nearly finished packing." I would not let him finish what he wanted to say, I said my piece and left him, I went back into the bedroom to get ready and pack. If I would have given him any time of day, he would have tried anyway possible to weasel his way out of it. I returned to the bedroom and finished packing my suitcase, Pauline was getting all her bits together. We both could not believe what was happening, but I did feel a sense of relief, I was happy I was leaving. I had a shower and got myself ready, all my things were now packed up and Pauline was also washed, dressed, and packed, we took our cases out to the front by the veranda.

When we went to the veranda, Eddie was sitting there with the money out in front of him, he handed me over the cash, I had never seen

American money before. When I was holding the money it felt like paper, it reminded me of monopoly money, so I thought it was fake. I said to him, "don't try and mug me off, you are not in a position to do that, I will send these recordings, don't test me." I could see he was worried, he kept saying if it were fake money, he could get arrested for fraud so he would not do that, the money is real, the way he went on made me consider he was telling the truth. I counted the money out in front of him, he had given me fifteen hundred US dollar, I took a moment and thought this isn't right, does he think I am stupid? I gave him fifteen hundred pounds, I told him he owes me more than this because of the exchange rate. I looked on google and I got the exchange rate up, I told him he owes me two thousand and thirty US Dollar. I held onto the cash and told him to get the rest, me and Pauline were waiting on the veranda. By this point you could tell Eddie really did not want to give me his money, but I basically left him with no other choice, actually, I convinced him he had no other choice, because we always have a choice. It helped that I had recordings of him, and that he did not want his family finding out, because if he did not care, he would not have given me all my money back. It also helped that Simon the other guest was in the house because it gave Eddie even more incentive to get this out of the way as quickly as possible, so his image was not destroyed, which made him give into my wishes.

Eddie had come out with the extra money he owed me, it was suddenly all so tense, I had not given him any time to think or dwell on what was happening, I was emanating so much energy that it must have thrown him off balance. I bombarded him with all this information and conflict with only one solution, my solution, I only gave him just enough time to fulfil my wishes. He may now reflect and wish he had done things differently, but the time frame I gave him did not allow that. This is why sometimes it is important to keep your plans quiet, if I would have told him how I felt straight away, he could have used that time to prepare himself and figure out a way he could leave me without accommodation, and without having to pay me my money back. The way I handled the situation put me two steps ahead the whole time. He was clueless, all because I held my tongue and used the time, I had given myself, to my advantage. He underestimated me, maybe because I am a woman, maybe because he knew some stories of my past, maybe because I was young and was going to be alone, whatever the reason, it made him lower his defence, which in turn made him vulnerable and allowed me to prevail. The rule of the universe is change. With time always comes change, you can use the present to your advantage or not. You can either be ignorant and unconsciously aware, underestimating your surroundings and get squashed like Eddie, or you can choose to be aware. Consciously accepting and never underestimating, this will allow you to make decisions and take steps to help you be prepared for anything.

We were all standing around the table, you could tell he knew he was in the wrong and was worried about the evidence I had on him. I could not believe the cheek of him, telling me he did not have the money before I exposed the recordings. He had the extra five hundred cash in his hand, but he did not want to hand it over to me, he kept asking me to listen and wanting me to go through the accommodation agency. I kept telling him, "I do not want to listen to what you have to say, I want my money so I can leave." I walked round the table closer to the exit, he said he will give me the cash, but he wanted me to cancel the booking before he does. He wanted the room to appear available online, so he could rent it out when I leave. I did not trust him, I thought as soon as I cancel the booking, he will pocket the cash and leave me with what I had already. I told him to hand the money over to Pauline and then I will cancel the booking on my phone right in front of him. He hesitated but he gave Pauline the money, I asked her to count it and she said that it is there, so I cancelled the booking in front of him like I said I would. I got the money off Pauline and counted it, there was only five hundred US, not five hundred and thirty, but I could not be bothered to argue over thirty dollars, so I left it.

After that situation was over with, he offered to give me and Pauline a lift to doctors' cave beach with our luggage, so we did not have to wait around for a taxi, Pauline was willing, but I felt very hesitant. All I could think was, what if he knows people, what if he gets people to run up in the car and take us or rob us or hurt us, I did not trust him. I did not know what he was capable of, I knew he surely did not like me anymore and he could possibly try to take this money back off me.

We decided to take him up on his offer, Pauline wanted to leave and so did I, but I did not go along all clueless, I put my money in my sock and then put my shoe on, so it was always safe on me. We put the luggage in the van and got in. I sat behind him with my hand and arm resting on the seat by his neck the whole time he was driving, I was ready for anything. He started driving but he did not take the usual route we were used to, this put me on edge, so I kept saying to him, "if you stop this van or try anything, I will snap your neck quicker than you can imagine." I do not know if I really would have snapped his neck, if I were threatened to save my life then maybe I would have. I do not like causing harm so it's possible I would have tried to find another way. I wanted to scare him so much that he would not dare do anything, I think it worked as he was shaky and nervous, he kept telling me to calm down and that he is not going to do anything. He was on edge, and I was glad, I wanted to intimidate him, I needed him to feel intimidated so I could complete my mission smoothly. I doubt I would have been able to break his neck since I do not know how, but he did not know that. Then again you do not know your capabilities when you are in survival mode, I felt like super woman. He dropped us off at doctors' cave beach and drove off, I was so relieved to be away from him and to have my money back. Luckily, me and Pauline got on well with the staff at the beach and they let us put our luggage in the cupboard by the toilets until we needed them. I did not mind that he shorted me thirty US dollars, especially considering I had taken that five thousand JA dollar from him, I felt like karma took it back, even if he knew or not.

The first thing we did was go straight to the shop where my friend Loz worked, I had to tell her everything that had happened. She asked where our cases were, I told her at the beach and she told us we should have brought them there, I said I will bring mine over when Pauline leaves. Loz was happy I was out of that house, I started looking for places to stay online and she was helping me. I was still buzzing from everything that had happened so I could not really concentrate, I could not believe all the money I had on me as well, it was surreal. I was on a high, not thinking, I told Pauline to get whatever souvenirs she wants and that I will pay. She took up the bits that she wanted, then Loz suggested that I wait and do not spend anything until I have sorted myself out with regards to accommodation, since I might need it. I agreed and apologised to Pauline, and I said I should wait just in case, I felt bad, but it was the smart thing to do, I can be too impulsive sometimes. I had a million thoughts going around my mind, I was looking for accommodation for most of my time. I told Loz that I had his credit card details, we both wondered if they would work. I never sent the email to get the Canadian address, all I had was the Jamaican one, so I was not sure.

I went over to doctors' cave beach to get the luggage, whilst I was there, I looked online and tried to book a two week stay at a five-star RIU hotel in Montego Bay. I filled out all the relevant information and the payment details and clicked book. To my surprise it had worked, I thought it might work but I was still in shock when it did, I did have the correct address details, I knew the payment went through as I received an email confirmation and a receipt. I took the luggage up to the shop and went to tell Loz straight away, I said, "Loz, you will never guess what I have just done, I booked a hotel room for when Brandy comes and it worked, you can stay with me the second week if you like, woii," we were both laughing. Loz was speaking with her boyfriend then came over to me and offered for me to stay at hers if I wanted to, instead of paying for a place. She said I could buy myself a bed since she does not have a spare one, then anytime I come back to Jamaica I can stay there. I was grateful she asked but I was not sure at first, it is not like I had known her for a long time, but I did get good vibes around her, I guess anything could happen either way. She told me that she lives with her sister, brother, and the kids, she insisted that I am more than welcome and told me that I would not get no trouble from anyone.

I decided to go with the flow, to not resist what the universe had planned for me, I thought that if I did not like it or it did not work out, I could leave whenever anyways so I might as well be positive, there was no reason to think negative. The time had come for Pauline to get into a taxi and go to the airport, she was glad I had somewhere to stay, we said our goodbyes and she got into a taxi then left. I was chilling with Loz at the shop then got a drink and went to sit on the beach for a little bit.

I wanted to ring my mum and let her know what had happened, the last time I had spoken to her was earlier that morning. I rang her via WhatsApp as soon as she answered I told her everything that had happened. I explained about Loz and that I was going to stay there, well at least for a few days and see how I got on. I told her that Eddie gave me all my money back, my mum chuckled and said, "of course he did, only you would get it back." She was glad I was away from him and safe, I could not help but wonder, so I asked, "mum, what would you have done in this situation?" She replied saying "I don't know, I would have probably cried and tried to come home." I thought that is sad, all because of the actions of someone else, we spoke some more, I told her I would keep her updated and said goodbye.

After I got off the phone to my mum, all I could think about was all the girls and women out there who may not have the courage, self-confidence, self-esteem or even self-worth, to stand up in these situations and say no. Unable to think to do something which could help them get out of the situation, I felt like I could relate as I used to be exactly like that myself. What happened with Eddie was sexual harassment and sexual coercion, I could imagine so many girls going along with it for a safer and easier life, especially when he makes it out, its their best and only option. It is sad, those poor girls, they need their self-respect, their confidence, their power! Then I began to think not only about the empowerment of women but the empowerment of men as well. I thought about every individual who does not have the knowledge, of how to take their power back from people and institutions that try to make them feel weak, vulnerable, submissive and want them to conform to their beliefs and ideas. Something had to Change!

Irie

The rest of my time on the island was amazing, I moved in with Lauryn, got along with her family so much it felt like we all connected straight away. I loved that all the kids had this energy to life that made me feel happy to be around. I bought a bed and we put it up at Lauryn's place, she lived in Norwood paradise. I submerged myself into the culture, lived just as the locals in a completely different environment and I loved every second of it. I think I was the only foreigner within the area I was staying, but I could not have felt more at home. The circus came to Montego Bay, all I could think was to take the kids and Loz's sisters to go see it, to say thanks. The kids had never been before and neither had I, not to one like this. Being in that circus tent was exciting, the show was amazing, the acrobats and the magician, the dogs performing loads of tricks, along with stunt bike performers. I will never forget looking to my side and seeing all the kids, seeing Tally's and Kaneile's face beaming with joy and amusement, all smiles. It gave me the warmest feeling inside, the thought that I could bring that much happiness to people lit up my soul and made me feel like that is a part of life worth living for.

Everything I wanted to do, I did without the help of any man, I wanted to travel around the island, so I did, I wanted to rent a car so I could get around easier, although I did not have a license, I can drive, but I did not pass my test before I had arrived. Luckily for me Loz's sister Tally had a license and was willing to rent the car using hers, I was so happy, I could not believe it, I felt so grateful. I would go everywhere, alone or with people, it did not matter to me, I went to the local food shops and market

124

many times alone and with friends. I was fine, this is a place Eddie had told me not to go trying to convince me that it is cheaper to buy take out every night, one of the many lies I naively believed. Having the car allowed me to explore the island for myself, Loz told me about the Digi cell sim card, I bought enough internet for google maps and was on my way.

One morning I drove to Falmouth, dropped Antonne at the pier where she worked and then made my way exploring, I found a public beach and sat to smoke a joint, then I drove up to the Martha Brae River. You can go down the river on a bamboo raft with a guide that takes you along, it costs $60 US for a foreigner, but I love nature and trying new things, so I gave them all the money I had on me and paid for it. I went to the raft and sat down then we made our way down the river, I had a joint and sparked up. You could only hear nature, the trickling of the river, the birds and insects, the silence, no civilisation, no cars, it was amazing, my soul felt completely free. I walked up and down the bamboo raft with no fear, looking up seeing the trees curl over to each other, it was magnificent, peaceful, and calming, I felt home, safe, I felt like I was exactly where I wanted to be. It took 2 hours to go down the river although it did not feel that long, time was not on my radar, I did not feel any need to rush or go faster, I was simply enjoying the moment.

I went and picked Antonne up from work and we made our way back home, stopping off at KFC on route. I really got on with Antonne, I have love for her, she is crazy like me with a good heart, I loved it. I went to a funeral with Antonne it was her friends baby father's funeral, she asked if I would go and support her, so I did. I ended up meeting her friends of friends, who I developed friendships with. Anvi and Monique, I will never forget them, I still talk to them to this day. I would chill with Anvi, we would go to the night beach together, I love her vibe, you know when two souls connect, that is what happened with us. I travelled to Negril with Louie, I went to ricks café a few times, once with Louie and again with Loz, Antonne, and Kaneile, and once with Anvi and Brandy. I done everything I said I wanted to, plus more, I travelled to Ocho Rios alone and went to the blue hole where there were waterfalls and lagoons, it was beautiful. I drove and stayed in Port Antonio, whilst I was there, I met a woman called Abiba who owned the accommodation with her mum and sister, we hit it off straight away, a cosmic connection was evident before we had even met. She came to Reach Falls with me, and we went to Winifred beach and French man's cove, she showed me around Port Antonio, it was amazing all the things I had done.

I became so used to the island that I even began doing tours for the other tourists to make some extra cash, I took some people to Flava's on the beach in Trelawny, I drove some people to Kingston, the Bob Marley Museum and to the mausoleum down the nine-mile strip. The hotel I booked for me and Brandy got cancelled, as Eddie must have reported it as fraud. I was happy it got cancelled because I did not want to get in trouble, I only booked it spontaneously in the moment as I felt I needed too.

I booked and paid for an apartment room for me and Brandy to stay in when she arrived, as me and Loz did not see eye to eye on some things. I wanted to give Brandy the best holiday as she took her time out to come, because she wanted to see me out there and experience a piece of it with me. I had booked up her whole week with things to do. I showed her around everywhere, we went to Dunn's River falls, blue lagoon in Ocho, Ricks café, Pier One to watch Chronixx, we went to Doctors Cave beach and Hard Rock café, we got the best weed, and my guy even gave us some freebies, and we also got a day pass in the RIU hotel. The week was amazing, a full holiday to end my travels, when Brandy flew home, I had one more week left, I chilled mostly at the beach and got high. I reconciled with Loz, and I even booked a flight for another 3 months to go back around her birthday. I spent time with her sisters and the kids and my other friends before I left to fly back to England, feeling accomplished, powerful, healed and untouchable.

Before my trip everything in the world was telling me to not go alone especially being a young woman travelling by myself, but I faced it regardless and went anyway. Then when I arrived, I had men haggle me trying to tell me, I need a Jamaican boyfriend to show me around and protect me, that I could not do it alone. Then all that sexual harassment and sexual coercion happened with Eddie, but I still handled it and thrived. I managed to find a second family of whom I love and appreciate and made lifelong friends. Internal riches can be found anywhere in the world and personally I believe Jamaica has the richest environment and the people have some of the best internal riches. You should never judge because you do not know the history of whom you are trying to judge, you may assume things but until you experience a place or situation for yourself, you could never fully understand, you can only try to. I travelled to every part of the island that I wanted to, ALONE, without needing anyone. I experienced what I wanted and every time I would meet like-minded individuals along the way, when I was doing whatever activity, I wanted to do for my own enjoyment. I learnt that healing myself is loving myself, an aspect of healing for me is trying to bring as much joy and positivity into my life at any given moment, in each present time. We hold our own power, we can do anything we set our minds too, you must believe with every single atom in your being, that you can achieve, so, enjoy, apply, and live your life!

Once we all take the internal journey through our self, our minds, our thinking, facing all our inner fears, demons, and low vibrations. This will help conquer the negativity, to find the power and light we all possess, once this is achieved, we can work towards living our life on earth, without these negative forced conditions. We will be able to interact with each other on a deeper level, not noticing our physical realms, yet diving into each other's psychological realms. We must overcome our identification with form, to love all consciousness behind it. These are the visions and ideas that drove me to write this book, for the betterment of humankind, I have shown some of my life experiences no matter how hard or traumatic they were. I have shown the knowledge I have gained from my life lessons, in hopes that it will inspire everyone to look at their lives in a way of continuous learning, growth and development.

If you apply this internal journey, question the world instead of following, strip away any negative prejudices, stereotypes, discriminations, and stigmatizations, then it will allow you to grow abundantly within your own created prosperity. We are creators, inventors, visionaries, why follow a world of inequality and injustice when we have the power to create a new one.

Part 3

<u>Oppression</u>

Oppression comes from the evils of the mind,
discrimination and prejudice keeps the beast alive.

There are different types of oppression within society and the
world we live in, I have included references to some of the information I have acquired from articles and books, if followed
up, I hope these sources help you gain a broader understanding of what
is going on. I have not covered everything as there is a vast amount of
knowledge out there, and I am still learning myself, but I hope what is
included inspires you to do your own research and to end your own ignorance. As a white woman there are oppressions that I have no experience in, I am only highlighting what I know and can see from living on
this earth. I want to make it clear that we all have a responsibility to listen
to those who are affected by oppressions that we may not experience.
We must understand our own biases and subconscious internalised prejudices. I understand that I do not have all the answers and cannot understand fully what it is like to be oppressed by, for example the colour
of your skin. I understand the human mind and urge all of us to look
within to transcend these evil ideals, to make this world a place we can
all enjoy. I have used certain educational sources to show how the mainstream, whitewashed, education system, has in a way reinforced oppressions within the world. I have included these so we can learn, see the
biased information for what it is, oppressing, discriminatory and dehumanising, so we can break the chain!

You do not control what you learn from, and what you have been exposed to, but when you reach a certain age, you become responsible over your life, thus your thoughts and actions. To put an end to oppression we need to unlearn or relearn prejudices, stereotypes, attitudes, and discriminations towards individuals that shape together the institutionalised oppressions. We need to learn these, accept them for what they are, ideas, theories, biased attitudes, power distributing, abusive, dehumanising, negative.

You must bear in mind all these negative prejudices, stereotypes, discriminations, and oppressions were created to benefit rich, aristocrat, higher class individuals, over others. These ideas no longer apply in today's world, the lower-class people are awakening to their own power, it is time we put an end to the past, we are more similar than we are different, we are all human!

Oppressions are institutionalised and systematic, intersectionality occurs within oppression as some individuals are subject to more than one type of prejudice. Negative prejudiced attributes, attitudes, and stereotypes are put onto individuals. Prejudice is the act of holding preconceived judgement on a group as a whole and its individual members. Discrimination is when a prejudice, an attitude in other words, is negatively, actively, expressed onto another group or individual that has been socially constructed as inferior. Prejudice is formed by the beliefs and information within the social world, it is not natural, it is man-made information, usually to benefit one group over the others.

"'Oppression' can be understood both, as a state of affairs in which life chances are constructed, and as the process by which this state of affairs is created and maintained. As a state of affairs, oppression is the presumption in favour of men, white people, and other dominant groups, which skews all social relationships and is encoded in their very structure" (Fine et al 1985 p34).

As you can see from this statement, in this world you have the oppressors and the oppressed. These systems operate through historically rooted beliefs, the information individuals believe, if you can convince people of certain information, you can create a powerful belief within them. Especially if you manipulate individuals into thinking they are doing the right thing, beliefs, negative beliefs, on other groups within society is what forms negative prejudice. These certain beliefs are formed into stereotypes, so individual members of the group will get treated in accordance with the stereotype of the whole group.

Colonization and the social construction of oppressions happened so long ago, it has had a snowball effect and that is why it is so large and present in the world today. That does not mean we cannot change this, create our own new ideologies and for those to also have a snowball effect for the future.

It is important to realise that many individuals are consciously awake of the impact that negative prejudice, discriminations, and oppressions have on themselves and others and decide to not follow the stigmas and labels. Many actively fight the injustices of oppression, not everyone is held down, many are empowered, we all have the power within us to conquer this negativity, this disease of the mind. Institutionally oppressed individuals, from within all socially constructed groups within society that have been deemed inferior, have stood up for the right of everyone throughout history, Ghandi, Martin Luther king, Rosa Parks, Nawal El Saadawi, Yuri Kochiyama, Malcom X, Frida Kahlo, Emmeline Pankhurst, and Nelson Mandela. Some knew the only way forward is with love, you cannot achieve peace from negativity, you must give out what you want to receive. Then some also knew the corrupt powers of the oppressors and knew inflicting fear and conflict was also a way you could face their power structures. The only problem with fear and violence is that it hurts all of us, not just the oppressors, but when the oppressors make sure we are all getting hurt anyway, does that really matter?

Oppression shows itself in our institutions, in our workplace, our social environments, places of entertainment, restaurants, in most social situations, so you are constantly finding it more impossible to escape. Fortunately, we can control how it psychologically affects us, you could either get sad and believe you are the label the oppressors are trying to put on you, or you can change your perception. You can view them as childish and immature, being ignorant, having a lack of education, instead of feeling anger, feel pity, that this person or place tries to oppress people to make themselves seem better or more important. Another way to combat oppressions is the cancel culture, be loud and express the discrimination, on social media, anyway you can, so the people can come together to cancel discriminators and highlight their ignorance. Some individuals do not see a problem with their prejudice, those that probably benefit from it in some way, either through material or ego gain and sometimes if it does not concern them, they do not care. Even if a lot of people in the world want to stay with their attitudes and prejudice, then let them stay. You do not need them to reassure you that you are great, be great anyway, let your light shine through. Put your energy into experiences and companies that reside with your beliefs and that bring you joy. Surround yourself with people who lift you up and show you kindness, love yourself so fiercely that another person's hate cannot penetrate you. If you can change your environment to rid yourself of toxic people then do it, do not fear the change, do not stay in a situation that brings you so much pain. Not one white person alive today should be proud of the history before us, how can you be proud of murder, genocide, enslavement, thieves, rape, torture, dehumanisation, and abuse. No one should ever feel proud of that, the only reason some countries are so privileged is off the back of the humans our rulers enslaved and profited off. New jobs arose, stock coming into the countries, money to build schools, all of this was from the labour enslaved human beings were doing. Anyone who is born into privilege, should try and use their privilege to bring as much social justice and equality to the world as possible, in their own way. We all must take responsibility for our part to play, and we all must actively fight within ourselves to rid the earth of discriminations.

Oppression gets more strength when individuals stay quiet when they are witnessing it, not speaking out and saying, "stop you can't do this!" That allows more of it to happen. You cannot stop racist, sexist, homophobic or classist individuals being prejudiced, you can educate but some may not be willing to listen. You cannot completely stop systemic oppression but what you can do is change how you let their actions effect your mind. Everything starts from within your mind, if something can convince you that you deserve to be treated in such a way, then you will allow yourself to believe their actions and corruption, you hold ultimate power of what you invest your energy into. What is already within the world are not your only options, we are creators, we can create our own options not just choose from the ones that are in front of our eyes. Stop feeding into the oppressor's businesses and start feeding your own ideas and your friends and so forth. The most important thing for everyone is self-love, when you love yourself truthfully and completely, nothing can shatter you.

Oppression stems from wealth, it could be argued that you could not have a hierarchical society without oppression. In other words, you could not have super rich and super poor without oppression existing. If we look back in history, the gold standard of a human being was the White Western Male, even in psychology. So, anything that is different to this gold standard deviates from the preferred norms in some way, that is how we have white male superiority within society. It is a constructed ideal that was created by let us guess, white men.

In the early years of academic psychology tools of measurement were created, these measurements were completely biased towards white males, a lot of research completely left out women and men from the other socially constructed groups who were also deemed inferior. This made all empirical research have the white male as the average golden standard, so when intelligence tests were introduced, everyone who was not a white male deviated from the average, statistically speaking. As they were able to label this as scientific evidence, it gave birth to theories that oppressed women, socially constructed racial groups, LGBT individuals, the poor and anyone with any kind of disability or so-called mental health issue. This is because mainstream psychology paved the way for the bi- ased tools of measurements that are used in modern tests, whether that be intelligence, academic, or any scientific test, it will be biased if the old, biased tools of measurement are used. It is not just intelligence tests that were formed, theories of eugenics were created and tested to try and 'prove' white superiority, these theories accumulated vast amounts of re- search, labelled as evidence. All this so-called evidence they acquired is completely invalid, biased, racist and was created in such a way it gave them the answer they wanted, much like a self-fulfilling prophecy. When you have a biased tool of measurement, the truth will never be found, only what the researcher intends to find, which was white males are above everyone else. When you have a gold standard of white male for empirical research, you are setting individuals up to fail before they even start, as not every human being has been born a white male.

I believe that this was not at the hand of ignorance, the individuals who were funding this research done it intentionally. If you want to stand at the top of the pyramid, you must get the levels below you in check and make them believe they belong at that level. They achieve this through physical abuse, coercion, and psychological brainwashing. When you can fund psychological research, you can control the manipulation of education put forth onto the masses of individuals. Most people were fed information that worked for the status quo, the information was a manipulation, so individuals could get away with the atrocities they were committing.

Eugenics and Phrenology were theories that justified slavers and the government selling human bodies as slaves. Evidence was created that would suggest African's are less intelligent, more animal like, in need of a master and aggressive. We do not actively choose where or what body we are born into, we are born and then we must grow and deal with our external environment, no matter how that may be. We are energy in human bodies which is also atoms, particles, frequencies, and vibrations, we all can create life, love, think and feel. White elites needed an excuse, the elite needed to convince the masses of white people that effectively black individuals are not human.

This has led to a spiral down effect of generational ignorance, prejudice, discrimination, oppression, and stereotypes. Even when some try not to live through the prejudice they were born into, it can be innate, you learn from subtle actions in childhood, any remark, any fear, you can pick it up and internalise it without your knowledge.

Allport (1954) states that prejudice is, "an antipathy based on faulty and inflexible generalization. It may be felt or expressed. It may be directed toward a group as a whole, or toward an individual because they are a member of that group."

Hilton and von Hippel (1996) states that stereotypes are, "cognitive schemas used by social perceivers to process information about other."

This means that individuals hold categorizing beliefs that are thought or taught to be a typical trait of the group members, these constructed traits are believed by individuals of a different group. They shape the belief of the in-group social roles and the degree to which in-group members share certain group qualities. Having a positive or negative attribution connected to these schemas, come from the agreed socially constructed consensus, it is not natural.

Jones (1972) explains discrimination to be those, "actions designed to maintain own-group characteristics and favoured position at the expense of the comparison group."

This statement shows that individuals that belong to one group can discriminate against the other group to maintain their socially constructed superiority, or favouritism.

Sherif (1954,1958,1961) The robbers Cave experiment, can highlight how prejudice is formed between groups that are labelled and treated to be different. The experiment suggests a realistic conflict theory, where individuals would get attached to their group and be discriminatory, verbally, and physically to the other group. They also suggested that making the group work for a common goal reduced the prejudice.

Individuals who are deemed superior get better social and more growth orientated options compared to individuals in the groups that are deemed inferior. This shows that it is not the individual that is superior but the constructed system and group we are born into, this is what says they are better, this gives them a head start or a better chance in life.

That is why it is best to stay humble because it is what is on the inside which equates to real power, so you will never know the realest of the real if you judge by societal materialistic covers. How can anyone genuinely enjoy their privilege when it is being denied to so many? Why is it being denied to so many when we have enough technology and resources for everyone to be comfortable? Maybe because we have 1% of the world's population enjoying 99% of the worlds wealth, in a capitalist system we are not ever going to be free, until we change!

As human beings I believe it to be important to transcend the aspect of discrimination that is internal, within the individual, how it shapes beliefs, confidence, bravery, an individual's self-esteem, and self-worth. I want to show that when we take control of our consciousness, we can be more aware of the influences we allow in, and we can be more aware of the emotion's discrimination tries to illuminate, like fear, unworthiness, submissiveness, and sadness. When we become consciously aware of what is in our environment and the true intention of these things and what emotions they try to create within us, we can then decide to change our perception and not feed into it the way it wants. If someone is trying to create aggression within you, because you know their intention is to make you feel low and gain a reaction, you can consciously decide not to give them what they want and stay calm.

With regards to the social aspect of oppression, prejudiced and corrupt individuals in places of power need to be replaced, effective immediately. There needs to be an extensive and rigorous investigation into mainstream education programs and to get all whitewashed information abolished and the TRUTH to be put into mainstream education, along with positive psychology to combat prejudices and discrimination. Teaching and psychological training to combat prejudices and discrimination needs to be full focus of workplace environments. Staff completing at least 1 hour of group activity a week and staff having to complete educational activities to help put an end to ignorance, the workplace needs to have a zero-tolerance attitude with regards to any forms of discrimination. There needs to be a direct consequence when people act out discrimination in all areas of society, education, emergency services, politics, law, social environments, and work-place environments. The consequence should be determined by the severity of the discrimination, but all forms of discrimination should not be taken lightly by anyone who is giving the judgement. There needs to be a limit on the amount of money one human being can make, 1 billion pounds is more than enough, any money that is made after that, should go back into the world, this will help put an end to greed and will share the worlds wealth more productively. Laws need to be put in place so companies cannot exploit their workers, no matter the country they live in. ALL workers should be paid comfortably and should have at least a minimum of 3 days off work per week. A critical crackdown on companies using slavery and extreme exploitation in areas like chocolate, diamonds, metals, materials, clothes, sneakers, gases, oils, corrupt individuals need to be removed, and companies must follow strict guidelines or be shutdown. A golden era of recycling needs to happen, with regards to the earth's resources we have taken enough! There is more than enough to recycle and produce what we need. The earth is a living organism, she provides food, water, oxygen, everything we need to survive, if we keep digging to the core she is going to explode. Just like us, if you give too much of yourself you become drained, we need to love ourselves so we can put that out for others, we need to love the earth so she can give the love and prosperity back to the earth and to us.

Racism

We are more than just our body, but some do not seem to know. We may fight discrimination but that is not the path many chose.

A s I have previously mentioned I do not have any direct experience with racism, as a white woman I cannot speak on having racism happen to me. I have witnessed racist acts, I am aware, I hear, I see racist actions in our environments, within the world we all live. I think it is disgusting, I think racism is a lead cause in one of the biggest human mass killings, we have ever seen in this world. For example, "Hitler killed around Six million Jewish people" U.S.H.M.M (2020), in the name of eugenics, in the name of their race. "King Leopold | | killed around Ten million Africans in the Congo." Hochschild, A. (2022). People with a darker skin complexion have been murdered continuously for years, even as we speak, due to the colour of their skin, the race individuals prescribe. This abusive, barbaric, dehumanising, genocide must stop immediately. In all areas of society this disease has spread, we will look back in the future, and see the abuse we put onto our fellow people, you will either be on the side of the abuser or of the brave individuals who have fought these injustices. We must stop the discrimination between race, we must have direct severe consequences for those who abuse others, over factors they cannot control.

The way anti-Semitism is perpetuated within society, (being racist to Jewish people) it is completely off limits and if people are being discriminatory, there are direct serious consequences. For example, a UK rapper was expressing his opinions on how the Jewish community own most corporations within most industries, he got called out for anti-Semitism, and got completely wiped off all social media platforms for supposedly spreading hate. But then a white UK media personality, can be openly racist to people with a darker skin complexion, and have absolutely no backlash. We can see throughout history there has always been an unfair outlook or advantage with regards to people with a light skin complexion. I have drawn educational sources to show how the education system has in a sense reinforced racism, how psychological research was used to justify racism and slavery. I want us to look on these to break the chain, see the mistakes of the past and stop repeating them. I urge all of us to look within and strip yourselves of this disease within the mind.

Scientifically there is no logical reasoning to racism. All human beings share the same chemical compounds, just at different degrees, based on genetics or environmental influences. The oldest human remains are found in Africa, it is theorised that all modern humans alive today, evolved out of Africa, no matter how different we may look. Human beings have created an oppression (racism), based on the colour of an individual's skin, this is a social construction. "Skin cells called melanocytes make melanin, all people have the same number of melanocytes. Some people make more melanin than others genetically, and the sun with UV exposure will also create more melanin, individuals who produce a small amount of melanin will look very light." Lin, J.Y. and Fisher, D.E., (2007). When we can understand that we are more similar than we are different, is when we can let go of the pain and the hate. When you learn to love yourself truthfully, and fully, you will have no room left to hate another. We are all amazing if we let ourselves be!

Labelling and discriminating physical differences are a man-made social construction, natural is to let things be, how they are without holding any pre-conceived beliefs about it. This becomes easier when you understand what you are doing, and then allow the person or situation to be what it is. There are many people who live in this world who see it completely differently, they let the conditioning take over in forms of labels, stereotypes, prejudices, judgements, and stigmatizations. All these ideas they hold within, reveal themselves through their thinking, actions, and reactions. It is not easy to not live through our conditioning, but it is possible, you must take responsibility and educate yourself, instead of following what you have always been told.

When researching racism within psychology, there was a theme I saw emerge, an analysis of how racism 'operates' instead of where it 'originates' from. Mainstream psychologists would try and explain racism through individualistic approaches. The cognitive approach and the personality theory towards racism both puts blame on the individual, expressing the behaviour and ignoring the socially constructed discourses, behaviours, and institutionalised attitudes, that must have existed prior, for an individual to learn to exhibit such behaviour in the first place.

I believe we grow through imitation and learnt behaviour, we learn from our environment and the information received. Many of us need to leave behind the white lens we have been conditioned to look through, and begin to see from an unbiased, ungrouped, unlabelled view.

Traditional approaches have in a sense reinforced racism, by allowing racism to be reduced to an individual pathology. Yes, the individual has full responsibility but its more than individual, its societal, it is a man-made social construction.

There are words that many people do not realise are derogatory. For example, the word caste comes from Latin which means purity, so to call an individual half-caste or quarter-caste, you are saying that person is half pure or a quarter pure, it is an extremely discriminative term that many people are unaware of.

The traditional cognitive approach within mainstream psychology argues that racism acts in terms of mental processes, these are said to construct our perceptions of the world, actively functioning behind what we say and do.

"This approach suggests that a cognitive perceptual readiness is apparent at the moment of perception, which is already an interpretation of the world." (Bruner, 1957).

This does make sense if you only look at it through a cognitive point of view. However, if you consider the social aspect, that argues we have socially constructed groups and norms, which is one reason as to why humans are divided by skin colour and not by eye colour. Also, if this were to be taken as significant evidence then why does racism have negative inferiority labels prescribed to them? If it were cognitively conceived then individuals would be placed into groups based on similar attributes, there would be no need to have a negative nor positive attribution.

The cognitive approach along with the personality approach was developed to try and understand the discrimination and inequality of Jim Crow in the American south. This was a socially constructed system that regulated and segregated individuals based on the colour of their skin, thus the group they had been pre-prescribed too. Jim Crow maintained

138

white superiority, but thanks to the Brown vs Board of Education supreme court case in 1954, there was a chance of social justice and change.

The cognitive approach has been criticized for, "naturalizing racism by explaining it as the outcome of universal mental processes of racism and stereotypical association." (Hopkins et al 1997).

When race categories are theorised as representing natural attributes of racial difference, it allows negative prejudice from a cognitive point of view to be theorised as a natural outcome of cognition, due to dealing with difference. This approach cannot account for the historical patterns of exploitation and misrepresentation. It does not consider the constructed networks of power relations that socially created one group to be superior to the others.

The other traditional approach is the theory of personality, this approach explains racism through susceptible personality traits, the authoritarian personality trait was theorised by, Fromm (1941) and Adorno, Frenkel-Brunswick, Levison, & Sanford (1950). Explaining racism via a personality trait, creates racism to be individualistic and takes blame from social constructions, this is dangerous. I believe that no one is born racist, they learn racism. If we allow ourselves to believe in individualistic theories, it enables racism to be reinforced, which is wrong.

The authoritarian personality trait was theorised to explain racism and why individuals would be susceptible to exhibit racist actions. Adorno et al (1950) theorised that an authoritarian personality trait is developed in childhood, factors that assist in this development were included, "rigid discipline at home, an emphasis on strictly prescribed roles and duties, interrelationships of dominance and submission and conditional affection." Individuals are not born with this trait; it is shaped by the environment of in which they spent their childhood. This suggests that it is not an innate personality trait that guides racism, although the research around this topic did try to guide academics towards that theory. If different racial groups were not socially constructed then individuals with a so-called authoritarian personality would not be able to assert their built-up aggression on others, as society would not have deemed others inferior in the first place. A way racism is possible in our society, is by the individuals within it prescribing and accepting that everyone should be placed into groups based on their physical attributes, and then deciding or conforming to discriminate the groups who are socially constructed to be inferior.

What if we did not have a group? What if our only group was human beings? Instead of dividing us into subgroups, the evidence is in the history and economic status of the world today. The fact that one group of race has more privilege and more resources available to them, suggests that the groups have been constructed to benefit one group over the other.

"Authoritarianism was accordingly understood as a historically specific personality syndrome linked to the fear of freedom that was produced by modernization." Fromm (1941).

This theory labels racism as coming from an individual pathology, most theories within this era would individualise social issues to maintain the status quo. This theory neglects to account for the fact that racism does not just emerge from an individual, but also in a variety of social situations and institutions without evidence of any pathology present.

Critical psychologists consider the social aspect of racism and try to answer the question of where it stems from. This branch of psychology explains that racism is a social construction, it came from the era of colonialism, slavery, and apartheid. When individuals started colonising the planet, theories were created of race and race superiority, so that the race with more gun powder could assert themselves at the top of the pyramid. Theories and rumours were spread that Africans were savages and are not human, when Africans were spiritually superior and had vast amounts of knowledge that modern science is finding out today within western society. "The African Moors had many advances like mathematics, astronomy, art, and agriculture, when they migrated to Europe, they helped elevate Europeans out of the dark ages. They brought their intelligences to Spain and over centuries these lessons propelled throughout the rest of Europe." ABS Contributor. (2013).

One notion in South Africa from the ancient teachings of a Zulu tribe was not savagery but to become the perfected human being. "We try to eliminate from ourselves all base feelings such as jealousy and anger, and within the limits of our tribal laws, we have sorted out the truth – the truth about mankind, the truth about the universe – and we have pursued art in all its forms for many, many generations." (Mutwa 1996, 2003). This is what a Zulu shaman believed the African ancestors strived for, the only savages were those white men who came with fear in their heart and spread the most unimaginable amount of evil onto the African people. Out of ignorance, out of having no willingness to learn what these people were about, instead assuming they are uncivilised and tried to make them in their image.

When colonising the world, the white English, white Europeans, Spanish and Dutch constructed labels and races, individuals were placed into such groups based on geography and physical attributes. Instead of allowing to be without labels, one had to divide the individuals into groups, so one group could dominate another. This led to a false ideology of superiority. Slavery was already at large in Africa, the Arab slave trade had been around before any Europeans came into the picture, but instead of helping their fellow people they decided to dominate. "John Hawkins was an English naval commander, he developed the British slave trade, by getting permission from the royal family, to capture and trade human bodies." N.P.D (2022) & M. Sherwood (2007). The rich aristocrat Europeans took full advantage of what was going on and decided to profit as much as they could.

It did not stop there, for some reason the white individuals felt even more of a need to assert superiority over their slaves, they committed atrocities to these individuals. Slave owners would rape the men in front of their families, this was called sodomizing. They raped the women as they so pleased, many children were sexually abused at the hands of those white perverted slave masters. Beaten, lynched, body parts cut off, mauled by dogs, sexually assaulted, treated as less than a human, no right to an opinion as they were seen as property, so it did not matter. Those white people were walking around like they were better than everyone else, but they acted in the most sinister of ways, and they deem themselves superior? They were never superior to anyone, none of us are, no matter your wealth or status, you are no better than anyone, as no one is no better than you! This does not even comprehend the type of abuse these white people enacted on the human beings they enslaved and completely dehumanized. It is one of the worst things that has ever happened in the world and yet it did, and yet there are still people to this day, who think it is okay to still behave in such ways, it is disgusting!

This racist history which stemmed from slavery has led to a spiral down effect through generations, today we have individuals who internalise the constructions. You have white people who believe it is okay to say racist things but deny being racist, you have some who do not even think racism exists anymore, then you have white people exhibiting blatant racism and not seeing any problem with it. You have individuals with a dark skin complexion who internalise the white European standard thinking that is beauty, for example wearing long straight European style hair, when natural afro hair is just as beautiful. Some people with a dark skin complexion are influenced to bleach their skin, some thinking that being a lighter complexion and having straight hair makes them more admirable, look less aggressive, and more likely to get a job. The fact that individuals can even feel like this, shows the injustice and how much society has failed people with a darker skin complexion as they are made to feel as if they are inadequate and unprofessional, as if there beautiful melanated skin is not admirable or enough. Due to this spiral down effect, you also have many white citizens who make up institutionalised systems like the police force, psychology, law, government, and education who are riddled with prejudicial thoughts. Biases come out in these institutions, prejudiced police officers racially profile and target individuals that belong to the racial group that they hold the prejudiced thoughts towards, this is a way oppression is exercised within the system. Once slavery was abolished the ruling elite created systems to enslave black people in other ways. Prisons were built and they made being black a criminal offence, black individuals get arrested and life in prison for ridiculous crimes that a white person would not face any time for. This is how slavery evolved instead of being abolished, as in prison you are doing labour for either free or extremely cheap. Racist individuals work within the very power structure that we all live in and call society, they take up high level positions within society and conduct their decisions, which are influenced by all their prejudices and biases. All the biased, corrupt, discriminatory, individuals need to be replaced and removed effective immediately.

In the media and advertisements, race has been tokenised for years, this coheres to a white superiority. In most advertisements and movies, you would have 3 white people and 1 or 2 individuals from a different prescribed racial background. When you are constantly tokenising race in television and film, constantly having more of one race compared to others, it will indirectly make the viewers undervalue the races that are less illuminated. These oppressions can move into everyday life with individuals feeling like they have no self-worth and others feeling like they can take advantage, some give away their power to external influences and allow themselves to feel, as the label states. One way to change a racist society is to end our ignorance and change our thoughts, how we think, question, do not just agree. Our pattern of thinking has been passed down from the generations who created these situations. If your ancestors were the ones who committed the negatives and evils of the world then why would you not want to break the chain, why not think for yourself, why not be better.

Maya Angelo said, "you can do your best until you know better, when you know better you can do better."

This is true, you do what you know until you learn and know better, then you can start to do better, do not halt your own growth because of an attitude, because of stubbornness, because of pain, because of family, even because of the law, if you want better, be better. Being pre-prescribed a race with the prejudice it holds, effects an individual's ability to receive quality education, health care, employment, land ownership, and housing.

Anybody who is oppressed or anybody who lives on this earth deserves to have life in their favour, if favours are not matched between different groups within society, then instead of resulting to discriminations and violence, we should level up, demand equality, and find a comfortable middle ground that keeps everyone happy, it is called sharing and compromising, not greed and destruction.

Critical psychologists have developed theories of how racism is conducted in the world today, they outline the extent of which our racist history has impacted the psychology of individuals today and our distributed mind, this is our shared knowledge of the world. Racism has been warped and interchanged throughout time, it has led to a subtler type of racism, that for most may be unconsciously aware of, in countries like the UK for example. Then again in other parts of the world racism is still very blatant and active in a more extreme way, such as China. The racial stereotypes that have been created, gives rise to racial profiling which happens all the time. It can range from a woman clutching her purse a little bit tighter when a black man sits next to her, compared to what she would if he were white, to security guards and police officers aiming their attention to dark skin individuals, as the stereotypes label individuals that are within this socially constructed race group as more criminal and aggressive.

Due to these man-made stereotypes which hold negative connotations about different race groups, for some individuals it creates a belief and an attitude of a negative nature, this is the prejudice. Then when

143

individuals exercise these beliefs within their behaviour, this constitutes as discrimination. As you can see this prejudice is only available after you have learnt of the negative knowledge from external forces with regards to information. When we allow ourselves to conform to these ideologies, we allow ourselves to become prejudiced. These beliefs can be acted out in a variety of ways, some are extremely subtle, some do not even realise what is being said is discriminatory and some are very blatant, violent, life threatening, and institutionalized. This knowledge also gives us opportunity for change, as when we take responsibility, we can consciously do things differently. As we learn prejudiced and discriminatory ideologies from external information, whether that be giving or receiving. We can also learn motivational and helpful knowledge from external forces. Once we enlighten our minds and stop living through the damaging ideologies of our past, then we can all move forward progressing into a more peaceful future.

These theories in a sense are still reinforcing racism as something that is natural, in our environments, that we always have to live with. These theories still ignore the social constructions of how racism was created and is maintained. The mainstream education system reinforces these negative prejudices as they say it comes from the individual, how will we ever make a real change unless we hold the system in place accountable?

When ignorance is high, interactions can produce problematic consequences between the individuals involved. After time, certain habits and behaviours are continuously carried out, they get passed down from generation to generation almost automatically. These behaviours start to shape how we interact in the social world, a lot of the passed down behaviours have a long history of biases in favouring men over woman, biases of favouring race groups over the others, and other multiple complex prejudices and behaviourisms, that have been passed down through generations.

Individuals have accumulated certain ways to do things, within our daily activities and experiences, we elicit subtleties that can be unconscious processes. It is a learnt behaviour; this is the doing knowledge, like riding a bike, some do without even thinking about it. We need to bring ourselves into consciousness, acquire knowledge and we can slowly but surely change the learnt actions for generations to come.

Bourdieu (1977) suggests that we learn certain bodily dispositions, these are learnt ways of relating, response types, avoidance patterns, the way

144

we facilitate our physical proximity, how we show our respect to others. We may never have technically sat down and learnt them like for example the way we are taught our ABC's. It would be the social code you had grown up within, you pick up social cues when developing from within your environment, immediate and social. This theory concentrates on the importance of how we hold ourselves in social situations, our behavioural and interactional styles that forms social life including the racist aspect. This theory exploits the non-verbal aspects of social life, from proximity to unfriendliness. These behaviours can underpin racism and show how it can be accounted for on an institutionalised level.

Segregation used to be a blatant act of learnt behaviours of proximity distribution, this was institutionalised to the point that it was law in some countries. Although it is not law now, racism still gets used with regards to proximity in many real-life examples; even from choosing a seat on the train, preferring to sit next to someone of the same race, this preference is the spiral down effect of racism. Assuming black guys are only good at sports or rapping is also an effect as if they are for entertainment purposes only, when black men and women are intelligent human beings and are more than capable of anything any white person can do. Preferring Caucasian workers due to a stereotype that others are lazy is also an effect of the institutionalised racism, black people only became lazy in societies eyes when they stopped working for free.

Another aspect of the distributed mind theory is our accountability for our actions and the things we say and do within social contexts. Individuals like to give accountability to the background knowledge of social life that is passed down through generations, they distribute accountability away from them and say, well that is how it has always been, or that is how we are supposed to act, or I was doing as I was told. This resistance to accountability is what allows individuals to conform to the norms of social life as it takes the responsibility away from them. It is like the German soldiers of the holocaust, when interviewed and questioned how they could kill those millions of Jewish people like they did. They resisted accountability and put responsibility on the social norm and government saying they were doing as they were told, following orders, perhaps that's why so many act out racism but deny being racist. Maybe because they act out learnt social behaviours from an institutionalised racist system. Deep down everyone knows racism is not right, but some keep conforming to the accepted norm, but underneath they do not really agree, or maybe they do?

Individuals are accountable even if they feel like they can defer blame to others or generational and societal influences, everybody is accountable for their individual actions, even if they try to put blame onto other things. Ultimately, we decide how we act, and saying that, we all know what is morally wrong, we all know what could hurt another and we all know what to do to love another, platonically or romantically. Having a negative pre-conceived social environment inhibits growth, especially the individuals who are subject to all the oppressions within the world, but growth is not impossible. The strength of the ones who can defy the odds of oppression is inspirational. One way to understand and alter our obstacles is to work within our own mind, this takes time, instead of partying all the time or watching television, or spending time online, why not work on your-self, own, and write down your flaws, your conditioning, the things you do not like about yourself, and then find solutions. This could be a change in your environment or a change in your own thinking and perceptions, as most time we can be our own worst enemy. There is enough knowledge out there for self-love, self-help, and societal growth, we must look in the right places, firstly that means looking within!

Racism is not only black and white, but also against anyone who is deemed a different race and made to feel inferior because of it. Being Asian holds racial oppression, Indian, Hispanic, Australian aboriginals, basically anyone who is not white Anglo descents. You can see race privilege in talk, for example Anglo-Australians have been reported to have concerns that the aboriginals are taking advantage and are taking more than they need off them. The fact that white Anglo-Australians can give, and the aboriginals are in the position to receive, shows that the whites have the privilege, the upper hand, having enough to give others as well. "In Australia, continuing forms of colonization have resulted in dramatic disparities between the health and wellbeing outcomes of Indigenous and white Australians. Produced by the disadvantages experienced by the indigenous people are privileges according to the white people. Understanding how racial privilege functions today, is an important aspect of challenging racism." (Riggs & Augoustinos, 2004, 2005).

Race privilege exists, that is why it is incorrect to say white individuals are subject to racism, they can be subject to discrimination on an individual level due to their skin colour or geographical location, but not racial structured oppression or institutionalised racism, as the institution has white as superior. White individuals do not receive racial oppression from workplace environments, the education system, law, health institutions, and the police. Race privilege comes from systems that work in favour of one race over the others and false ideologies that have convinced our minds that this is how it is meant to be. To change this, we must fight for equality in all areas of society, and change our thoughts, behaviours, and attitudes. Never let anything put you in a negative state, you are power, you are pure light, if it did not bless you, it teaches you in some way, you must try to learn the lesson.

IMAGE 1.

Misrepresentation is systemic, these stereotypes are in the highest parts of society, for prejudice to be eliminated we need to end the whitewashing of the education system, stop white washing sciences and having the gold standard as white being the norm. For example, in image 1. You can see governmental discrimination in this UK police chart as you can

POLICE
RACIAL CODES

CODE	CLASS	RACE	DETAILS
IC1	White European		White skin, Caucasoid, highest life value, pure blood, Aryan, Nordic, straight blond - blonde hair, blue or pale eyes, not visibly contaminated with non-white blood?
IC2	Dark European		Olive skin, Melanochroid, lower life value, straight dark hair (no curls), dark eyes, visibly contaminated with non-white blood?
IC3	Black		Black Skin Negroid?
IC4	Asian		Brown Skin Asianoid?
IC5	Chinese		Yellow Skin Mongoloid?
IC6	Arab		Mixed Heritage, Mixed Race, Half Breed, Mulatto, Semite, Latino, Hispanic, visibly contaminated with Black blood?
IC7	Unknown		Not Stated (NS

Race Equality Secret Service (RESS)

see it fully states that whites have highest life value and anything else is lower, labelling white as pure blood! The words they use, half breed, or visibly contaminated with black blood under IC6, under IC2 it clearly states that individuals of that colour have a lower life value. This is wrong, this is in our systems due to the prejudice, discrimination, and education of the past, how can you deny someone their worth because of the colour of their skin. Especially considering we know a lot of research was manipulated to justify an agenda, so white people could turn a profit. This insidious act needs to stop, and education needs to be updated and adjusted, if we are to progress into a more liberating future! How are the police supposed to serve and protect the public when they consider some people's lives less valuable? How can we trust them to do what is right when this is the information they are exposed to, and educated on? In a capitalist society the policing system is only there to serve and protect the rulers of that country by keeping everyone else in line, they are not here for the people, they are here to help oppress the people!

All the psychological literature on racism will never make us understand how it feels to experience it as the person who receives it, unless of course you are an individual who receives it. Maybe quantitative interviews could help people understand more but no matter how much evidence is acquired, it will never reach the extent of being subject to the actual experience of racism. If anyone tries to undervalue the experience or say it does not exist, you are completely insensitive and ignorant, because you may not have experienced it, it does not mean it does not exist. Individuals that do experience the brunt of racism have a right to express how they feel, and individuals that are privileged enough to not experience it, have a responsibility to listen, to become aware, to understand. To take responsibility in knowing that their silence is compliance and to use their privilege to encourage and bring about social justice and change. Although racism is happening, know your power, nothing can control our thoughts unless we let it. Even if it beats you in the face or burns you a thousand times, even if it feels like it rips your soul a part, the only way it wins is if we submit to it, if we do not and we stay with what is right, then we win.

Race oppression is even more insidious than any other because human beings are being completely dehumanised and made to be seen as inferior. Racism effects the education system with most of the history being whitewashed, credit of inventions being misplaced. The health care system is whitewashed with most empirical research for medicine being for white individuals, we are only just starting to get good prosthetics for black and brown individuals. Even if a person has the privilege to not experience oppression via classism, or sexuality, or mobility, or gender, there is no escaping racial oppression. Whilst travelling, white privilege in western society is being able to travel anywhere without people staring at you, without people giving you abuse because of your skin colour. Without people wanting to be violent or exclude you from certain places and without security or police treating you as you are a criminal before you have done anything wrong.

Race oppression was not just about slavery and discrimination. White scholars completely tried to change the classifications of humankind, to construct a hierarchy of race, when we all belong to the human species, but this did not stop the oppressed. Even living within the worst circumstances, we had fellow human beings break the boundaries of their time and achieve unimaginable accomplishments, when all the odds were against them, like for example, Madam CJ Walker the first black female self-made millionaire. Due to the oppression of race, a lot of individuals have been left out, or ignored, or have had their spotlight stolen, by the so-called superior race, but the truth is the truth, and it will always be revealed. The real intelligent minds behind the inventions within the world have been uncovered, and when prejudice and discrimination is no longer an agent in society, we will see the truth in mainstream education. This does not take away their creativity, intelligence, bravery, and inspirational motivation to overcome any obstacles, that were designed to hold them down. If anything, oppression only should show us how strong we really are as human beings, especially when we look to the people who defied the oppression put unto them.

I believe we should take inspiration from the individuals who have fought this oppression, who have stood up against all odds and said, 'I am more than what you say I am', 'I deserve more than what you offer', iconic individuals like miss Rosa Parks, an inspiring woman who stood up for her right, for her life. Mr Martin Luther King who fought within the civil rights, for the many individuals he knew were just as worthy, as anyone else. Mr Mandela who fought for the right of the people who were wrongly oppressed just like him. Every single person today no matter what shade, that defies the boundaries that were set forth, who refuses to feed into these labels, ideals, and continue to be their true selves. In the media it is perpetrated that individuals of African descent only fare well in sports or entertainment, but there are amazing scientists, revolutionaries, inventors, entrepreneurs, artists, authors, composers, intelligent individuals. Do not let society or the media lower your capability because we are all limitless, as we transcend our bodies and believe in our minds, we can achieve anything. Look at Oprah Winfrey, a successful businesswoman, look at Katherine Johnson with a brilliant mind for mathematics, a brilliant scientist and without her, America would never have gone to the moon when they did. There have been many individuals throughout history that have contradicted the ideals of stereotypes put forth due to racism, and these are the people you should focus your energy on, and who you should derive your inspiration and motivation from. Black Lives Matter movements and all the individuals that are within the organisation and the individuals who support the movement. It is giving them a voice to dismantle the systemic racism that still exists by highlighting oppressions experienced today, empowering those individuals to see their worth, their power and offering a new path of thinking. You are more powerful than you may believe and once you finish your internal journey, discover, recognise, and take hold of your light. You will realise what these great individuals have realised, that you are enough just as you are, and more than powerful, once you change your thinking, you change your life!

Sexism

Your eyes are clouded by what you are told I should be, let me be free.

Sexism is when individuals are oppressed and receive discrimination due to the sex they are born into, whether that be male or female. These turn into gender roles which come with defined behaviours, gender stereotypes, beliefs and attitudes about masculinity and femininity. Both sexes get oppressed but in different ways, women more so than men, due to the institutionalised western society having male superiority as the norm.

Men are oppressed in the sense of their feminine aspect, from an early age it is taught that boys should not cry, to avoid all their feminine qualities, to gain status, success and to be confident, to "use aggression or violence if you need too – never let anyone get the better of you" (Brannon, 1976).

Within sexism, the severity of oppression differs between women and men, this is due to other socially constructed groups thus oppressions, they may be subject too. For example, white women have less oppression than any other woman, just like white men have less oppression than any other man, this is what the white superiority complex is within society. Black women have oppression and stigmatizations completely different to other women around the world, due to the insidious accounts of slavery, eugenics, and phrenology. What the education system and society has labelled them as, and how they are treated, these beautiful souls and minds, have been subject to invisibility for many years. These brave wise souls have been breaking through boundaries, we can see some amazing movements and accomplishments, for the longest time. Ignorance needs to end so we can love and treat others how they deserve, ignorance will end when you take an internal journey, try to learn, and grow. The stereotypes have been passed down which implements subtle generational

151

racism and sexism from ignorant, uneducated individuals. It does not stop there, as with racism black women endure sexism, and diving even deeper within the complex of being a black woman, oppression is further divided. In history darker skinned black women have received more discrimination and oppression than lighter skinned black women, this could also be due to the white superiority complex.

When the white lens has faded and we all look through the same eyes, we will be able to see the evils of the past, we would be able to hold hands and turn around standing in love, standing proud that we all overcame it internally and externally together.

Young girls are being subject to female genital mutilation, around the world, because they were born with a vagina, because within their culture which is intertwined with their religious beliefs, the male believes the woman to be purer this way, by 'preserving their virginity' for marriage while men are allowed to do as they please without judgement. It is ridiculous that girls are getting mutilated to impress men and the religious and cultural practice support's the notion of sexism and male superiority, at this extreme expense of young girls.

Hispanic women experience racism and classism, Mexicans are seen as trespassers instead of people, also poverty oppressions, if you are black, Hispanic, and poor you get intersections of oppressions. Women in Mexico are oppressed for being a woman, countless amounts of Hispanic women are raped, murdered, and tortured. Girls are scared to walk alone in the day and night because the men keep asserting their dominance, aggression, and abuse, because I assume they think they can. In India, young girls are being put into brothels or forced into arranged marriages and getting sold by their families to old men. This is paedophilia, but it is allowed as it is seen that the girl belongs to her parents, instead of being an autonomous human being herself, she is seen as some sort of property. Asian girls within places like Korea are subject to horrific oppressions, being treated like a machine instead of a human being. Young girls get taken from third world countries that are said to be poverty stricken, they are taken by westerners and sold into sex slavery, being promised jobs in foreign land with the promise of being able to send money to their families, not knowing that they will be drugged, beaten, and sexually violated for the rest of their lives.

Within child sex slavery and exploitation, racism still exists, with little white girls with blonde hair and blue eyes being the most expensive to buy, and every other race differing. The reason child sex slavery happens all the time with hardly any arrests, is because they are not being bought by the poor paedophile in the neighbourhood who mostly looks online. These children are being bought by some of the wealthiest elite, these are called white collar crimes. As they have money and power, they manage to keep themselves out of the light, that is why you mostly get the traffickers and the sellers who are arrested, not the actual buyers! For example, look at "Jeffery Epstein the billionaire paedophile who committed suicide", D., Mangan., (2019), because he was caught. Which also shined the light on his co-conspirators and due to them all being rich and powerful, even though there are pictures of them with the victims, none are getting punished for their evil crimes! "Royalty have been one of the alleged co-conspirators" C. Contreras. (2020), he does not even have to go to court, this rich elite make is so that they are above the law as they created it, we need to make a new law, so no one is exempt! Now getting into royalty, "the royal British empire has committed so many genocides and crimes against humanity," P. Gregoire, (2017), I do not know how or why the people have let them rule for so long, due to ignorance, I guess. "The British empire killed native Indians to take over America" D.L. Fixico (2018), "the British empire enslaved Africans and beat them, killed them, raped them, and made them carry out forced labour." A. Mohamud & R. Whitburn, (2018). They sold their children in front of them, imagine someone selling your child and you having no power to stop them. "The Royal British empire sanctioned and led the genocide and major famine in India." Major, A., 2020. The English people are subject to being owned and paying a percentage of everything they make to this scam artist family; you call the royal family. Being associated with them is shameful and disgusting, they give you a small amount of privilege and many think they are better than others because of it, well you are not! We are all here together and we all can work within to better ourselves, and create a richer life for ourselves, internally and externally, no one is above anyone. You are not above someone because of your colour, you are not above someone because of the country you were born into, you are not above someone because of your wealth, you are not above someone because of your sexuality, and you are not above someone because of your status. You must remain humble if you will ever strive to be the best you can be.

The violence against women that is exhibited in this world seems to be due to seeing women as inferior beings, objects, that sometimes are only viewed to be good for pleasuring men, as sexual objects. Some societal practices such as religion, can be very oppressive, some practise female genital mutilation, stoning, and arranged marriages from a young age. The only regard they give these women is an explanation from their religion, which says they will sin if they do not obey the laws of this religion.

For me, I believe in God, Allah, the Almighty, energy, the universe, the most-high, whatever you want to call it. All religions I see them as signposts, Buddhism, Christianity, Islam, Catholics, all religions try to give individuals a set of instructions on how to live a prosperous life without sin, in hopes you will be rewarded after death with salvation. I believe that Buddha was not a Buddhist, Mohammed was not a Muslim and Jesus was not a Christian, they were individuals who found there divinity, as we all can. For me, I do not feel that we need religion to reach God, the most-high, God is a creator, we have Godly essence within, we are creators, we can find the divine within each of us. God is within us all, the powerful energy that spreads across every human being, every animal, every piece of land, that is how we have been created in its own image, because of our consciousness, our abstract realm is all connected, it is the same. We have the light within us all, that connects the whole universe together, it is up to us to recognise it and cultivate it, to let it grow within, we hold ultimate power over our lives. The problem with religion is that it limits us and gives our power to the religion rather than our spirituality. This happens by separating us and passing judgement to people who are different, do not match their standards or are in a different religious group. This is not living in light or close to God, this is living in division, in negativity, away from our higher self.

We know right from wrong by how we feel, if something hurts or causes pain, we should know it to be wrong to inflict that onto another. It is the same with love, if it feels good and loving we know we can give that to another. Unfortunately, our feelings can be manipulated and groomed, so some individuals can do things they have been told and made to believe are acceptable, although it inflicts pain onto others. We are all energy, vibrations, frequencies, when vibrating on a higher frequency like love, it is hard for a low frequency to penetrate you. When vibrating on a low frequency like depression, it's hard for you to pick up or be penetrated by a high frequency. You are your ultimate power; you just have to let yourself be.

Asian women and their oppression are expressed in Asian feminist theology, which shows how they too endure interconnections of racism, sexism, classism, and colonialism. Indian women suffer a great deal of sexism, oppression and abuse, an example I will use is of the planned rape attack on an eight-year-old girl named Asifa. God bless her soul, several men took part in this horrendous act including policemen, the officer even washed her clothes to destroy the evidence. The national crimes records bureau in India showed that in 2016 the rape of minor girls had risen by 82%, there is vast amounts of literature on feminism in India that show the oppressions they face.

Many women from third world countries and some men endure sex tourism. For some the only way they can have money or look after themselves is through dating a westerner and receiving money from them to maintain their life, as in their own country no matter how hard they work, the pay is so low its extremely hard not to live in poverty. This is disgusting, these poor individuals selling the only thing these westerners would want. They have so much more to give than their body, yet this is blind to the over privileged. Intersections of oppression make talking about sexism so complex as it is not just sexism we have to deal with. Each group of women have their own oppressions they experience, some more than others in extremity and severity, and each is just as important, especially our women who have the most amount of discriminations piled up on top of them. I am grateful for those who see the truth and want to help lift the layers off, that is what we need to do, break boundaries, lift the layers clear for each other and let all women stand on one level, hopefully men too.

Men oppress themselves by trying to maintain this superiority complex, they suppress themselves of their feminine qualities, their nurturing side, their emotional intelligence, the ability to allow themselves to be vulnerable and to accept help, the ability to surrender. This keeps most men in a stagnant state of built-up tension and aggression, feeling like they have something to prove. It is important to remember that not all men fit into this category, some do see through the conditions of the world and do break the boundaries of the social norms. Some men, when they allow themselves to be, are fantastic nurturers for their children and loved ones, some are very loyal and respect women as equal. Some men do not live up to the male superiority norm, we need to raise our sons like this and to embrace every man that is like this. Gay men and trans men are also oppressed as they do not fit into the stereotypical male norm, this can cause violence for them, abuse, oppressions within the workplace and being seen as inferior in the historical white straight male superiority complex. In another way some women live up their masculine qualities, expressing emotional detachment, aggression, what they think is strength, maybe to feel less inferior to their male counterparts, or simply because they reside more with their masculine qualities. I believe it is healthy to find a balance of both femininity and masculinity within both of the sexes, although it will be uniquely different to each individual. Where we are oppressed with regards to our genders, sexuality, and sexes, I feel that individuals feel the need to break out and make a statement that we are all different yet the same, apart yet simultaneously connected, these individuals that completely break the norm boundaries, being themselves, are paving the way for a more open-minded, freer future.

The information I have included does not even touch the surface of what really goes on in these women's lives, the day-to-day oppression they endure, some with more oppressions than others, some enduring horrific abuse and violence every day. Each woman experiences it differently and in her own intensity, we must be compassionate to all, we must be compassionate to ourselves and love ourselves, especially when no one else has shown us love. There is so much to talk about in so much depth with regards to these topics, I wanted to state their existence and to get everyone thinking of the horrors, in hopes it will motivate you to face your own horrors. In hopes it will inspire you to be the best you can be, because once we work on ourselves and become the best we can, that is how the world will change. It starts with each one of us taking responsibility for all the bad things we do, and have been through, so we can consciously grow and to learn, forgive and be better. The first step for anyone would be to learn self-love, once you fill yourself with so much love, you will not have any room left to hate another.

Critical psychology talks of sexism and gender equality in social and academic terms, the only problem with academic literature is that it leaves out some groups of women from the research as like I said, some groups of women are more oppressed than others. These may include the poor, oppressed race groups and the location of where you live in the world. I have been over my psychology of women notes and have noticed that when they study the psychology of women, it is predominantly women from a white middle class background. Women from other races seem to be left out of a lot of empirical research, this renders their research invalid for all women, as evidently not all women are from a white middle class background. Without women from different backgrounds, psychologists who are not white, that have recognised this injustice and have tried to grow a body of research for women that have been made invisible, then we would never have been able to get closer to significant real scientific psychological study for all women.

Science and psychology could never really get close to figuring everything out because individuals are complex due to the diverse backgrounds, histories, cultures, and their subjective and social experiences. A way we could disentangle the strings of intersectionality is to recognise the differences, listen to each other with understanding, respect, and love. Then to embrace our differences with respect and positivity, each woman no matter how diverse from another, each woman is just as important and just as powerful as the next. Our feminine quality is our power, our compassion and willingness to love, to show kindness through evil is our strength, and that is what will help change the world.

It is important for any reader to recognise that any woman who is not white, rich, or middle class, this research will not apply fully as they will have various other discriminations to face as well as sexism. It will apply in a sense that every woman can still get treated differently because they are a woman, but women who are not white and rich will have a lot more intersections. So, when reading the research consider the racism, classism, sexuality, religious discriminations and their birth location, factors that many women around the world have no control over, but must endure, as well as the oppression from being born a woman.

Psychology in a sense reinforces sexism, it leaves some women out of research witch oppresses them further. It upholds the male superiority norm, psychology was used to keep women at a certain level, creating research which would deem women hysterical and unable to form logical reasonings. When looking at the research it is very individualistic, stating how some men act out or think sexist thoughts, it does not draw to the social constructions of sexism, it does not account for the thousands of years European males have tried to assert dominance over the women. Women have not always been treated as second class citizens. In Africa before colonisers rule, women were held in very high regard, as extremely wise, loving, powerful individuals, who men should listen to and take advice from. Also, native American Indians held their women in very high regard. It was the euro-centric view that women were less than the man, this view has spread through countries and cultures, to the point that women are being disrespected daily, by the men who supposedly love them. With true love comes an abundance of respect, if there is no respect, there is no love, respect and love will conquer all base feelings, such as lust, desire, jealousy, envy, and possession.

"Gender is seen to be a social construction particular to a specific sociocultural historical period, a result of shared cultural knowledge and language use rather than of internal psychological or biological processes." (Bohan, 1997).

This social constructionist approach holds two key components, firstly anti-essentialism which simply means that gender is NOT a stable permanent feature, that resides the same way for all individuals, as something that is seen to originate from personality or biological attributes. Secondly social categorization, this states that gender is unnatural, this complex arrangement prioritizes and emphasises gender difference. The way masculinity and femininity are performed within society is from the culturally repeated and socially accepted actions. For example, social products such as make-up, at one point in time it was normal and acceptable for men to wear, in a different point of time it is seen as taboo for a man to wear make-up. This approach suggests that gender is what you do rather than what you are, it gives more freedom for individuals to act in ways that resonate with them personally, rather than what their social environment tells them to do, gender is seen as an experience.

"Women are seen to embody gender – men just are. This reflects a long history in psychology where men are presented as normal and women as 'different' and their difference needs explanation." (Tavris, 1993).

This is due to women being extremely oppressed when psychology was originated, thus left out of most empirical research, the male superiority put themselves as the norm and everyone else deviating from that.

Juliet Mitchell (1974) and her writings on men and women are made in culture. She proposed the idea that sex is not all physiology and biology and that what is more important is the way in which we learn information. What we take in from society, what it means to be a man and to be a woman, within our culture, our family groups, and the view of how gender is played out. Either being the traditional sense that a man is strong and does not cry, takes care of his family and that a woman is emotional, nurturing and is better at tending to the house and kids. Some people may be raised in a more liberal environment, so it is more fluid in what men and women are expected to do, more equal. Each able to live as an autonomous human being with their own likes and dislikes, whilst influencing and adding to each-other's lives in a productive manner. Juliet Mitchell opened a space for challenging the notion that a man is this way, and a woman is that way. When we theorise, that gender is a social construction it gives us an opportunity for social change, we can rebel against it, we can change it to make it better and fairer for everyone.

Society pays women less than their male counterparts; they are offered more traditional jobs whilst men progress to higher levels within the workplace more rapidly. Why?

Rudman & Glick (1999) found that women who are trying for jobs and career advancement are often confronted with a virtually impossible dilemma, they are seen as more worthwhile if they present themselves with stereotypically masculine traits rather than feminine. These can be manipulated into coming across as aggressive, they are also perceived as less socially skilled and attractive which could in turn cost them their job or career advancement. So, either way women can find it harder to progress within the workplace.

Glick & Fiske (1996, 1997) outlined the attitudes individuals hold towards women and the discrimination they elicit, they explained it through hostile, benevolent and ambivalent sexism.

These theorists suggest that these factors complement each other and reinforce the traditional gender roles. That it preserves a patriarchal social construction of women being inferior, being subject to a lower social status. The main points of hostile sexism are a hatred of women, of which is expressed through blatant negative views of women, for example, believing that a woman is incompetent, unintelligent, and over emotional. Benevolent sexism is when a man evaluates a woman's worth in a somewhat positive but very stereotypical way, like for example, admiring a woman for being a good wife with cooking and cleaning, or viewing her only in terms of her being a great mother, having a strong belief that men need to protect women and that women are weaker without men. Ambivalent sexism is defined as the simultaneous presence of both hostile and benevolent sexism.

Glick & Fiske (1996, 1997) discovered that the men they researched only showed signs of hostile sexism, for example they believed, "women only ask for equality as they want special treatment, that women go over the top with their problems and exaggerate. The men felt that women liked acting as a tease then deny the man his pleasure, that women are offended too easily, and that they do not appreciate all that men do."

As you can see these attitudes have extremely negative impulses towards women and is very much egotistical and in favour of the man. You can see that men who hold these beliefs are unable to think objectively, incapable of showing empathy and to put themselves into a woman's shoes. These hostile attitudes of prejudice lead to discriminations within society, these negative thoughts of discrimination materialise as actions of segregation, exclusion, demeaning comments, harassment, and violence.

Benevolent sexism is described as men having a protector attitude towards women. This type of sexism is demeaning towards women, it treats women as if they are not a powerful autonomous human being like a man, the same but different.

Men who exhibit benevolent sexism have shown to express these attitudes: "women are wonderful no matter how accomplished they may be, a man could never be truly complete without having or experiencing the love from a woman, believing that women have a purity that most men cannot possess, that women have a higher moral sensibility and are classy and cultured." Glick & Fiske (1996,1997).

As you can see, they seem positive, but it creates the woman to be this stereotyped being, as something to be gained and possessed instead of being autonomous human beings all with varied likes and dislikes, behaviours, and anti-social behaviours. Men can be just as pure as women; we are all the same in the sense that we all can grow and develop within ourselves, it depends on the information we allow ourselves to follow and live by.

Benevolent sexism results in a subtler form of discrimination, it comes out in over-helping women, praising minor accomplishments, like it is a big deal for a girl to achieve something that a man could easily do, praise instead of promotion and a denial of her autonomy. As you can see the theories of sexism can point out the blatant sexism within society, but it puts it down to an individual pathology, ignoring the socially constructed norms of sexism, ignoring the sexist social ques, when this is ignored, more individuals can learn these ways and continue the cycle of sexism.

Benokratis & Feagan (1995) suggest that sex discrimination materialises in modern society through politics, education, mass media and employment, organisational, judicial, and governmental organisations. These theorists suggest that women are kept in their place at various levels in societal systems, and that all important decisions within society are still made by men. A perfect example would be politics, a board of white men passed a bill in Alabama to make abortion illegal, they state they are trying to protect human life but there are asserting their dominance and control. I believe it is down to the individual to decide, as who knows what events may have occurred for them to become with child.

Benokratis & Feagan (1995), express sexism as materialising in three ways, there is blatant sex discrimination, subtle sex discrimination and covert sex discrimination. Blatant discrimination is shown through unequal, harmful and intentional ill-treatment of women which is visible even if there are laws against it. It can manifest in ways of sexual harassment, sexist humour, sexist language, physical violence, unequal treatment within areas like home, family, employment, religion, and law.

Subtle sexism is a prejudice that has been internalised, by what an individual has grown up around, and learnt from within their environment, it is an unequal treatment of women, a conditioning that some may not be aware of. Subtle sexist actions have been acquired which then in turn gets normalised. It could be either innocent or manipulative depending on the person, unintentional or intentional, it could be well intended or malicious. It is down to the individual and how aware they are of their environmental influences and how they decide to view women. An individual can act in a sexist way without having any negative intentions, purely because they are unconscious of it, and think what they are doing is correct due to the knowledge they have acquired, as they have grown and developed from birth.

The theory explains that covert sexism, is the unequal treatment of women that is hidden, purposeful and malicious, it can take form of tokenism, containment, manipulation, taking over a woman and revenge.

Sexism is declining in some countries, but women still get paid less because they are women, and due to the preconceived ideas of child rearing, women are still seen to be the main caregiver of their child compared to their fathers. If men and women were seen as equally responsible, for all the care of their children and household, then maybe the progression and pay gap would be more equal. If the employer expected both men and women to care for their child, they could offer equal wages and progressive opportunities. This is mostly in western society, around the world in some country's women are still seen as second-class citizens, as less than their male counterparts, this is wrong, untrue, and unjust. We as women need to be here for one another, through any pain, not fighting against each other, but helping lift ourselves and each other up.

Even though sexism is prevalent within the world and has been for many years, we can transcend it, even when there are still many countries, where women are more oppressed compared to their male counterparts. We all need to work together to help each other, women are no different to men in the sense that we are all human beings. Yes, our anatomies may be different, but we are still human, we all have the same chemicals and atoms within us, just at different degrees. There are women who experience disgusting traumas because they are women, such as being sold into sex trafficking, women who are extremely oppressed through their religion, women that are still seen as less than their male counterparts, society still oppressing women with their pay wage. All of this we can transcend; we must come together as a collective and take our power back and decide not to stand for it anymore. If a business discriminates women, we should be encouraged to expose these institutions and businesses and show them there is no room for discrimination in our society, we must fight together, we must say no more together.

Women who have challenged sexism are women like Emile Pankhurst who ran the suffragette movement in the UK. Women like Kirthi Jayakumar who founded the gender security project. Women like Xiao Meili who is known for her campaigns that raise awareness for gender inequality. Women like Gloria Evangelina Anzaldúa who was an American scholar of feminist theory, queer theory, and Chicana cultural theory. Women like Winnie Madikizela-Mandela who consistently fought the apartheid and persistently committed to South Africa's liberation and advancement of women's rights. Women like Angela Davis who fought sexism in the US, but she could not face sexism without facing racism as well. Since most feminist psychology never took the time to understand racism concurrently with their own oppression of being a woman, most likely because they did not have to. Black feminism was created to show the barriers of fighting sexism, because of the oppression they must face

162

with racism as well, there are numerous intersectionality's with regards to women who are not white, these intersections make fighting sexism even harder, but not impossible!

Regardless of this, we do have women and men of all variety, from all around the world standing together and standing up for themselves and each other, no matter where they are from or what they look like. We need to take this knowledge and power and let it spread through to every woman and man like a virus, so we are all infected with the idea of being equal. Claudia Jones was a revolutionary feminist with her mantra, that no peace can be obtained if any women especially those who are oppressed, are left out of the conversation. Her viewpoint is exactly where we all need to be, and when all women around the world stand up for each other, we can put an end to the abuse women receive, we can show them our strength, our power!

Some women have made strides to be treated as an equal to their male counterparts with regards to being a fully functioning, smart, human being with full abilities and potential for growth just as men are. For some women it is harder, as the violence they endure whilst trying to fight for their right is so severe it can kill them. We must not give up, the more we help each other, the more each of us can move forward. Men need to be taught as well, they need to learn the feminine aspect of themselves and how to embrace it, not repress it, the system teaches men to bury their feelings and compassion and are manipulated to carry out purely logical actions. Life and people are not purely logical, we are all emotional as well, and decisions need to be made with feelings not just logic, feeling is what makes us human.

There are a lot of gender equality campaigns that are trying to make strides for women everywhere, HeForShe is a campaign on Instagram that wants to create social change with regards to gender equality, #ENDFGM is a movement trying to bring awareness and change for the violence put onto young girls. If we embraced and followed more campaigns or created our own that are close to our hearts, which help's individuals we know, as well as the millions of others across the world. Then we are taking steps closer to positive social change, we need to stop doing what we think is right and start doing what we feel is right.

You have movements like the Green Tide, which is an amazing movement from Latin Argentinian women, who received numerous amounts of support for woman's rights and the ability to be able to decide the actions they could take with regards to their own body. For example, fighting the right to decide for abortion, as wealthy Argentinian women could pay for it whilst the poor could die if they tried. I know it is a sensitive subject but as human beings we should be able to decide over our own bodies, especially when it comes to the cases of rape, women should be given a choice, it is a decision only the girl who is pregnant should be making! Stemming from the #MeToo movement, women in Pakistan and Bangladesh have been standing up for their rights, trying to eradicate rape from within marriage, trying to bring more and more rights to every woman that is going through pain and unjust experiences, simply because they have a vagina. You have young women like Xiaowen Liang fighting for women's rights in China, trying to activate feminism and show the injustices put unto women from governmental bodies, even now having asylum she is still trying to make the world better for everyone! Sojourner Truth and Harriet Tubman, fought for women's rights along-side fighting for the right to be seen as an equal with regards to racial oppression. It is impossible for any black woman to fight solely for women's rights as the racial injustice is still so prevalent. It is a factor that must be considered, until systems and people in the world destroy their historical racial prejudices that have been conditioned into them. These women are brave, fearless, strong, powerful, full of light, being something great, trying to change the world for everyone, follow these women and their mantra, be the change you want to see!

Sexuality

You tell me how I am supposed to feel, you tell me if my desires are acceptable, but I do not care because they are real, it is not my fault they are flexible.

"Western Societies' notion of sex and sexuality: men, masculinity, and male sexuality embody activity; women, femininity, and female sexuality embody passivity." Fox et al (2009).

Mainstream education suggests how strict our society is with regards to sexuality, it has no fluidity which is ridiculous considering human beings are naturally fluid. The time era will also determine wrong and right within sexuality, for example in ancient Rome nearly everyone was bisexual, this was seen as completely normal. We vary amongst a vast spectrum of sexuality that may never end, you cannot help what you feel naturally, does that mean we should suppress it? "Same-sex behaviour ranging from co-parenting to sex has been observed in over 1,000 species with likely many more as researchers begin to look for the behaviour explicitly. Homosexuality is widespread, with bisexuality even more prevalent across species." J, Bawagan (2019). Some sexual fantasies such as paedophilia and bestiality are not a sexuality, they are a fetish, a complex one, that is usually groomed into an individual. If it is not consensual from both participants and they do not have to be groomed or manipulated into doing it, it cannot be classed as a sexuality whereas two people who share views are taking part. Also, with paedophilia adults are taking a child's virginity which should only be given by a person who has developed enough internally and externally to take that step.

Sexuality is furthermore oppressed within the heterosexual norm, requiring women and men to act out or cohere to a standard of heterosexuality. It used to be more prevalent in western society, for example, women were not allowed to wear trousers and boys could not wear makeup as it was viewed as feminine. Sex and sexuality are a crucial part of who we all are, it shapes our likes, dislikes, and desires, we are all sexual beings, we have a sex identity along with a sexuality. We make sense of this on an individual personal level and a societal collective cultural level. Sex is something that we do, and this action is at the core of a range of processes including cultural, power and language. If you look up the meaning of sex in the dictionary, most of them, use two terms, these terms say that sex is "that by which an animal or plant is male or female" and "sexual intercourse," one is the idea of having a sex and the other is the idea of performing sex. It highlights a dual notion of sex as something we have and something we do with other people, the sex we are in modern terms is our gender, whether that be male or female. Sexual intercourse is a very narrow term for sex, especially considering it is not the only form of sex you can have. Sexual intercourse is defined as penetration for example, oral sex, is performed without intercourse. Mainstream education tries to perpetrate the idea that sexuality should be a certain way, for individuals to be normal. The term normal is only a shared consensus between people. I believe mainstream education reinforces discrimination with regards to sexuality, due to the way they try to assert that men and women should be a certain way, from what they are assigned from birth. It does not account for cultural influences, the time era, and other conditionings we may be subject to. It also does not account for the natural feelings millions of human beings on this earth have, not every gay, or trans, man or woman, can be wrong.

There are different types of sex that use different actions, sex for reproduction can be performed differently from sex for purely pleasure, sometimes sex is just to obtain some form of intimacy, not always reproduction. In society there is a tension and prejudice with regards to an individual's physiology and who they desire sexually, their sexual fantasies. Western society assumes all to be attracted to the opposite sex, from the sex they are born into, if not, the stigmatizations within society infiltrate their minds judgement and belief system. Sexual desire and fantasy come from within, but another aspect of what shapes desire is the cultural aspect, notions and standards of beauty and desirability.

In western society there are tensions with regards to what is considered normal and abnormal sex, what is acceptable and what is unacceptable, decent, and indecent. The way laws have been shaped and constructed,

166

sexuality has shifted, for example, it was against the law for same sex marriage and now it is not in some parts of the world. As the law changes it seems that morality changes for some individuals, so what we deem acceptable and unacceptable can change. There can also be tensions between our psychology and sexual identity, how desirable we perceive ourselves to be in the social world, how these aspects are shaped by society, our families, our cultures. The way in which there are cultural rules for what is right and wrong, in how to act like a man or a woman. For example, within the heterosexual norms, if a man pursues a woman, it is seen as natural, but then if a woman pursues a man, it can be seen as she is easy or desperate. This is one example of how male and female sexuality is constructed differently within society, these norms exist before we are born as they are socially learnt constructs. These constructs can be different to our inner sexuality and preferences, and this can cause inner conflict.

In modern day we are prompted to think of ourselves as either bisexual, heterosexual, homosexual or transexual, and with these labels a whole heap of stereotypes, moral prejudices, beliefs, and expectations all come with the label itself. All of this is real but at the same time it is constructed socially in our environments, through shared agreement of certain information that has been embedded within our society. It seems funny to think the simplest way to change the world is by changing our minds.

There are so many theories and ways to look at sex and sexuality, this is due to many factors being involved, especially when discussing or studying the subject for example, power, our identity, pleasure, reproduction, gender, culture, relationships, marriage, intimacy, sense of worth, intersections of other oppressions, being wanted in a sexual way. These are all influences of sexuality, and we must consider how our close and societal environments influence us. The problem with psychology is that each theorist, thus each theory, embodies the morality of their environment, this carries a bias of historical and cultural views. With morals, comes beliefs and ethics and since morals are tied within the theories you cannot find an unbiased theory. So, when reading and researching, it is smart to remain critical, especially considering these professors are human beings, like all of us, their opinion is not necessarily more valid than yours.

There is an intersection between sex, morality, and the law, traditionally the morals of sex have come from religious systems. All the world's leading religions have something to say about sex, with regards to what you should do, and what you should not, and when it is right to do so, for example, only when married.

Particularly in the west, another major shift of secularisation took place with individuals moving away from religion, far fewer people in the west attended church compared to 100 years ago, statistics show that only around 4% of the UK attend religious institutions. Secularisation has resulted in a backdrop of religious morals, especially culturally, and a rise of secular morals. Morals are still there, with regards to what we believe to be right and wrong with regards to sex and sexuality, but without the religious rules and prejudices, for example I view paedophilia as wrong, as it is aimed at innocent young people that cannot even comprehend what sex is, or, defend themselves against predators. I do not believe homosexuality is a sin, because you are attracted to the same sex, there are two adults that are consenting, there is no victim in the situation, unless it is rape.

With sexuality you may be attracted to someone of the same sex, but your first contact with the subject of learning about attraction is heterosexuality or that same sex attraction is morally wrong. Then you may associate your desire with feeling ashamed or that you are doing something wrong. This is the external environmental influences telling you that you are wrong, you should stand strong, go with your gut and be proud. The problem with having heterosexuality as the norm and being gay as deviating, is people who are attracted to the same sex may feel ashamed as society does not agree that it is normal. Children may have not yet developed the sense of strength to be proud of who they are regardless.

The main point of Freud with regards to sexuality, is that the socially constructed aspects of sex and sexuality that exist within the world before we were even born, the meanings and representations that circulate within our cultures, have and always will be there. They do constantly change but meanings and representations are there, and like a sponge from an early age we soak it all up, we absorb the meanings and they come out in our psychological processes. These socially constructed meanings get into our psyche. If we are naturally against the norm then we either have to stand our ground and just be our true selves or act accordingly to society and end up being a product of our environment, instead of a powerful, intelligent, autonomous human being that we all

168

have the potential to be. The message from this is that our families have a big impact on us, sometimes for the better and sometimes for the worse and most often both. They are not fully to blame as their social environment also had a big impact on them and their parents and so forth. As we grow there are beliefs and behaviours we learn, when we are older, we may let go of them, or we may embrace them and grow with them. When we are young, we cannot do that, we hold onto everything we are taught like unremovable luggage, these early years are the most crucial.

In South Africa, the knowledge from a Zulu shaman, Credo Mutwa states, their spirituality says that sexual intercourse is a gift from the Gods, it is not something that should be deemed taboo or sinful. (Mutwa 1996,2003). He suggests that sex should be celebrated and appreciated.

Judith Butler (1990, 1993, 1994), suggests that sex and sexuality are acted out as a performance and that we are given certain scripts prescribed accordingly to the social category of which you fit into, these scripts are made and distributed by society. We learn how to be male or how to be female, she says that gender is tied up with genitals but how we act it out, whether that be acting like a boy, or a girl is from a social construction, from how society says a boy and a girl is meant to behave or act. We know from the rise of knowledge that what it means to be male, and female is a lot more complicated and complex especially when we hear accounts from trans individuals. Judith says that from an early age we learn how to inhabit our bodies, there is nothing natural about learning how to perform and act out what it is to be a man or a woman. Especially as we have heterosexuality as the norm, it does not give children the space to discover their own preferences, it labels and penalises individuals who do not fit into that category, which can lead to a spiral down effect of depression and other psychological issues like being in denial with your true self. I also feel as though no sexuality should be forced onto a child; they should discover their own self but if you think about it. Heterosexuality is forced onto everyone from birth due to the logic that it has reproductive purposes. Criticising anything that deviates away from that norm is not fair.

Within psychology, theorists trying to find a reason or cause for homosexuality or transgender gives a superiority to heterosexuality, as they all exist simultaneously why can't they all be regarded as normal, why does one have to be superior to another? It happens because of a shared attitude of heterosexuality being the norm, the more people that agree and feed into it, the more real and essential it becomes. Instead of individuals being allowed to just be, I am sure the majority would act out similar masculine and feminine qualities instead of conforming to just one. We all have shared attitudes of prejudice that have been passed down through generations, historical knowledge given by those who control the education systems, any one of us can break the chain, resist biased information given, think critically and learn for ourselves.

Sex and sexuality are a subjective experience, when we let our environments tell us how to be instead of acting according to our own likes and dislikes, we can develop an incongruence within ourselves that can cause negative emotions like depression and anxiety for example. We need to come away from the ideology and oppression of what is normal and to just accept that most things are as normal as the other. Why should anyone be the judge of what is normal to what is not normal, when it is personal and does not inflict any harm.

"When two people meet, a male and a female, or even two females, or even two males, meeting and deciding to live together, why should we interfere with them, so long as they don't by so doing destabilize or harm to others in the process? Why should we interfere with the private lives of people? If we insist that relationships must be one way only, aren't we leading to tyranny." Mutwa pp.167 (1996,2003). This statement is from a South African Zulu shaman and healer, this is what his perception is with regards to sexuality.

In society sexuality is oppressed, we know this as LGBT individuals are mistreated, receive violence, and could potentially lose work or be in danger travelling to certain countries within the world. Why do some people think that is okay to be prejudiced with regards to sexuality, it is a natural phenomenon, if people really did choose who they are attracted too, do you not think they would choose the easy option? The option with less risk, but no, the only thing they choose is to live their truth! When you are genuinely heterosexual, it is hard to understand being attracted to the same sex because you do not experience that. This is fine, but it is extremely selfish to think that is the right and only way to be. If individuals are not hurting anyone or themselves then why do you think you deserve to pass judgement with who they are attracted too. Another aspect of sexuality is the way in society we can express our sexual preferences and how we are empowered by our sexual body. A good example of women's sexuality being oppressed is the major backlash Cardi B got for her song WAP. Women, confident and comfortable within themselves showing their boss moves, then many men and women completely shunned them as if they were doing something wrong. Many men want to be superior and in power even sexually, look how the media portrays their sexuality. An example is from the movie pretty woman, she is a prostitute, and a wealthy man comes and saves her from that life, she is portrayed to be on the streets, not classy, giving it away to whoever would take it. Then you have the film Deuce Bigalow, a male prostitute within this film is portrayed as a bachelor, driving Lamborghinis, wealthy, giving the women an offer, they do not want to refuse. Both are prostitutes but, in the media, women are portrayed as degrading and the men are portrayed as heroic.

Patriarchal society has historically been governed by men as they have held the power, they have shaped women into fitting the image that patriarchy requires. Women can make themselves attractive for heterosexual men, that is why some feminists refuse to shave or wear makeup as it is a constructed patriarchal beauty standard. Power shapes what it means to be beautiful, desirable, regulating bodies and reproduction, the notion of right and wrong, the notion of law, all of this intersects. Also, many men do not mind the idea of lesbians, as they like the thought of two women sleeping together. Then they will completely shun the idea of two men, in love, sleeping together. This could be due to straight men, asserting their ego and dominance onto the situation. Instead of living with an unbiased, non-judgemental view.

There are many individuals who have fought to transcend the heterosexuality norm, it is different within each culture and subculture, and it can be harder for individuals who belong or were raised within a religion. Religion tries to emit the idea that being homosexual is a sin. Growing up within a religion, must make it even harder to accept what is inside you, is fine and pure. It is easy for someone who is born heterosexual to say it is a choice but unless you are attracted to the same sex and have the experience of feeling it within yourself, you could never completely relate or pass any kind of judgment. You cannot understand what it is like to live with this aspect of yourself, constantly being judged or feeling different or less than anyone else, over something you cannot control, unless you experience similar oppressions like for example racism, and even then, some individuals will still live with negative judgements. It is like all other oppressions and prejudice's; they have been around for many years and individuals have fed energy into it by believing the ideas and believing the discriminations are just. So, one way we can transcend these ideals, is to look within ourselves, to not pass judgement and to be proud of who we are, and others regardless!

Classism

Am I lazy? Or am I born into a faction, that has been given hardly any chance of elevation.

C lassism is oppression given because of the socio-economic status an individual has within society, in other words their class, how much wealth and power an individual and their family has. The class oppression can be seen in terms of discrimination, exploitation, poverty, lack of nutrition, lack of food, lack of education, lack of loving and quality upbringing. Exploitation is giving your workers the bare minimum, for example, the UK minimum wage is nine pounds fifty per hour, whilst the owners take millions of profits for themselves. It is important to acknowledge that there are different degrees of exploitation, in some cases people are extremely exploited, where it could be deemed as slavery, and in some cases around the world slavery and forced labour is still happening!

Then there are the less extreme cases where the government maintain the poor by putting systems in place to keep them poor, this is the same system that keeps the rich, rich, maintaining the status quo. Exploitation can keep individuals at the same level, by giving someone minimum wage and them having to work at least 40 hours per week to pay for the expenses of their lives, for example, rent, food, and childcare, it makes it impossible for them to save or to invest in their own ideas. This is what maintains the status quo, opportunities to make a decent monthly wage are not so readily available for individuals, who are not born into a wealthy and powerful family. This keeps the system in a vicious circle, somewhat of a trap, you are given goals and material desires which keeps you working, in hopes you will afford it one day, but your daily living expenses are so much you can hardly save. If you try to save, it will only amount to a little, due to the amount you get paid and the amount you must pay out.

This is a way society creates criminals, the easiest way for individuals from a lower class to make the same monthly wage as someone from a higher class, is to sell drugs or commit crimes. If more opportunities were available and less exploitation existed and people were given a wage which they could enjoy and live their lives with, as well as work, then individuals may not feel the need to make money illegally. Exploitation is even worse in other countries such as Jamaica, the minimum wage is eighty-nine pence per hour in UK money, expenses to live in Jamaica are still high. A factor of this is due to other countries around the world and their own government, oppressing them via trade, it is more expensive for things we take for granted, like meat, vegetables, dairy products, snacks, perfumes, trainers, gas, electric, internet and other materials. In Jamaica because it is hard to get things into the country, they have to pay more, even socks gets sold separately whilst in western society we can buy a pack of seven. People in Jamaica work extremely hard, mostly 6 days a week to earn the bare minimum, while business owners charge western prices, the owners take profits over the people. This exploitation is systematic and is termed as oppression due to the government allowing businesses to get rich, while their workers live in poverty. If wage was increased and people were making enough to enjoy and live their lives, crimes are more likely to be dramatically reduced in all areas of the world. Third world countries are exploited and oppressed even worse, and western people aid it, maybe unknowingly, getting cheap phones, shoes, clothes, appliances, and cosmetics. Many of these companies that trade these products exploit third world countries drastically, to enable more profits for themselves. We need to take a stand and stop spending until they give their workers decent pay, we need to take responsibility for our input and try to make it right.

"Classism is the composite of attitudes, beliefs, behaviours, and institutional practices that sustain and legitimize class-based power differences that middle and high-income groups have at the expense of the poor and working classes." (Bullock, 1995)

"Psychologists and social scientists are often part of the machinery of control (e.g., schools, universities, and mass media) created and maintained by the ruling elite, and their job is to perceive and conceptualise the realities as defined by the interests of the dominant political system." (Mehryar, 1984: pp.166)

These are aspects of classism we need to consider; the way generational attitudes, beliefs and systematic influences legitimise the class hierarchy and how it normalises the fact of class difference but does not highlight exploitation! Opportunities of higher socio-economic positions within the workplace are more readily available to individuals who are born into a higher class. Whilst individuals who are born into lower classes have less opportunities, less quality education, and less resources available to help them progress, also dealing with various discriminations put onto them for being born into a lower class. It is not just society that does not help individuals within lower classes, it is their immediate environment also, their family. If society has convinced their family members that this is all they will ever achieve, it is all they are capable to achieve and it is all they deserve, then that information will be put unto the child, maybe unknowingly and unwillingly. This is not their families blame as they have learnt it from their environment, whether that is being uneducated or having been exposed to the same information. Although as individuals, when we reach a certain point from childhood, we should take responsibility over our lives and stop repeating our families' mistakes. To learn from them and grow, so we can pass productive knowledge down to our children instead of repeating what we learn from our environments. To uplift a child, motivate them, build them up to think they are intelligent, kind, brave, and able to achieve anything they set their minds to, so when they grow up, they genuinely believe and know they can!

Class has been perpetuated to be normal, a natural thing, that if you work hard, you will be able to live a wealthy life. While this is true in some occasion's, individuals can jump classes, if you have a great idea or start your own business, but this is a small percentage of people, compared to the majority within the world. To build great wealth you need to be financially literate, which mostly the rich only get taught by their families. The general population either live in dept, on minimum wage or just above, all because we do not have the links with regards to the people our families know, or the opportunities more readily available to us. The social world severely lacks for individuals who have no money, who have been placed into a negative stereotype of a constructed race category, individuals who do not meet the heterosexual and gender norms, being treated differently or less than, because you are born a woman, as if any of us have a choice what body we are born into?

Cozarelli, Wilkinson, & Tagler, (2001), suggest that there are two main ideas with regards to class inequality, one is individualistic, and the other is structural. Individualistic ideas when it comes to class and poverty suggest that it is the individual's fault or responsibility for where they are on the economic spectrum, whether they are extremely wealthy, extremely poor, or anything else. Individualistic explanations tend to point at ideas such as individual laziness or lack of talent. Ignoring the idea that being born into less opportunities and poorer parents results in a poorer education, bad nutritional foods, and a low-quality social environment, which in turn can help create a psychologically negative life. Structural explanations highlight the facts of societal structures like obstacles poorer classes have to overcome, compared to their wealthy counterparts, for example, low wages, discriminations, psychological and physical abuse.

It was found in Cozarelli et al (2001) that individuals with greater power in the world such as wealthy white men, favour individualistic explanations. Whereas individuals with less power, for example, people who are put into negative attributed race groups, women and individuals from low-income groups tend to favour structural explanations.

Individuals from higher classes, although they have vast amounts of opportunities and resources available to them, some still fail internally and develop negative behaviour patterns. Wealth does not bring psychological growth; it makes it easier to acquire materialistic growth. Growth within the mindset is down to the individual, growth materialistically is harder or easier depending on your class, due to the knowledge we are exposed too. The same goes for individuals from lower classes, some break the chain and do the opposite of what they were born into and acquire vast amounts of wealth. The fact is that the percentage is low on each side, so most wealthy individuals stay wealthy, and flourish and most poor individuals stay poor and diminish within the system. This is because the class you are born into shapes nearly every aspect of your growing life, as you grow you learn from experience, and information that is within your environment. These can either be detrimental to you or can be great tools for growth, society is extremely flawed for many individuals. Only we as a collective can change it by changing ourselves, we must be the change we want to see in the world, the more of us that will do this, the more we will see a difference.

Some of the aspects class effects within our lives are our parent's knowledge, their parenting skills, the nutrition that is available to us and our recommended diets, our education system, our health care system, our sense of confidence and well-being. The way we are treated from the social world, our value, our positioning, the resources available to us, the knowledge that is exposed to most of the world, for example, not teaching us about critical thinking, or nurturing our creative minds, for us to invent or create business, instead teaching us how to follow rules and obey, or crunching numbers. Our parents teach us the best way they know how, but so many parents are still lost themselves. They do their best but do not realise the effect and impact it has on their child, if treated negatively it can create negative behaviours in an individual. You cannot blame these parents as their environment and parents have severely lacked them in support for psychological growth. It is a continuing vicious circle that rarely breaks, unless a person questions life, what they know, then decides to do and be better.

The societal system does not give classes or teach individuals how to be good parents and how to help develop their infants to be the best they can possibly be. Even though there is a wide variety of child developmental psychology, knowledge which would highlight good parenting skills. Unfortunately, it is not taught in mainstream education so the parents either learn from their parents, their environments, or act through their own experiences and sometimes the lessons they have learnt. This can be detrimental to the child, if society offered more support and proactive knowledge, our children could flourish. Some parents put far too much pressure on their children which could also be detrimental and could even lead to suicide if they feel they cannot live up to their expectations. Pressure and expectations to become a lawyer, doctor, psychologist, pressure to study, pressure to be a productive member of society. The parents are manipulated by society and because they love their children, they think what they are doing is best. Why not let children follow their own path, find their own passions that lift them up, love unconditionally, teach your child how amazing they are, at being them. Putting pressure on them is not going to help them get anywhere, of course motivate and inspire but do not cross the line, because as parents you may think your child needs materialistic gain. Not wanting them to struggle, that is not the most important thing, them being healthy within, must always come first.

Our health care system is shaped by the class we are in, with regards to the quality of health care we receive, if any, in most countries compared to the UK, people do not receive free health care and if you are in a poor class, you may not receive any. This effects individuals and even children who have no choice with regards to what class they are born into, a case highlighted by Otto (2007) is a perfect example. It is of a young American boy called Deamonte Driver, he was a young 12-year-old boy from the US who was born into poverty, he died because of an infected tooth that had spread to his brain. A charge of $80 could have paid for an extraction and would have saved his life, with his family living in poverty and homelessness no dentist would accept Medicaid and the young boy passed away. This is something that would never happen in higher class families as they have the wealth to treat such illnesses as soon as it arises. Who gets to decide that their life is more relevant than his? We are all born a tiny baby, a human baby that needs nurturing and loving, we do not decide if our parents have money or if they have the means and opportunities to make it. Yet it is the children that suffer because the outside social world also does nothing to aid or help these situations, even if they did, why should the wage gap be so big? Why do these individuals need so much money, whilst people lose their lives as they have none?

It is like how there is an epidemic of starvation and obesity within the world at the same time, some people are dying because they get too much food, and some die because they do not get enough. There is more than enough food to go around to satisfy everyone, but it is not distributed in a way that preserves all human life. This must be pointed at the individuals that are in control of manufacturing and distribution, the ones who decide what goes where, who deserves what.

It is the same with class, there are individuals who decide who deserves what, and only gives most opportunities to their friend's children or individuals who they can relate to, who have the same kind of background. This does not mean individuals who are born into lower classes cannot succeed because they can, but they will have more obstacles and oppression to overcome than those in higher classes. Also being born into a lower class can condition your mind into thinking that this is all you can achieve and deserve. Especially if your family are the same because some cannot see any options of how to get out of a situation and cannot think to create some of their own options. When you think you cannot achieve great wealth you do not set yourself high goals, maybe some people will set themselves goals to be a manager instead of a business owner, because they feel that it is more attainable.

Whatever goals we set ourselves, we can achieve no matter what class you are born into; it may be harder for some than others or it may take longer but you can achieve it, your only limit is your mind. If society can convince you that you cannot achieve you will not be able to, if your family can convince you that you cannot achieve then you will not. You must believe with every fibre of your being, that no matter how hard or how many times you fail, you will succeed, do not let doubt get the better of you! Even if your dream or goal is so grand and you have no clue of how to achieve it, you can, if you right it down, research and find steps to take towards it, you will achieve. I love this saying, 'the universe helps people who help themselves,' because it is so true. When you believe you can do something even if you do not know the way, when you start trying to actively take steps in that direction, it is like the universe feels your intention and will start placing opportunities within your life to help you achieve it. It can be subtle signs like an ad in the paper, or a course you can do to get you closer to your goal, you must keep your eyes open and have faith.

Class shapes the nutrition and diets that are readily available in western society, if you are in a higher class, you can afford quality meats and fish with organic fruits and vegetables. Whilst lower classes are given cheaper options of chemical pumped meats, fishes, vegetables, fruits, and processed foods. Fatty foods that shorten your life span and make you less energised and aware. Western studies have shown that mothers from lower classes tend to take into consideration how much the food will cost and how many they need to feed over health; Hupkens et al (2000) shows this in their study of the differences in social class food consumption.

The fact that some individuals must consider their kids health over what they can afford is disgusting, these processed fruits, refined sugar, crisps, all processed foods, meats, and fish that are factory grown, they are all cheap for a reason because they are detrimental to your health! You get lazy, less confident and motivated within yourself, it kills you slowly by taking years off your life. Why are freshly grown fruits and vegetables which have had no chemical trail so expensive? Why are foods that are good for your health hidden, there is a whole network of people that

benefit and make money off your bad health, food companies, pharmaceutical companies, and charities. Disease creates monetary benefits!

The only person who does not benefit is you, except for that slight
feeling of contentment or happiness when you eat it, other than that,
there is no benefit. We need to train our brains to benefit and find happiness for things that are good for us, good for our health, good for our
psychological health, things that make you smile, things that make you
feel proud. Food that comes from the earth without being modified with
chemicals for 'shelf life'. Food from a tree or the ground, like fruits and
vegetables are called live foods. Before they are cooked, they are at optimum health with actual living organisms inside of them, that are full of
vitamins and proteins that help the body. When cooked the vitamins become less frequent in the food, it operates on the organs like an enhanc-
ing potion that gives it the energy and life to run the body at its best and
full capacity. We are genetically designed to consume live foods from the
earth, plant-based foods, our atoms and receptors and the nutrients we
need to keep our brain levels at optimum health, match up with what
fresh foods have to offer, like iron, potassium, magnesium, niacin, and
all the other chemicals our body discrete and eats, all of these are waiting
for us in food provided by the earth. Foods that are man-made and mass-
produced, like processed foods, crisps, biscuits, cakes, cheap noodles,
sweets, nuggets, cheap meats, cheap chemical ridden fruits and vegetables, take-aways and frozen foods. It is all lower health and nutritional
value and in time could be detrimental to your health and the way your
body works. When you consume live fresh foods, you are more aware
and able to concentrate for longer periods of time, your body is running
on optimum health and has more energy for daily functions.

Our nutrition is shaped from childhood, the influences of our parents
and the options available to them depends on their class, some individuals around the world are even more so oppressed. They are oppressed
by the amount of food they get distributed to them and what is given to
them. The lower the class you are in within western society, the poorer
the dietary habits you can adopt. Most third world countries have home
grown foods, of which is very nutritious especially when it is not mass
produced, their nutritional value would be a lot greater than that of westernised people. Then also some areas in the world, people must deal with
scarcity of food, resources, water, and starvation!

In westernised society, schools and primary schools contain foods of extremely poor nutritional value in significantly poorer areas, compared to foods served in private, paid, higher education schools. Freeman (2007) shows us that schools in low-income areas cannot deny fast foods, as they are sponsored by the companies. The companies buy materials for the schools, in exchange to sell their products on site and to advertise on site. This results in individuals from poorer neighbourhoods being predisposed to unhealthy foods, of which can create life-long habits. They have no choice but to live in this environment and yet the blame is put onto the individuals instead of the controlling system! When you develop unhealthy eating habits in childhood it generally grows right into your adulthood and is then passed down to your children. A vicious circle that may not stop and when nutrition shapes so much of your health and psychological well-being, we would all benefit from a healthier diet. To achieve this, it makes sense to start with the children, show the children of today how to be healthy. Teach them how to grow food and how to reach their full potential, this will in turn create a better tomorrow for us all, and future generations to come! For countries which are oppressed extremely with regards to food, how can we help them? I mean really help them, not by giving to a charity that will take 90% of the money for themselves but to actively create something. To make food get distributed to areas of the world that desperately need it, or to build and develop their land so it is easier for them to grow their own, because right now they are being severely neglected. Chakabars is doing amazing work with helping these individuals, the money he raises goes to the people that need it, if you want to help, give to his charities, not the other charities within the world that are renown for raising hundreds of millions, but only giving a small percent to those who are in need.

Class also shapes our education system, the knowledge that is exposed to us as individuals and the efficiency of which we receive such knowledge. In the UK we have two types of education systems much like most of the world, we have free government funded education schools (state schools), then you have private schools which charge fees that enable you to study there. Within schools that charge fees, there are further hierarchies, schools that charge low fees and schools that charge high fees, all of this and the amount you pay if any, will and does affect the quality of education you shall receive. Within some countries like India some children do not have any school to go to, some schools are so full, or their parents are so poor, that many children do not receive a good, if any, education. Luckily for the people at the bottom of the hierarchy, it is what you think and how you think, which will enable you to make it in this world. Belief, confidence, creativity, critical thinking, seeking knowledge, and growth will surely put you on the right path to achieve whatever you set your mind to. Unfortunately, our environments can be so stressful we can make mistakes, and we must think about having enough income to survive, we do not use our intelligence and creativity to its full potential, but just because it is harder, does not make it impossible!

Education is funded and like anything else that is funded, the main decisions and what is generated and permitted from the funds, come from the decisions made by the person or persons giving the money. This is how education works, you have individuals that decide what is permitted into mainstream education. Luckily for this generation we have the capability to research and teach ourselves whatever we may desire, as education has become more readily available, due to us having online resources. The wealthier class have quality education, an education of which teaches them and cultivates their entrepreneurship, being taught business economics, how to cultivate ideas and put them into action, how to lead and have employees. The poorer class have just enough education to be able to follow orders and how to think to be the best employee. It is rarely taught how to cultivate your own business and how to make your own money, to be your own boss. Unless individuals learn it from their own families or their life experiences, the mind-set of the rich is profits not salary, and vice versa for the poor.

Universities were only accessible by the ruling class 100 or so years ago in the UK, anyone from the working class was not welcome to study at higher education. Even calling them ruling reinforces their power, they are not elite, they are human beings like us, they have cultivated society over many years to serve them and oppress us. It has got to the point that education shapes our decisions and how we view ourselves throughout our lives. What we learn in childhood and adolescence can determine what we believe we can achieve, it can determine our ambitions, our self-esteem, and our confidence in our ideas. Some can break through this conditioning and defy the odds, but many will follow and live a docile life, not ever recognising the power they hold inside. The infinite possibilities that they can make come true, the creator inside us all, the only limit is the limit we set ourselves and the limits we allow others and the system convince us are there. Class also shapes the way we value and view ourselves; it teaches us from a young age the position we have been given within the world, some are more favourable and healthier than others. It is the same with all the other oppressions I have previously mentioned, all of these create a complex system of intersectionality.

Class also shapes how the social world views us and the value it assigns everyone, it shapes the resources that are more readily available to us, it shapes how we can advance with regards to our wealth and ideas, it shapes almost all aspects of our lives yet is left out of conversation and psychological study, maintaining the status quo, maintaining class naturalization. For example, in Liu, Ali, Soleck, Hopps, Dunston and Picketts (2004) study, they expressed that class is one variable that is hardly ever taken into consideration, even though it shapes so much of our lives. They carried out a content analysis of 3,915 published articles and found only 98 studies included class as a variable.

Rothman (2005), states that elites control major institutions and hold most of the world's wealth, it is explained that this small group acquires their wealth, status, and power from ownership of business, stock, property, or from very high-level government and corporate leadership positions.

Porter (2006) shows that the top 1% of the world's population holds nearly 40% of the world wealth, while the bottom percent holds 1.1% of the world's net worth of wealth. Wealth is so unevenly distributed because in most cases, the wealthy exploit the poor to obtain their money, earning billions while giving their employees minimum wage. Why does it have to be like this? Why can we not all have a comfortable living standard, not one that is based on surviving and limited living?

Class is a social construction, it is not a natural occurrence from hard work, it comes from generational wealth, quality education, inheriting large businesses, becoming famous, or on the rare occasion you will have some individuals jump classes. You cannot change class just by hard work in a normal job, you must be motivated, have great ideas and the knowledge of how to succeed or run a business, if anything you must acquire such knowledge on your own. Due to the hierarchical world, it is harder to create wealth for the lower classes than it is for the higher classes, but we all have the chance. It is down to each one of us as we ultimately shape our own lives, even when it is harder for the oppressed due to the obstacles they need to overcome, it does not mean they cannot reach higher heights.

Another way class level is kept in place, is by the banking system, a term I like to call dept-slavery. We live in a system where lower or working-class individuals believe that they should get a credit card to gain good credit, to be able to purchase properties or get a mortgage. Without ever being educated how to make enough money to be able to pay for these things themselves. It is taught that if you stay on top of your card, then you will receive good credit, this is true for some, but the trap is that, where life is getting more and more expensive to live, many individuals cannot stay on top of their credit card. If they do stay on top of their credit cards and have paid back all their credit card dept at the end of the month. Most people will still have hardly anything left to live off, thus rendering them unable to survive on their own earnings, having to resort to using the credit card once again, keeping them in this cycle.

Unless you can make double or triple your salary in one month then you will stay in the cycle of using your credit card. If life is harder for some and they do not have the means to pay all of what they owe back, they will then have to pay interest. Many individuals spend their whole lives trying to pay back the interest they owe to the banks, therefore its dept slavery, you become a slave to the bank, forever working to pay back the interest you owe them, or the money you have used on credit, in the form of cards, loans and mortgages. Vulnerable people are more susceptible to fall into this, individuals in low-income families, individuals with lack of knowledge, working class single parents who need to care and pay for their children but work in a job that does not pay enough. This system inhibits individuals from progressing, advancing from their position within their economic status. Due to them constantly paying the money they earn back to the bank with regards to the credit cards they must pay off. The banks are owned by the ruling elite, a family, it's a company, it is an exploitative trap, a systematic scam of great intellect, to the point where it has been manipulated and advertised, to make individuals believe that it is there to help them!

There have been individuals throughout history that have tried to expose class oppression like Karl Marx, Max Weber and many more, but even though individuals speak of social class, and independently speak of exploitation, not a lot of social justice occurs. Classism used to be a lot more blatant 100 years ago, the royals would be the higher class and commoners and peasants were seen as lower class, inferior. Many individuals who are living comfortably, would not see an issue with socio economic class, since they have so much privilege. Some individuals like not having excessive amounts of money, they are happy with what they have and that is fine. There are also millions of people who die because of their social class, as they do not have access to resources like food, water, health care, and this is not right. There are more than enough resources to go around fairly, the only reason they do not is because of profit. There are individuals who struggle significantly, and on another point of the spectrum there are individuals who struggle to simply be happy, because they are always working. We are human beings, we thrive on life, creativity, passion, love, happiness and nature. Life does not have to be so down and hard, it can be easier, less hours of work so people can have family or alone time, and holidays. Higher pay so individuals can have access to quality health care and do not have to stress over food and bills. There are some countries like Jamaica, Haiti, any county deemed third world, that need some serious TLC from the rest of the world. It is time to stop paying less in these countries just because you can, they deserve more! Businesspeople go to these places as they can take more profits and pay less wages than in the west, this is wrong, exploitation at its finest, it's time to uplift one another, to stop holding each other down! If we start creating a new society together, it can be done! Individuals need to stop being so selfish and just thinking of themselves and their close ones, think of everyone!

If the major corporations would raise minimum wage to a level that ensures the ending of the suffering for the masses, then a hierarchical system may not be so bad. But they pay individuals just enough to survive, as most individuals still need to live through credit cards to be able to sustain their lives. This is unjust, we need social justice to mend the weak and restore integrity into this world, if everyone in the world was to protest and stopped working, a change would surely come. I think individuals forget that nature gives us everything for free, lost are the days that our ancestors never had to pay a bill, or worry about putting food on the table. Self-sustainable living had died out but is slowly coming back, if we all grew our own food, collected our own water, built our own homes, what would we really need money for? Unless you cannot live without all those materialistic objects, if you want to make money you can, but why not create business ideas that help you and your workers instead of exploiting them. We all need to be the change we want to see in this world, that is why it is imperative to start an internal journey. To strip yourself of the manipulations and conditionings of the world, to find your true purpose, your true passions. Sitting at a desk or working in a fast-food place is not your life, not if you do not want it to be!

ıntersectionality

The Woven Intricacies of oppression, entangled together to make life, what a life, the oppressed power
of these people, when they rise, they will rise.

Intersectionality is a word that was termed to describe groups in
society, that are not subject to only one oppression and discrimination but live with multiple oppressions, that have been prescribed to them from birth. This is one way you know that oppressions
are social constructions, as they exist before we are even born!

Intersectionality describes individuals who have multiple oppressions,
for example, a gay, physically disabled, poor, dark skin woman, must endure and grow up with five different types of oppression. The sad part
is that none of us ask or choose to receive these, they are apparent when
we are born and we must deal with it, but ironically, we all have the power
within us, to transcend any discrimination and to change our conditioning as a collective, to make life fairer for everyone. Individuals who are
born into privilege, could be less likely willing to acknowledge that these
oppressions exist, as they do not have to live through them and the un-
comfortability. This is selfishness and pure ignorance, anyone who is
born into privilege is obliged to end their prejudice, or at least listen to
others, so they can make sure they do not live through ignorance or allow
discrimination to happen. Individuals that live through intersectionality
can find their power more readily but in the same breath can lose it just
as quickly. When we walk through the darkness, it can enable us to discover our light, having to walk through conflict can allow us to recognise
true peace and strength. Each one of us has the power to shape life on
earth, but most of us feel powerless due to the position that is assigned
onto us from birth. We need to look within and understand our own
divinity, to make any real social change and justice.

Harley (1978), Truth & Painter (1998), outlines in their article the concept of intersectionality arising within the nineteenth century, it was birthed because of the relationship between the discrimination of both race and gender. Anti-racism activists such as Anna Julie Cooper and Sojourner Truth, highlighted the importance of intersectionality, at a time when only one or the other prejudice would be discussed at one time, never together. It was of upmost importance to show the fact that some individuals deal with more than one oppression, to create social justice. We must first understand the true mechanisms of what is really going on in the reality we live in.

A critical legal race scholar Kimberlé Crenshaw (1989,1993,1995), openly termed intersectionality when speaking of the intertwining of multiple factors and categories of oppression. Dhanoon (2001) speaks of how this generates a space that recognises how, various oppressions act together to inflict a discrimination, different from one that is solely based on either gender or race alone.

Through working within the sensitive factors of rape and domestic violence within broader society Crenshaw (1995) identified 3 aspects of intersectionality.

There is structural intersectionality, this shows the differences of experiences of sexual violence for women of socially constructed labels of colour in macro-level systems of race and gender; the broader society, the stereotypes and labels that come with it, it was shown to be a significant difference of experience compared to that of white women. Women with race and gender oppressions are more likely to become a victim of sexual violence, this could be due to many factors, but the most prevailing would be of a systemic manipulation that these women are of less value. Which in my opinion is disgusting and false, unfortunately because of history, the education that was perpetuated and propaganda! It has been conditioned into society that certain races are of less value as well as women being of less value. So, these women are susceptible to extra discrimination and mistreatment due to society's misrepresentation of them.

Political intersectionality speaks of the way's communities and towns, the meso-level of the anti-racist and anti-sexist politics can wipe away the experiences of women with a darker skin complexion. This is done by undervaluing and propelling the view of it not being true or that all women are suffering, not just women with a darker skin complexion, this

IM SO WITHIN IM NEVER WITHOUT

shadows the actual experiences as if they are not valid. Whether individuals are racist or not, the experiences are happening, and they deserve to be heard, so we can completely understand, take whatever responsibility we should, forgive and try to make the situations better.

Representational intersectionality speaks about the cultural imagery or stereotype put unto women that are not white. This representation is on the micro-level which means the images represented in the mind of yourself, your families, your partners, your neighbourhood. Like for example feminist theology highlighting the exploitation of being a housewife whilst excluding the fact that many black women were active workers and did not stay at home. The representation these individuals hold of people can influence how individuals view themselves, the stereotypes people may have of you is learned from their own experiences, and what society and academic education has told them. That is why it is best not to take things personal even when they are aimed that way, because it says more about them and their hatred and ignorance, than anything you are.

Intersectionality was created in its time due to the need to explain the multiple oppressions experienced, and to hopefully help end the inequality experienced.

Patricia Hill Collins (2000) also talked about intersectionality to refer to forms of oppressions, for example, race and gender or sexuality and nations. Collins expressed intersectionality as micro-level (immediate caregivers, community, friends), an expression of our interpersonal perception and biases. It is an exchange of behaviours along with symbolic exchanges and cognitive explanations, it is all in conjunction by the processes within the macro-systematic structure, so the way the system treats and labels individuals. You can see the intersections within the system of race (white supremacy), gender (patriarchy), and other dimensions of equality (capitalism). 'These multi-level systems work together to shape oppressions creating a 'Matrix of dominance." Collins (1990, p.238)

Deborah King (1988) illuminated the factors of multiplication with regards to intersectionality, by this she states the character of oppressions - racism x sexism x classism x sexuality. She argued that black women, have adapted to define and sustain a multiple consciousness essential to challenge and survive the structure of these oppressions. Social identities of race, of gender, of class position and of sexuality are simultaneous and

189

multiplicative. Individuals face homophobia, racial profiling, poverty, sexual violence, and harassment all in one complex matrix within their day to day lives.

Black women show the power, strength, and resilience of the human spirit by the way they overcome all these dimensions. The magnificence of these individuals is inspiring. All women, even white women can have multiple oppressions to deal with, but the way black women were broken down and tarnished within history, it is empowering the way they bounce back, and you can feel the strength of every black woman that has rose above any label, or stereotype, put unto them. To be honest it is inspiring when all of us break through our cultural and oppressive boundaries, when we all wake up within, but with black women its amplified because of the horrors they had to overcome compared to other women around the world.

Anyone that rises through an oppression is admirable, anyone that contradicts or tries to expose injustice and create justice is inspiring. The fact that some individuals have multiple layers of oppression and injustice they climb through, that creates power, strength, and determination that not all of us can say we have to experience. These individuals deserve the upmost respect, they have the hardest lives to conquer, yet some do it with ease, some still prevail and some like all of us fail but keep pushing forward. Our struggles are limited compared to the struggles of the individuals who are born within the matrix of intersectional oppression.

A great example of an individual who combated intersectionality is of Sojourner Truth, 'it is the true story of Sojourner Truth, the famous statement she made of '"Ain't I a Woman.' Imagine it was a women's rights conference in Akron, Ohio, you have these white women there protesting the oppression and discrimination received, arguing for their rights. White male protestors were expressing stereotypical images of being a woman, saying they are too frail and delicate to comprehend and administer complex matters of political activity. Then Sojourner Truth stood up, illuminated in bravery, not letting the white women around her who wanted her silenced take her voice. She stood proud and tall, the women had no choice but to allow her to speak and the most inspirational, powerful speech came from her beautiful mind. "Look at my arms! I have ploughed and planted and gathered into barns, and no man could head me—and ain't I a woman? I would work as much and eat as much as a man—when I could get it—and bear the lash as well! And ain't I a woman? I have born thirteen children, and seen most of 'em sold into slavery, and when I cried out with my mother's grief: none but Jesus heard me—and ain't I a woman?'" Crenshaw (1989).

This statement gave me goosebumps when I read it, I was filled with pride, she shut down any sexist stereotypes those white men had, she was living proof that a woman can do just as much, if not more than any man. She worked harder, she endured racial discrimination and she suffered from beatings and abuse, she is true power, she made the white women look like fools in my opinion. Yes, they have oppressions to complain about, but it is nothing compared to what black women go through. White women should have used their privilege to help other women in society, not just themselves a long time ago! If we all worked together the possibilities of what we can achieve are endless.

Inner Growth

When you grow within, you can grow without

It is hard to be positive when people and the world around you are so negative. I mean think about it, every news channel mainly reports bad news, rarely any good news, inducing fear and negativity into the minds of the masses. It is hard and scary to show love when most of the world is full of hate, jealousy, greed, prejudice, discrimination, aggression, judgement, and violence. We must lead by example, it takes bravery to be kind and show love, especially when you yourself have been denied it. We are strong enough to tackle any obstacle, even the fear of getting hurt or being taken advantage of. These are negative thought projections into a made-up future. You must try and live in the moment, without your past conditioning taking control of your present thinking and experiencing.

Our entire existence from birth has been conditioned by our culture, society, country, time era, family, education, history, friends, the media, our governments, and experiences. If no one has taught us how to learn effectively and elevate our consciousness, then it is extremely hard to embrace new information and unlearn what we already know, especially when some beliefs make up so much of our self. Many beliefs we grow up with are negative, like do not talk to strangers, trust no one, do not cry, do not let people see your weakness, thinking you cannot achieve, feeling undeserving, jealousy, being manipulating and dishonest to get what you want. There is negativity everywhere in the world, but there is also positivity, it depends where and how you look.

I believe that the saying about the two wolves is true. That there are two wolves inside each of us that are constantly fighting each other, one called good, and one called evil, the wolf who wins is the wolf we feed. It may be hard to transcend the negativity, but it is not impossible once you become aware. Aware of your control that you can assess your

192

thinking, this helps life get a little easier. Think to yourself, who says being soft is weak, it takes so much strength to show love and kindness in a world that has little of it. You must go against everything you have learnt when you have experienced mostly discrimination, negativity, and trauma. Those who still lead with love by example and carry on, even if they get hurt or let down, that's true strength, that is a warrior. We must start with ourselves and pass it onto our children if we are to hope for any kind of future worth having, it is easier to teach a child than to re-teach an adult.

Everything I have mentioned would be found when you take an internal journey, you need to heal before you die, so you can truly live. This means that you need to heal all of the things within you that were put there from external conditionings, like behavioural issues gained from incompetent parents, low self-esteem from a system that tells you there is a certain way to be perfect, all the fears, discriminations, and the voice in your head that says you are not enough. You are all perfect just the way you are, being your true authentic self. You are more than enough, you can have so much impact over your own life, let alone others. You are one of the most powerful beings in the universe, you are a creator, and it is time to own it.

I have learned like so many others to hold an optimistic view to life. I try to see the positive in everything and everyone, even situations that cause pain, if you dig deep enough you can find the gold, the lessons. I do understand how easy it is to hold a negative outlook, I fell into that trap myself when I was younger, especially when all you experience is pain. So many people have it a lot worse, more than you can imagine, that is why we need to try to be kind and open, to others and ourselves, we do not know the impact we could have on a person's life.

Due to pre-existing structures within the world, where you are born and what family you are born into, can come with certain obstacles you will have to try and overcome or privileges you will reap. For example, being born into child sex slavery, abuse, a body that holds stereotypes and oppressions due to sex, gender and race, a negatively oppressed religion, being born into a country that has oppressions and extreme exploitation over the people. Governments that try to heard you like sheep, pre-organised standards of behaviour, beauty and perfectionism, economic classes, all of this will be different for each of you but just as powerful of an impact within your own lives. Recognise and emanate your own power, your own self-worth, to overcome all of these, and you can, only you can do it for yourself, books like this and other means in the world are here to help you help yourself, get closer to your own goal on your own journey.

What is true but unbelievable to many, is that we really do hold our own power and strength that can overcome our environment and our past, it is not easy, but it is worth it. We hold the power to create, actions from ourselves, reactions from others, emotions, abstract ideas to physical objects, life itself, we are all divine Gods in our own right. This means each of us have the ability and opportunity to create a better future for ourselves and the world, we do not know for certain that something or someone will do it for us, so we must start doing it for ourselves. If you look at the government for answers, look at their historical track record, they only look out for things that will benefit them. Politicians get paid more than the people, so they will never have the people's best interest at heart, only their pockets.

I believe there is a lesson in everything you go through, even if it is as simple as learning joy and trust from another, and then the most painful experiences can hold the most meaningful lessons. Seeing and feeling all the evil, dark and hatred in the world can show an individual how to appreciate true love, compassion, honesty, and pure light. Forgiving the world and people who have caused you pain, who are not even sorry, will create an unimaginable strength within you. Forgiving yourself for all the bad you have done, will allow you to set yourself free and to continuously try and do better in every future situation.

Regardless of where you are born in the world, regardless of the labels, oppressions and obstacles that have been set forth onto you and have been running for years before you were even born; regardless of all of this, you are still a beautiful being, you deserve love, to receive it and to feel safe to give it. You deserve more of a chance than the world you are born into gives, they say if you are born into a world that you do not fit into, it is because you were created to help make a new one.

Many people are lost in hatred and pain, due to a history of torture and corruption within our own minds and within our environments, people are loved for being fake and lying, people are being hated for being real and honest. Individuals are hated because of their skin, sexuality or position in society, everything is backwards and up in the air, that is why an internal journey is a must, bravery is a must. Be strong, positive, and better, no matter how many times you get burnt and hurt, move on. No one needs to stay in your life, you are not obliged to put up with constant toxic behaviour. Be good and keep getting better for yourself, people will see your happiness and will want that for themselves. Try not to hurt anyone with negative intentions along the way, you will end up teaching without even knowing.

Everyone is hurting each other and since it will always come back to you, because everyone is doing it, why not class it as self-harm, trust is being broken, a cold fearful outlook towards love has been created. The notion that it is better to be closed and cold, instead of open and loving, because it can protect you from feeling pain, this all comes from us. This notion has evolved so much and been passed down through generations, it is so embedded within some, that they cannot even be aware of the impact this subconscious belief has on their lives, on their self-worth, self-esteem, and on everybody else they encounter. It is a vicious cycle that will not stop unless we remove ourselves from it, looking within, learning yourself, will give you the power to stop repeating and start creating. Love is the purest, most powerful natural energy within us and every living thing, we should always try and live through love and know, no matter what heartache, pain and suffering we may go through, we are strong enough to overcome it. No matter what anyone tries to take away from you, they can never take your love away, unless you let them. Have faith that what is meant to be, will be, ask for nothing but what is meant for you, learn from everything, be strong, show love, lead, be brave and kind. You will impact people differently, some will feel mistreated, some people will not like you and that is okay, go with the people that do, if there is no love in your environment then you can always change environment. Whether that be across the world or a few hours away, but the most important thing is that you love yourself and to create love for yourself. Let love flow through you and you will naturally attract it back into your life.

Self-development is an internal journey. Society can inhibit many individuals from taking that journey, because they put false developments into the world, which people think are more worth striving for. Instead of developing and working on yourself to be the best you can be, people are convinced that working towards a mortgage, a family, a career, a car, designer clothes, celebrity status, or money, is more important. Developing and maintaining external materials are made to believe to be gains, but spiritual development, empowerment and true gains are developed within. How can you be involved completely with having anything or anyone and embracing its full potential, if you do not fully have yourself? If you have everything in the world externally, but you are not developed within, you are not winning, and you may feel incomplete.

It is sad that ego is sabotaging essence so much that some individuals can feel more entitled than everyone else. If you lived through your essence, if we all did, the world would shine, it would be beautiful, it is going to take a process, a journey that we have already begun but the fruits are going to be sweeter than any of us could possibly imagine.

Not all but a vast number of children who are born into a low economic status, either working class or below the poverty line, will receive a poorer education, chemical ridden foods, judgement, pressure, abuse, negative thinking patterns, trauma, discriminations, stereotypes, and stigmatizations. All of this can come from family and societal environments, you cannot even blame the family because parents had just the same inadequate teachings and upbringings from society. Most people do their best and do not realise that their best is not as good as they have been led to believe, or it is an improvement from what they have experienced but is not completely beneficial to their child.

When some parents want to do better, because they are consumed by trying to make money to clothe, shelter and feed their children, the self-development gets lost due to the exploitation that is allowed in society. If individuals were given enough wages to sustain living costs and have enough time at home, they could work on themselves, their own happiness and life, then there may not be so much negative thinking and negativity within the world. Some parents have their era, their parents, histories, traumas, issues, and negative social conditioning that they had never become aware of, let alone tried to work on. When they have children, it can get passed down, it is sad because it is like a cycle that does not end. Until someone decides they want better, they become aware of the negative patterns within their family, and they work within to break the chain. If you are strong, you will teach your family, if they are ready to learn, and not by telling but by actions, from leading by example. It is hard to break the chain whether you are the parent, child or whoever but it is not impossible, this should give us hope, if you realise your power, you can be the change you want to see.

There are so many of us, if we all realised and recognised our worth, took responsibility over our lives, took back our confidence, independence, our power, then the people who create oppressions and poor socio-economic classes will start to crumble. Eventually they would, if forced, give into having less profits so we can enjoy our lives fairly, they will have to get used to a less profitable and consumer-based world. There is more than enough people and resources for ALL of us to live a happy sustainable life. We have the technology that would enable us all to have free heating, electricity and hot water, solar power alone can achieve this. The reason it is not so, is because we live in a society that is governed not by the quality of life we can give and achieve, but rather the amount of profit a small percentage of people can make. The individuals who exploit millions of people to gain billions in cash, have so much power within the world we live in, due to them absorbing and using our own power against us. Different corporations do it differently, depending on what they want the consumer to buy or feel. Corporations can make individuals feel worthless, making people feel like they need them and their service or product to survive and to become better.

With regards to our physical appearance, the possessions we own, our education and the way we allow our minds to work, taking orders instead of thinking we could do better for ourselves. Some corporations take our power, by making us feel ugly, creating idealistic beauty standards, which most human beings deviate from, on purpose of course. Advertisements use an individuals' emotions against them, they make people feel like they need their product, to be better and more attractive. These factors create individuals to strive and try to reach this beauty standard, of which most of them cannot as it is unrealistic. This is one reason why so many people wear so much make up, take slimming supplements, or even go as extreme to undergo plastic surgery. Think about it, the pictures are photoshopped, so even the actual models do not look like that. This standard is unattainable, on purpose, as they want to create consumers. You consume their products because they create a feeling of ugliness, or maybe, the standard makes individuals feel ashamed of who they are. They buy products and spend loads of money to make them seem or feel better. All along they are being controlled by the narrative that has been created, that standard of which they so crave.

They show off these luxurious lifestyles but make it impossible for most individuals to attain, this creates the masses of people to continue to consume and try to create this lifestyle for themselves, it is unrealistic as you cannot achieve this working minimum wage or even on a middle-class wage. People are working themselves to death. Missing out on vital life moments like family time or time to themselves, self-development and travelling because they believe they are working for a better future. Unfortunately, the way the system has been created for most people, that future will never come. Unless individuals decide for themselves that they want better and deserve better, then you can create better. Bear in mind once you take an internal journey, that better may not be what you once thought.

You can achieve a better life by taking your power back, loving yourself. Not giving your energy to people, situations, materialistic objects, cosmetics, and ideas that want to drain you. Instead give it to yourself or others you love, realising you need nothing brings everything. When you believe in yourself fully, when you love yourself fully, when you embrace your confidence and be brave, when you find beauty in your perfect imperfections, when you find power in your uniqueness. This is when you will be the most powerful person in your life, this is when bad energies, anything or anyone will not make you doubt yourself, or turn on yourself through fear or intimidation, you will be a conscious powerful autonomous human being.

You could grow your own food or buy locally grown food, manage, and store your own electricity with solar power and other forms of free renewable energy. Stop relying on other people to sustain your life in every aspect, psychologically and materialistically, start living for yourself, start living through independence and love. Do what you enjoy and follow your own passions, walk your own path not the one that has been given to you.

The system goes even deeper than what I have previously mentioned, negative patterns of thinking are conditioned into most individuals from childhood, it could be simple things, from getting bullied for not owning a pair of Nikes. On the other side of the spectrum some people grow up learning how to deal with racial abuse, traumas, sex slavery, police brutality and the poverty low class living brings, like drug addicted parents, no support, the ideals of be strong or get squashed. Many children never learn what real, pure, unconditional love is, this negative pattern can follow individuals all throughout their lives. Some have realisations on their death bed, some before, but many will die never realising they controlled whether they got better or bitter, rather viewing their ambitions as an impossible dream. Always seeing themselves as the victim not the victor, I do understand why, I was once the same, thinking 'why do bad things always happen to me? ` Until I decided I wanted to be happy, I wanted better. Then I actively tried to accomplish that, every single day, trying to improve so I did not only face life but enjoy, embrace, and thrive to be the best I can be. It is the same with many of us, we must decide and believe that we want and deserve better. Some do not even bother to dream at all, this is what inhibits their power, the negativity, the thought that they can never be more than what they are born into. Belief, faith, love, motivation, joy, gratitude, optimism, these positive feelings will bring you what you want.

The internal journey I speak of is real and it works, it did for me, and I am sure it will for many of you, only we can heal ourselves and when you do, you will see your light, your power, your strength. I do not know your purpose or the lessons you need to learn to grow into your higher self, it is different for everyone as no matter how alike we are, simultaneously we are all uniquely different, and we all have different battles with different severities. Therefore, only you can do it for yourself, it is good having a healthy support network but even if you do not have that, you are still more than capable to achieve healing alone. That is something I am certain of, no matter how hard or, how many external things and people, try to convince you that you cannot, if you believe, truly believe in your mind that you can, then you can. You can find your peace within; you can take your power back over your own life. You can choose to say no, you can create something new, something better, equal, with no negative ideals with regards to your life and institutionalised systems, organisations, education, and progress. Every single moment we live and breathe, we have the power to create something better, so start creating.

Everybody can live a life that is unique to them, we all have different passions, beliefs, ideals, and histories, some like to help others, some like to perform, create music, art, buildings, theories, and some like to cook, plant, travel, learn, grow, read, take care of animals, play sport, write, and teach. We all have different unique paths every person has a chance to follow if people live as their true authentic honest self. If instead individuals always follow other people or ideals and unjust systems, they are not living out their own life, it is living out the idea of life someone else had created. You can live your life walking the path that your environment, society, or family has laid out for you, or you can follow your own unique path which is specifically tailored to you. For your benefit to learn and grow within yourself, to develop psychologically as well as physically, to find your happiness and to leave your own unique imprint within the world. More individuals will make a positive imprint if they work within, find your power, love yourself and then it will show within the environment. It requires consistency and I still fall back into old habits, trip over past constructs, get lost, losing sight of my path but I always take responsibility, try to make it right, learn and grow, then move forward. Do not feel despair if you feel like you are failing, it is a lesson in disguise, showing you what you need to work on, so own it, see it, feel it, and then do better. I feel like I became aware of my path and life lessons when I was around sixteen, before I was oblivious to the impact life had on me, but when certain things changed in my mind, I could see an external change in my life, that is when I discovered growth, psychological growth.

I could see significant points in my life timeline, where certain life experiences would teach me a vital life lesson, if I truly learnt, it would change me within, and I would see progression. When my life would get better internally, it would also get better externally.

If lessons were not learnt, I could see similar situations as before, enter my life-experience, until I learnt what was needed to progress into the next stage of my life. When you are on your path, things in life will try and distract you, throw you off or intimidate you, so you fear moving forward. Sometimes you want to do something, then your mind takes over and convinces you not to do it, usually due to negative reasoning like fear and doubt. This is getting distracted from following your path, letting fear stop you from acting out your realness. You want to go somewhere? Then go, find a way, any way, if you want to say something, say it, you want to do something? Do it!

You can do whatever you think of at any given time, do not let fear or anxiety stop you from living the life you are truly destined for, live your best life! Just 'go with the flow', if it comes, let it, if it goes, let it, then you are on your path, stop resisting! Learn what you need when you are supposed to, do not put excuses in front of it, see it for what it is, understand the background of everything. Everything and everyone have their own history, that is the background of all their actions, many people are not consciously aware, so they act through their histories rather than their true self. You cannot blame them for this, all you can do is help

200

where you can, leave when you are supposed to, have faith that they will learn and show love. Teach them how to be better by being better yourself, be everything you did not have, everything you needed. You have yourself, that is all you ever truly need, and most people have not even got that.

You should only want what is meant for you, the good, the bad and the ugly, because no matter how bad an experience, it can teach you strength and growth, so you become less bothered and at peace with minor things. Any pain from betrayal can teach you not to betray, this would be the positive lesson, a negative impact could be thinking that you are not worth enough to be loyal to, this is false. You are just as worthy as anyone and it is not your fault someone treats you less than you deserve, but it is on you whether you stay and let them. There are billions of people in the world, do not be scared to leave the ones that treat you less than you deserve, explore, the right ones will come and stay. Any love not felt should show you what love needs to be given out, by knowing what you want to receive. At the same time, each of us know when we do not receive it back, you can let it affect you negatively or you can turn it into a positive and move on from that person or situation, that is on you, you control your response.

Not all lessons are bad, some people will come into your life and teach you true love, joy, and happiness, but first it should be yourself that teaches you this. If you learn and grow within yourself you will gain a true appreciation for the positive, loving, good things in life and you will appreciate the people and situations that offer it. You will not resist due to past pain, you will accept without judgment, and feel feelings you could not have possibly felt before as you were blocking it. You will be able to develop powerful, deep, trusting relationships with the people you meet.

Fear stops people from doing most things they want to do, the fear that it will not work out, or fear of danger and pain. Facing your fears is a crucial step in your development, it is something I started to put into practice when I was twenty, a friend let me down with a trip to Amsterdam we had booked, so instead of not going, I decided to go alone. I had a lot of fear within the build up to go, but I wanted to prove to myself that I can do it, so I booked an all-girls hostel and went, it was my first solo trip. It ended up being an amazing experience and showed me why we should face our fears. Now I have no fear to travel anywhere around the world, I have ventured alone to Amsterdam, Mexico, Jamaica, Egypt, Lanzarote, I have met amazing individuals, and have received very empowering lessons.

Each piece of land should be ours to share, without some having a fear of traveling and some not, due to privilege. We all have just as much right as the next person to walk freely across this earth, that being denied to many is one of the many injustices in the world and will be changed. It is significantly more dangerous for individuals with a darker skin complexion to travel, it is disgusting that they receive racial prejudice, being stared at constantly, feeling unwelcome, having a fear of the possible violence put onto them, being mistreated in restaurants, by police, establishments, security, and the public of countries they may visit. Especially considering we do not choose where we are born, whether that be into privilege or not, we should live by the rule of one earth, one race, who all have just as much right as the other. Bad things happen everywhere, no matter what people look like, but if we all stay positive, we can create the change we all want, not being led by fear but led by bravery, integrity, understanding and positivity.

I grew up with a fear of love due to love and pain, disappointment and heartache always coming together in my life. It was an extremely hard obstacle to overcome but I did it, mostly because of Kellise, the one person who showed me interest, effort, love, attention, someone who wanted me around and put in the effort to have me there and spend time with me. I was so scared of love and what she had showed me, I was never able to return it fully, I did not want to expose my weaknesses. That is what I used to think anyway, I thought I was protecting myself from future pain. Then after she died, realising I will never get another chance to show her the love she deserved, the love and compassion I had inside, it broke me. The pain I had inside was unimaginable, regret, disbelief, if only I was more open and loving it may have changed so much. After getting myself out of the despair I was trapped in, I managed to strengthen myself a bit more each day since she died, I have learned to be open. I knew that if I could heal from this, I could heal from any kind of heart break because nothing could hurt or break me like that did. That's why I feel it is best to be completely open and loving because either way bad things can happen. At least if you are open and loving, people have a better chance of valuing themselves and their lives or at least will know that you value them. You never want to feel like it is too

202

late to tell someone how much you love them. I now choose to love deeply, honestly, with no regrets because love and kindness can do more for people than we give credit. I am not scared of anything anymore; I found my voice and I will use it; I encourage each one of you to discover yours and use yours too.

Empowerment

You are the most powerful person in your life, you just have to let yourself be!

O n this earth there are structures that are in place, before all of us were born these systems were created, it assigns us our position when we are born by what we are born into. If we are born with more melanin than others, we are considered different, sometimes threatening even if we do nothing wrong. We have negative labels, ideals and stereotypes put unto us that perpetrates an image of who we supposedly are. Without anyone spending time to try to discover who we really are. If we are born with a darker skin complexion we must deal with even more racism, abuse, and systemic prejudices. If we are born attracted to the same sex we deal with labels and prejudices put unto us from strict beliefs, if we are born a woman we are automatically seen as less than. If we are born without wealth we are seen as less than worthy, when true riches come from within, not from without.

When you are born into two or more of these categories that is when an intersect occurs and you have even more obstacles to overcome. The truth is that we are all born tiny babies, that need feeding, nurturing, and love, at this stage we do not know any concept of what the world tells us we are, we just are. Everything we learn after is from the social world and from our immediate families, it shapes how we view the world, and it shapes how we deal with our experiences. We are all born with a power inside us, the power to feel, the power to love, the power to grow, the power to create, if nurtured productively we all have the capability to reach our full potential. In this world babies are not always nurtured in a positive way; we develop and pick up unbelievably negative habits that follow us into our adult lives. Some individuals underestimate the impact our childhood has on our adulthood, individuals underestimate the impact love and positive reinforcement has on a child. Something not a lot of children are shown, a child that does not receive love can find it hard to give love in adulthood.

Everything we learn that is damaging to ourselves, we can undo this, but we must be willing, we must want it, many people if they live a comfortable life, they may not feel any need. We were born into a system that is designed to keep individuals at a certain level, that's why hierarchies exist. So, if you find it hard to better yourself, it is not your fault, the world around us is corrupt, and is doing a great injustice to most individuals that live on this earth. It is not right that individuals are born without a fair chance in life, but we can change this. We must change how we perceive life to be, because we ultimately control how anything can make us feel, so when you change your thinking, you can change your life.

The path we should all consider taking to undo our conditioning and to change our thinking patterns, is an internal journey and there are many ways to achieve this. Psychologically CBT therapy (Cognitive Behavioural Therapy) has discovered how to re-wire your brain, the more you give energy to certain thinking patterns the stronger and more automatic they become. Any automatic negative thoughts you have, you need to bring your attention to it, understand it, accept it, rationalise it, and change it into a positive thought. For example, if you are taking an exam or applying for a job and you automatically think it will not work out or it will fail or you will not do too good, then that is what you will attract into your life. If you think people are always thinking negative things about you, or laughing at you then change it into a positive, think that they could be thinking about anyone, why would they think badly about you? If you stop that negative train of thought and change it into, I am capable, I am deserving, and I can achieve, then you will attract this into your life. The more you interrupt the negative thoughts and replace it with a positive thought, the more strength you will give to positive thinking. After time of actively doing this, you can rewire your brain and neural pathways, to have more automatic positive thoughts.

To undo the conditioning of the world and the impact of all the negative experiences and propaganda we have experienced from birth, we must take an internal journey. This means a journey into your own mind, of which only you can do, a therapist can help, but no one knows you, like you know you. When taking this journey, you must start at the beginning, the root cause to all your negative emotions and negative behavioural reactions. This usually comes from experiences in child-hood, these experiences can be at varying degrees for everybody, even if you do not feel like it has affected you. You may think it is not that serious or others around you have normalised it. If it has made you feel a negative emotion at the time it happened, then more likely it has in-fected your mind and has created a conditioning or negative habitual pattern of behaviour. To do this you have to reflect, think back on all your experiences and actions, question all of it, ask why you did certain things, learn from the lessons of these experiences. Think about it, un-derstand it, know that you did not deserve the trauma, find the root cause of your pain, and in turn negative mind and actions. Forgive yourself and everyone involved even if they hurt you, even if they do not care or ask for forgiveness, even if they do not forgive you, let go and move on into a brighter more positive future that you can create for yourself, by de-ciding what you really want!

Empowerment comes from our awareness, we give our power away to things without even noticing, that is why when we allow ourselves to become aware we can take our power back. Beauty products for example hold so much power over many of us, how we value ourselves and see ourselves. Some are convinced that their beauty comes from these prod-ucts. Beauty comes from within; if you are pretty on the outside, but ugly on the inside you are not winning. We need to become aware that we are giving our power away to an ideal that comes from someone else, the belief that you are less without this product, the standard they create, rather than living by your own. This is the exact same moment that we can take our power back and say I do not need this, I am beautiful, pow-erful, and more than enough without it, I am stunning in my natural form, completely uniquely me. It is not just beauty products that have this effect on us.

Anything that makes you feel less than who you are or, tries to get you to conform to their way in a negative way, any person or situation in your environment that makes you feel powerless, this could even be friends, family, colleagues, teachers, media, literally anything and anyone. As soon as you shine your awareness onto it you can consciously decide not to put any more of your energy (your power) into it. It is the same as our family or your immediate environment, if we only listen and do as we are told, never questioning, then you are handing over your power of crea-tive mind. Your power to create the life which is best for you, your giving in to the person or system that is trying to map out your life for you. If you only ever do as you are told or only believe what others say of you and what you can achieve, then that is all you will ever accomplish. If you grow up with parents or carers that tell you not to dream too big, or that you cannot achieve something because it is harder than it looks. If you let them convince you that this is true, then you are handing over your power to them, and are living through their ideas and beliefs. If you disagree with them and think that you can achieve whatever you set out to do, and if you set your own goals instead of living through others. Then you are living through your own power and sooner or later you will achieve everything you set out to achieve, if you believe, with every ounce of yourself that you can, then you will.

Although all the discriminations I have mentioned are within the world, we can transcend them, yes, they are there, yes, we are aware of them, now we can consciously decide not to feed our energy into them, into the labels, into the stereotypes, into the prejudice. If individuals in the world are unconscious to their thoughts and actions do not give them your power by believing them, educate them and try to encourage them to think differently. Because it says nothing about you, and it says all about what is going on in their mind. You know your truth, you know you are more than your body, your shell, you know that their negative prejudices are a learnt idea that they carry, and it weighs them down. That is why they try to shift some of the weight onto you, do not allow it, move on gracefully ascending to be the best you can be. You are not responsible for trying to convince another they are wrong; we are all responsible over our own minds and our own happiness and our own empowerment!

Of course, if you have children, we are responsible for shaping their minds. That is why we should empower and teach ourselves to be the best we can be, before we even think about having a child. I remember when I was fourteen, I always wanted to be a young mum, I was convinced I would have a baby before I was 20. As I got older, and I took my internal journey, trying to become the best I can be, for me. I realised the only reason I wanted a child, was because I felt that my life had been without love. I felt like I had so much love to give, but I did not know how to give it to myself, and I was scared to give it to others, with the thought that they may hurt me. I thought I could only give it to my child and in turn I would have this being, that would love me unconditionally.

It was only then that I realised I wanted a baby for all the wrong reasons, and it shined a light on the fact that I needed to overcome my fear of showing love to others, and that I had to learn how to show love to myself. When you take an internal journey, you will discover so much about yourself. There is a reason behind everything and once you become aware of these reasons, you will consider that all the answers are within you. Once you become aware of that, you can understand and decide to be, and do better.

The first step within empowerment is to truly learn self-love, to do this think about all the love you would give another, maybe a partner or your child, the right person for you, think about all the love you would show them. With gifts, kind words, trips, anything you can do that would put a smile on their face and bring them some happiness and joy. Now instead of waiting for the right person to come along to treat in this way, make yourself the right person first, show yourself the love you hold inside, make yourself smile, take yourself on trips, give yourself gifts, bring as much happiness and joy into your life as you possibly can. Love yourself so fiercely, with so much certainty, that you set the standard of how you want to be treated. When you love yourself completely, you will not allow situations or people, that treat you less than what you give out, stay around, and drain your energy.

Another part of an internal journey is facing all your fears and demons, what makes you angry, what makes you sad, what makes you feel less than what you are. All the negative aspects in your psychological wellbeing, face the feelings of jealousy, ask yourself why you fear this person or situation. Ask yourself, why you have prejudices, why you think negatively about people, and continue to show yourself love and forgiveness, once you love yourself so much, you would not have any room left to hate another.

The thing is that every human being on this earth, no matter what we may look like, we are all the same whilst concurrently being uniquely different. We all have the potential within us, we all have the power to create, to learn, to grow, we all feel certain emotions, we all have a mind where we can reflect. We all have the power to take an internal journey no matter what our environment is like, and once we transcend within ourselves, everything on the outside will look different. Your perceptions will change, things that once hurt you will not hurt anymore, things that made you angry will no longer give you that response. I am not saying it is easy, it is a continuous journey of practise, reflection, discipline, positivity, and consistency that takes time and effort, but if you decide to take this path for your own betterment, I am saying that you will be unimaginably better off.

When the systems of the world no longer phase you, when the media can no longer manipulate you, when the opinions and actions of others no longer disrupt your own internal peace of mind, when your riches do not come from materialistic attributes, but rather riches within your mind, within the lessons you have learnt, then you will reach the embodiment of empowerment. You will be on the path of limitless possibilities, feeling happiness, peace, love, contentment. No longer getting frustrated over miniscule matters, having a low self-esteem, being doubtful, no longer feeling undervalued or having no self-worth. This is true empowerment and enlightenment; this is something we all have the power to achieve.

It is time to use these lessons for the benefit of everyone, we all need to spread the word and work within ourselves individually, healing ourselves. This helps the world, it benefits me, you, my future children and yours, the future of mankind. It helps defenceless animals and land, that we burn and torture, because once you look within and strip yourself of your inner demons like, fear, judgement, jealousy, negative thoughts, consumerism, addiction, toxic patterns, feelings of being unworthy or nothing. You can find your light, your courage, your strength, your confidence, your self-esteem, your love, and your willingness to let things be without judgement. It will illuminate a light within yourself and then all the earth, everything, and everyone, shall reap the fruits of our labour. We will be so within, that we will never be without.

References

- Abdul Mohamud., & Robin Whitburn., 21/06/2018. Britain's involvement with New World slavery and the transatlantic slave trade. https://www.bl.uk/restoration-18th-century-literature/articles/britains-involvement-with-new-world-slavery-and-the-trans-atlantic-slave-trade. 08/06/2022.
- ABS Contributor. 7/10/2013. When Black Men Ruled the World: 8 Things the Moors Brought to Europe. https://atlantablackstar.com/2013/10/07/when-black-men-ruled-the-world-moors/#:~:text=The%20Moorish%20advances%20in%20mathematics,Ages%20and%20into%20the%20Renaissance.&text=The%20Moors%20brought%20enormous%20learning,through%20the%20rest%20of%20Europe. 07/06/2022
- Adorno, T. W., Frenkel-Brunswick, E., Levinson, D.J., & Sanford, N. (1950). *The Authoritarian Personality*. New York: Harper & Row.
- Allport GW. 1954. The Nature of Prejudice. Reading, MA: Addison-Wesley.537pp.
- Benokraitis, N. V., & Feagin, J. R. (1995). Modems& (2nded.). Englewood Cliffs, NJ: Prentice-Hall.
- Bohan,J. S. (1997). Regarding Gender: Essentialism. Constructionism and Feminist psychology. In M, Gergen and S. N. Davis (Eds.), Toward a new psychology of gender: A reader (pp. 31-47). New York: Routledge.
- Bourdieu, P. (1977) *Outline of a Theory of Practice*. Cambridge: Cambridge University Press.
- Brannon, R. The male sex role: Our culture's blueprint for manhood, what it's done for use lately. In D. David & R. Brannon (Eds.), The forty-nine percent majority: The male sex role. Reading, Mass.: Addison-Wesley, 1976. Pp. 1–45.
- Bristow, J. 1997. Sexuality. New York: Routledge.
- Bruner, J. (1957). On perceptual Readiness. *Psychological Review, 64,* 123-152.

- Bullock, H. E. (1995). Class Acts: Middle Class Responses to The Poor. In B. Lott and D. Maluso (Eds.), *The Social Psychology of Interpersonal Discrimination* (pp. 118-159). New York: Guilford Press.
- Butler, Judith., (1990; Anniversary edition 1999) Gender Trouble: Feminism and the Subversion of Identity, New York: Routledge.
- Butler, Judith., (1993) Bodies That Matter: On the Discursive Limits of "Sex," New York: Routledge.
- Butler, Judith., (1994) "Gender as Performance: An Interview with Judith Butler," Radical Philosophy: A Journal of Socialist and Feminist Philosophy 67 (Summer): 32–9.
- Collins, P. H. (1990). Black feminist thought in the matrix of domination. In P. H. Collins (Ed.), Black feminist thought: knowledge, consciousness, and the politics of empowerment (pp. 221–238). Boston: Unwin Hyman.
- Collins, P. H. (2000). Black Feminist Thought: Knowledge, Consciousness, And The Politics of Empowerment (2nd Ed.). New York. Routledge.
- Cozzarelli, C. A., Wilkinson, A. V., & Tagler, M. J. (2001). Attitudes toward the poor and Attributions for Poverty. *Journal of Social Issues, 57,* 207-227.
- Crenshaw, Kimberle´. 1989. "Demarginalizing the Intersection of Race and Sex: A Black Feminist Critique of Antidiscrimination Doctrine, Feminist Theory, and Antiracist Politics." University of Chicago Legal Forum 1989:139–67.
- Crenshaw, Kimberle, 1995. "Mapping the Margins: Intersectionality, Identity Politics, and Violence against Women of Color." In *After Identity,* ed. Dan Danielsen and Karen Engle.
- Crenshaw, Kimberlé (1993) 'Beyond Racism and Misogyny', in M. Matsuda, C. Lawrence and K. Crenshaw (eds) Words that Wound. Boulder, CO: Westview Press.
- Cydney Contreras. 22/10/2020. Ghislaine Maxwell's Deposition Unsealed: What She Alleged About Jeffrey Epstein and Prince Andrew. https://www.eonline.com/news/1201123/ghislaine-maxwells-deposition-unsealed-what-she-alleged-about-jeffrey-epstein-and-prince-andrew. 07/06/2022.
- Dan Mangan. 20/12/2019. 'Missing' jail video from first Jeffrey Epstein suicide attempt has been found, prosecutors tell judge.

https://www.cnbc.com/2019/12/20/video-of-jeffrey-epstein-jail-suicide-attempt-is-found.html. 07/06/2022
- Dhanoon, R. K. (2011). Considerations on Mainstreaming Intersectionality, Political Research Quarterly, 64 (1), 230-243.
- Donald, L, Fixico. 2/3/2018. When Native Americans Were Slaughtered in the Name of 'Civilization'. https://www.history.com/news/native-americans-genocide-united-states. 08/06/2022.
- Edwards, D. (1997). *Discourse and Cognition.* London: Sage.
- Fine, B., Harris, L., Mayo, M., Weir, A. and Wilson, E. (1985) Class Politics: An Answer to its Critics London; Leftover Pamphlets
- Fox., D. Prilleltensky., I. Austin., S. (2009) Critical Psychology: An Introduction, (2nd Ed), SAGE, London.
- Freeman, A. 2007. Fast Food: Oppression through poor nutrition. California Law Review 95:2221-2259.
- Fromm, E. (1941). *Escape from Freedom.* New York: Avon
- Glick, P., & Fiske, S. T. (1996). The Ambivalent Sexism Inventory: Differentiating hostile and benevolent sexism. Journal of Personality and Social Psychology, 70, 491—512.
- Glick, P., & Fiske, S. T. (1997). Hostile and benevolent sexism: Measuring ambivalent sexist attitudes toward women. Psychology of Women Quarterly, 21, 119—135.
- Glick, P., & Fiske, S. T. (2001). An ambivalent alliance: Hostile and benevolent sexism as complementary justifications for gender inequality. American Psychologist, 56, 109–118.
- Harley, S. (1978). Anna J. Cooper: A Voice for Black Women. In S. Harley& R. Terborg-Penn (Eds.), *The Afro-American Women: Struggles and Images,* (pp. 87-96). Baltimore: Black Classic Press.
- Hilton JL, von Hippel W. 1996. Stereotypes. Annu. Rev. Psychol. 47:237–7
- Hochschild, A. (2022, April 5). Leopold II. Encyclopedia Britannica. https://www.britannica.com/biography/Leopold-II-king-of-Belgium
- Hopkins, N., Reicher, S., & Levine, M. (1997). On the Parallels Between Social Cognition and The 'New Racism`. *British Journal of Social Psychology, 36,* 305-329.
- Hupkens, C., Knibbe, R., & Drop, M. (2000). Social class differences in food consumption: the explanatory value of

permissiveness and health and cost considerations. European Journal of Public health, 10, 108-113.

- Jones, J. M. (1972). Prejudice and Racism. Reading, MA: Addison-Wesley
- Juanita, Bawagan. 2nd of May (2019). *Scientists explore the evolution of animal homosexuality.* Scientists explore the evolution of animal homosexuality | Imperial News | Imperial College London.
- King, D. (1988). Mulitple Jeopardy, Multiple Consciousness: The Context of a Black Feminist Ideology. Signs: Journal of Women in Culture and Society, 14 (1), 42-72.
- Lin, J.Y. and Fisher, D.E., 2007. Melanocyte biology and skin pigmentation. *Nature, 445*(7130), pp.843-850.
- Liu, W. M., Ali, S. R., Soleck, G., Hopps, J., Dunston, K., & Pickett, T. (2004). Using Social Class in Counselling Psychology Research. *Journal of Counselling Psychology,51,* 3-18.
- Major, A., 2020. British humanitarian political economy and famine in India, 1838–1842. Journal of British Studies, 59(2), pp.221-244.
- Marika, Sherwood. 2007. Britain, slavery, and the trade in enslaved Africans. Britain, slavery, and the trade in enslaved Africans, by Marika Sherwood (history.ac.uk). 08/06/2022.
- Mehryar, A. H. (1984). The role of psychology in national development: wishful thinking and reality. International Journal of Psychology, 19, 159–167.
- Mitchell, J. (1974) Feminism and Psychoanalysis, London: Allen Lane.
- Mutwa, V. C. (2003). Zulu shaman. Dreams, prophecies, and mysteries. Rochester, VT: Destiny.
- National Portrait Gallery. N.D. The Slave Trade. The Slave Trade - National Portrait Gallery (npg.org.uk). 06/06/2022
- Otto, M. (2007). For Want of a Dentist: Pr. George's Boy Dies After Bacteria from Tooth Spread to Brain. Available: http://www.washingtonpost.com/wp-dyn/content/article/2007/02/27/AR2007022702116.html, accessed 28 February.
- Paul Gregoire. 02/07/2017. Crimes Against Humanity: The British Empire. https://www.sydneycriminallawyers.com.au/blog/crimes-against-humanity-the-british-empire/. 07/06/2022.

- Porter, E. (2006). Study Finds Wealth Inequality is Widening Worldwide. *The New York Times,* 6 December. Available from http://www.nytimes.com/2006/12/06/business/world/business/06wealth.html?ref=business
- Riggs. D. W., & Augoustinos, M. (2004). Projecting Threat: Managing Subjective Investments in Whiteness. *Psychoanalysis, Culture & Society, 9,* 219- 236.
- Riggs, D. W., & Augoustinos, M. (2005). The Psychic Life of Colonial Power: Racialised Subjectivities, Bodies, and Methods. *Journal of Community and Applied Social Psychology, 15,* 461-477.
- Rothman, R. A. (2005). *Inequality and Stratification: Race, Class and Gender* (5th ed.). Upper Saddle River, NJ: Prentice Hall.
- Rudman, L. A., & Glick, P. (1999). Feminized management and backlash toward agentic women: The hidden costs to women of a kinder, gentler image of middle managers. Journal of Personality and Social Psychology, 77,1004–1010.
- Tavris, C. (1993). The Mismeasure of Women. Feminism & Psychology, 3, 149-168.
- Truth, S., & Painter, N. (1998). Narrative of Sojourner Truth. New York: Penguin Books.
- United States Holocaust Memorial Museum. 8/12/2020. "Documenting numbers of victims of the holocaust and Nazi persecution." Holocaust Encyclopedia. https://encyclopedia.ushmm.org/content/en/article/documenting-numbers-of-victims-of-the-holocaust-and-nazi-persecution. 07/06/2022